0075982

DATE DUE

RAKU

For Sandra, Lizzy and Jessica

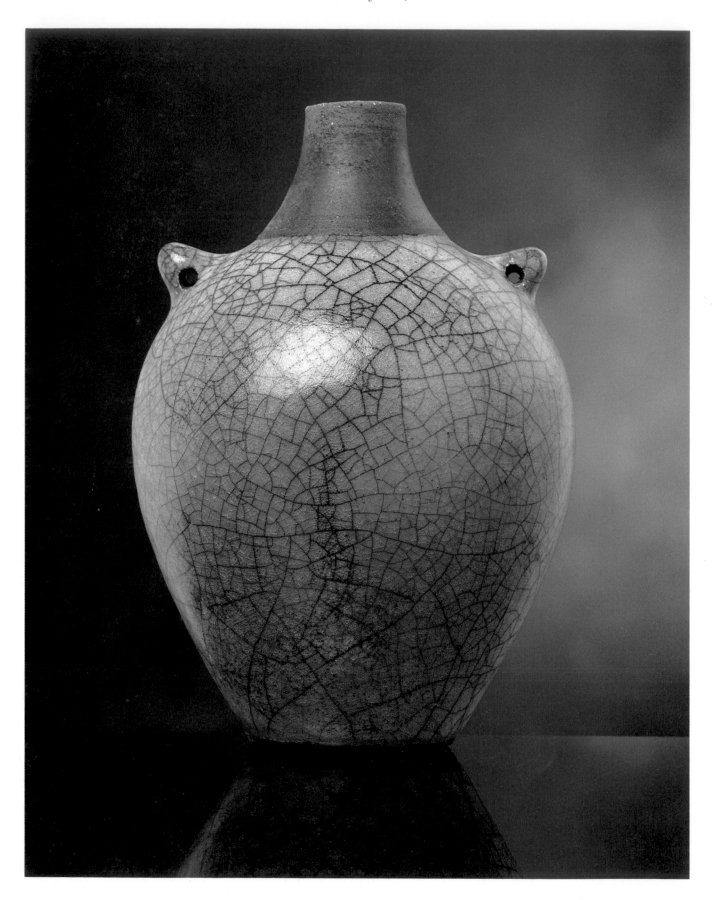

RAKU

A Review of Contemporary Work

Tim Andrews

A & C Black · London
Chilton Book Company · Radnor, Pennsylvania

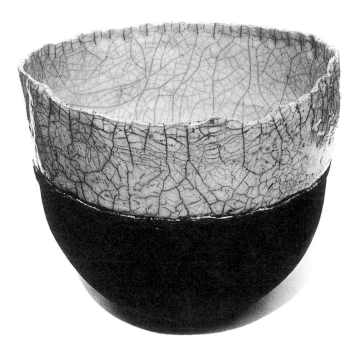

Raku bowl by Bert Mens.
Thrown and coiled. Smoked black with glazed rim and inside.
Photograph by Dick Elsenaar.

First published in Great Britain 1994
A & C Black (Publishers) Limited
35 Bedford Row, London WC1R 4 JH

ISBN 0 7136 3836 2

First published in USA by Chilton Book Company,
Radnor, Pennsylvania 19089

ISBN 0-8019-8633-8

Jacket illustrations
front: Tall vase form with fumed copper surface by Tim Andrews, h.15".
back: Reverse side of the tall vase on the front. Both photographs by Peter Harper

Frontispiece
Small bottle by Tim Andrews.

Designed by Janet Watson

Typeset by Selwood Systems, Midsomer Norton
Printed in Singapore by
Tien Wah Press (Pte.) Ltd

CONTENTS

Acknowledgements

To my parents who might have expected a biologist, a teacher, a parson or even a lawyer – at least someone with an income – but who instead have supported, encouraged, cajoled, worried over, and sympathised with my idiosyncratic arty endeavours.

To Harvey Bradley, my first pottery teacher who inspired and enthused and was responsible for the immortal line, 'I think Tim will do something with clay'.

To David Leach who gave me my first break, played Paul Robeson in the workshop and has always been available for advice and philosophical debate.

To my wife Sandra – the great enabler – who has given aid and succour in times of crisis and is also a very good speller.

To my two delightful daughters, Elizabeth and Jessica, for their patience and understanding. Yes, you can play with the computer now.

To Ann for her generosity which has made all the difference.

And especially, to my brother Martin for his fresh eye, his probing perceptive mind, all his hard work and editing skills, and for explaining how to use a semi-colon.

I would also like to thank Victor Harris at the British Museum and Cathy Niblett at Stoke on Trent City Museum for their help and cooperation.

Thank you all.

I would also like to thank all those who have contributed directly to this book. Especially all the featured potters who took the trouble to send information and photographs, gave interviews and generously supported the project.

Preface

By my 18th birthday I had already been smitten with clay and fire, and had abandoned (pragmatically I think) a potential university degree in zoology in favour of the strange notion of becoming a potter. To celebrate my coming of age and something of a U-turn in future aspirations, my parents, supportive as ever, offered to lay on a party. Bored with the conventions of my 1970s generation which to be honest were never very appealing to me, I opted instead for a raku event to be held in our Rectory garden.

Early April weather notwithstanding, the bemused guests duly arrived in requisite glad-rags of jeans and sweaters, immediately being ushered into the garage where awaited a selection of pots to be decorated and glazed. However, it soon became apparent the corporate gathering had quickly divided into proverbial sheep and goats with the larger portion, no doubt attracted by the faint but familiar strains of Simon and Garfunkel, making a rapid bee-line for the warmth of the house and, more importantly, the drinks table. There remained, however, a hardy rump of enthusiastic rakuers who, once hooked, could not be dragged away from the home-built wood-fired kiln which was by then yielding its magic. The power of this seduction was great, even tempting one young man to demand that he should camp out next to the kiln until dawn. My father – perhaps anticipating the difficulty he might have explaining what this malodorous lad had been up to all night at the Rectory – sent him home. But that milestone of a day spawned an excitement for raku that has never left me.

Researching and writing this book has been a learning experience for me. It contains a good deal of technical information, techniques, recipes and advice gleaned from potters around the world. But above all, whether you are a fellow maker, a collector, a student or just have an interest in pots and potters, I hope that this book may enthuse and inspire you to explore more deeply the magic of raku.

Foreword by David Leach

Interest in Raku has grown enormously in the last 10 to 15 years. The excitement and immediacy of the process has caught and fired the imagination of potters and public alike.

Perhaps it is a reaction against the precisions required by porcelain that makes Raku so rewarding. A much greater play with the unknown makes the outcome unpredictable. The direct handling of live flame fires the pyromaniac imagination to experiment. Some results are disastrous, others magical.

It is a gamble that appeals to emotions more than to rational intellect, and teaches us what to recognise as 'life' in a pot, the criterion that all art should have.

It is not pottery by the kiln load but pots fired individually. It therefore has a closer affinity to fine art values consistent with the general ceramic trend of the day. It fulfils the innovative urge in the modern spirit that is not necessarily satisfied by the results of skilled repetitive making.

I was fortunate to be in on the first introduction of Raku to the West from Japan where its first seed was sown at the end of the 16th century by the Emperor Hideyoshi after his conquest of Korea. It was brought to England in 1920 by my father Bernard Leach and Shoji Hamada. I have been privileged to be allowed to provide the bones of a chapter on this early experience at St Ives. The second Raku invasion came 40 years later from California via Paul Soldner who introduced the post-firing reduction techniques not practised by the Japanese.

Soldner once said, 'Not another book on Raku!' Well, yes, another book on Raku but one with a difference. There have been other books which have had clear and comprehensive technical sections and which have covered the early history of the subject. However, what makes this book so different and so interesting is its emphasis on the maker as an expressive individual.

In this book Tim Andrews has gathered the work of some 50 like-minded international Raku potters and explored their personal statements, motivations and methods. He offers an insight into the characters of the potters themselves as well as their work – how they integrate in their work an underlying way of life or philosophy of living. There is a recognisable thread that is common to the approach of most Raku potters and conveys the strength of this contemporary ceramic movement in the last decades of this century.

The historical and technical chapters are clear and comprehensive. In addition a range of more personal techniques are described under the headings of the various potters.

Tim's enthusiasm for Raku shines throughout the whole book and I am sure the reader will also be caught up in the magic of Raku.

This is a most readable book which should have a wide appeal to teachers, students, connoisseurs and collectors alike.

David Leach

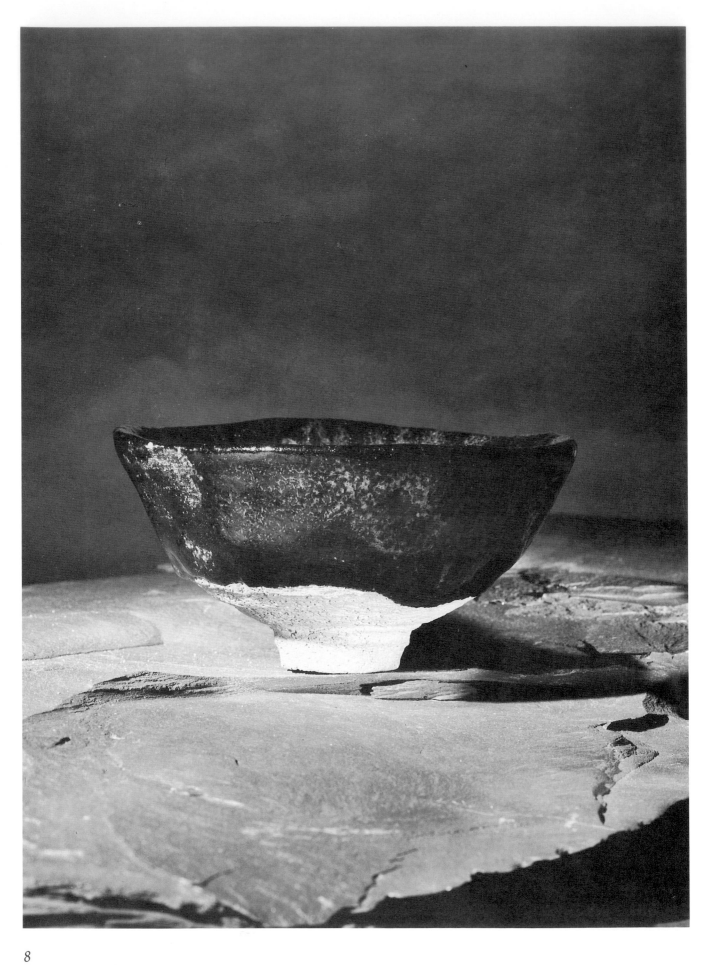

RAKU - ITS MEANING AND HISTORY

What's in a name?

The name 'Raku' first appeared in 16th-century Japan when it was bestowed by the emperor Hideyoshi upon Jokei, the son of a Korean immigrant potter living in Kyoto. The raku character, originally taken from the Chinese, was inscribed on a presentation gold seal. Roughly translated it meant contentment, enjoyment, pleasure and also 'the best in all the world'. It paid homage to the work of Jokei's father Chojiro who had been chosen by the influential tea master Sen-no-Rikyu to produce wares of refined simplicity for the Zen Buddhist tea ceremony.

For over 400 years the raku name has been passed down through successive generations of the family or to esteemed students of the tradition who became 'adopted sons'. Some of the most highly respected potters through the centuries have been Donyu (third generation), Sanyu (sixth) and Ryonu (ninth). The youngest in the dynastic succession and the present 'Mr Raku' – Kichiemon – is the 15th generation.

Recent history has seen the raku name assimilated by and attached firmly to the work of Western artists, and so has arisen some difficulty with its use. In a now famous craft conference held in Kyoto in 1979 a heated debate sprang up between the American potters, Paul Soldner and Rick Hirsch, and the present Mr Raku, who maintained that only he had the right to call his work 'raku' under the emperor's ancient 'patent'. It is an important point that the name 'raku' to this man was not, as is perceived in the West, a title or description of a particular technique, but the name attached to the potter producing such ware. Therefore, logically any work by other craftsmen should

Black raku tea bowl, mark Raku 19th century, d. 13.6 cm.
The seal is that of the 10th generation, Tanyu (1795–1854).
Reproduced by courtesy of the Trustees of the British Museum.

be made under their own names i.e. Soldner ware or Hirsch ware. Facing the daunting prospect of locking antlers with a man with hundreds of years of Japanese culture behind him, Soldner himself suggested a solution. As many things in America seemed to be done in an opposite way to Japan then why not call the work 'Ukar', the opposite of 'Raku'.

Unfortunately, Soldner was by then too late as the name 'raku' had, for better or worse, already entered the language of potters and indeed that of the wider appreciative public. It is important to remember however, that whilst acknowledging the influence of the Japanese, the varied techniques of American-style raku – many of which are shown in this book – are somewhat different to those practised in Japan for centuries.

Japan and Raku

To understand something of Japanese raku and the influences by which it came about, it is worth trying briefly to set it in an historical and political context. Going back into pre-history, the Japanese people, like so many other cultures were hunter-gatherers. For 10,000 years they lived in much the same way – a nomadic people who roamed the forests and mountains, the rivers and the coast. Pottery-making was widespread during this early period and consisted of coiled, low-fired unglazed ware simply decorated with incised marks and later a cord pattern. The rims would often have four raised peaks – [an undulating rim with five peaks is also a feature of much later raku chawans (tea bowls)]. Recent archaeological excavations near Nagasaki have produced pots which have been carbon-dated to around 10,000 BC – which makes them the oldest pots in the world yet discovered.

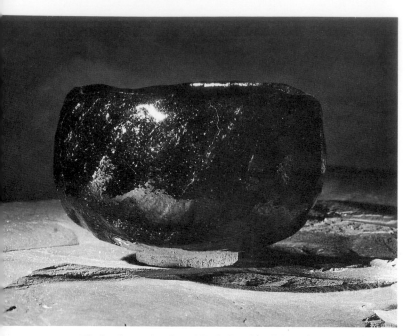

Black raku tea bowl, seal 'Raku' and 'Koki', 19th century, d. 11.4 cm.
The seal is that of the 9th generation, Ryonyu (1756–1834) and the inscription Koki was used by him after his 70th year.

Many of the arts which make up the cultural identity of Japan today – flower arranging, Nō theatre, calligraphy, ink-painting, architecture and the tea ceremony – were established at this time.

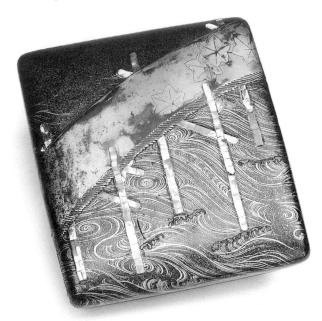

Japanese black and brown lacquer writing box with gold makie and lead and shell inlay, 23 × 20.5 × 4.5 cm.
The design is of the Koetsu School and is inspired by a classical poem.

A sudden worsening in the Japanese climate brought the population down to settle on the flat land between the mountains and the sea. There they turned to agriculture and a more permanent lifestyle. It is thought that the advent of bronze and iron manufacture at about this time along with the limited living space available, encouraged the emergence of the first warring states which were eventually to become dominant.

Strong influences from China and Eastern Asia over the next few hundred years brought about great changes in Japan. Technological advances and the adoption of the Chinese system of writing along with the introduction of Buddhism and other religious traditions were eagerly absorbed. There arose a scholarly aristocracy of Buddhist priests and a nobility which ruled Japan for more than two centuries.

Eventually dissatisfaction with the ruling hierarchy led to the emergence and dominance of provincial Samurai warriors who, from the 12th century, seized power under a military command led by the Shoguns. Internal power struggles between rival warlords made this an unsettled period in Japanese history. Later centuries (AD 1300–1550) saw continued fighting but also the rise of Zen Buddhism which became the dominant cultural force. Enthusiastically embraced by the Samurai, the influence of Zen was far-reaching.

The tea ceremony and Raku

The importance of the Japanese tea ceremony, or of the 'Way of Tea' (*Sadō*) – which embraces the philosophical and religious thinking behind the ritual – is difficult for a non-Japanese to appreciate. However, from AD 1550–1850 it was by far the most important influence on Japanese culture and even today its tenets are widely studied and highly regarded by many in Japan. The name 'tea ceremony' is actually an English invention – the original custom was a relaxed affair simply called *Cha-no-yu* or 'Hot water for tea' and it probably acquired its ceremonial connotations when later it was formalised into a more stylised ritual.

The religious and cultural roots of *Sadō* – the way of tea – stem from Zen Buddhism. The simplicity and austerity of Zen was attractive to the Samurai classes who had rejected the ostentatious trappings of the imperial court. It also related well with the pursuit of personal enlightenment which was encouraged through military discipline and an emphasis on an expertise with weaponry.

In the Zen Buddhist temples of China, tea drinking was considered by the monks to aid meditation. The simple bowls used for this were much appreciated by the Japanese who soon began to copy them for their own use. Throughout the 15th century Zen spread widely in Japan, penetrating more and more into secular, as well as religious, culture. Tea ceremony began to assume importance with the building of the first tea house (*chashitsu*) by the Shogun Yoshimasa. The practice of *Cha-no-yu* consequently became a mark of high fashion and good taste for the elite.

The rôle of the tea masters was all important. They attended to every detail from the design of the tea house to the choice of vessels and utensils. They also were responsible for setting the mood of the ceremony itself and its peripheral activities. Above all, the desired objective was to achieve an integrated harmony of all the physical elements in a peaceful atmosphere for the chosen guests.

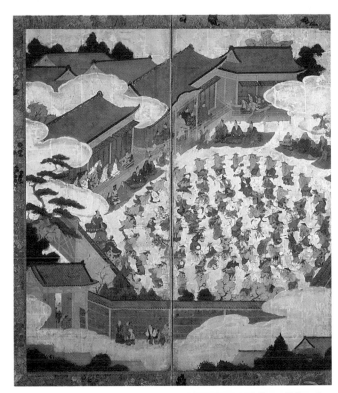

Red raku tea bowl with buff pine tree on the side. The seal is that of the 9th generation, Ryonyu (1756–1834), d. 12.6 cm and black glazed tea bowl with buff form of Mt. Fuji on the side. Mark 'Dohachi', 19th century, d. 12.2 cm.
The latter bowl is by the versatile potter, Takahashi Dohachi (1795–1854), who also made Kyoto-style enamelware.
Reproduced by courtesy of the Trustees of the British Museum.

Sixfold screen; ink, colours and gold leaf on paper, 103 × 216 cm. This screen of the Kano School comes from the early 17th century Edo period and depicts scenes of Kyoto city life. *Reproduced by courtesy of the Trustees of the British Museum.*

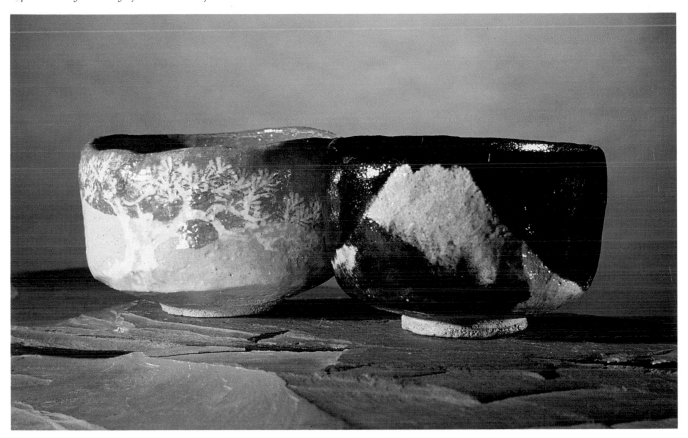

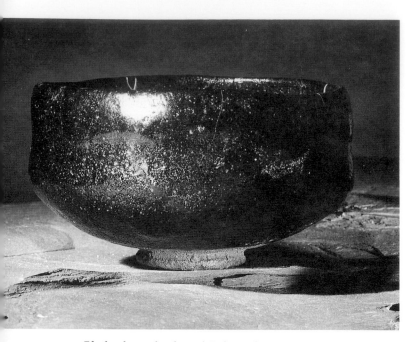

Black raku tea bowl, mark Raku 17th century, d. 12.5 cm.
The bowl has been repaired with gold lacquer. The seal is
that of the 4th generation Ichinyu (1640–1696).
Reproduced by courtesy of the Trustees of the British Museum.

Perhaps the greatest of the tea masters was Sen-no-Rikyu (AD 1522–91). It was he who established the concept of *'wabi'* which is loosely translated as austerity or simplicity. The spirit of wabi and its many nuances was sought by Rikyu in his choice of tea ware – tea bowls (*chawans*), water-jars (*mizusashis*) and the tea caddy (*chaire*). Imported Chinese tenmoku tea bowls were replaced at first with Korean pots which were prized for their simplicity but it was Rikyu who then commissioned Chojiro to make the raku ware which he felt best represented the idea of wabi and was most befitting for tea ceremony use. Since that time many other types of ceramics have been used for tea ware including Shino, Oribe and Bizen pots, but there is an old Japanese saying: 'Raku first, Hagi second, Karatsu third.' That is, only raku ware possesses all the qualities looked-for in the perfect tea bowl.

Early Western Raku

The first introduction of raku to the West came via Bernard Leach. In his famous *Potter's Book* he describes being taken to a garden party which included a tea ceremony and also participation in a raku firing: his first pottery experience, in Tokyo in 1911.

David Leach here describes some of his father's experiences in Japan and subsequent raku firings in St Ives:

Bernard in Japan

In 1911 in Japan, Bernard Leach was taken to a tea ceremony. In the first place, one wonders why my father went there. Was it an invitation from Yanagi who thought that the tea ceremony would provide an interest for him? I guess, mainly along Zen lines, the pursuit of the inquiry was nothing whatever to do with pottery, but with a greater knowledge of the part the tea ceremony played in Zen thinking. Therefore, I think it was a considerable surprise to my father to find part of the afternoon's activity involved an itinerant raku potter. All the guests were invited to participate in the decoration of unglazed raku pots in the Japanese manner, mostly consisting of characters, forming perhaps a poem or verse.

My father, confronted with this opportunity, and without any knowledge of Japanese characters, felt the best thing to do was something decorative along the lines of his earlier artistic training. So he decorated one or two raku bowls which were fired in the course of the afternoon. I think it is interesting to remember that his very first introduction to pottery appreciation and direct experience was this one with raku. After the pots had been decorated, they were taken away and dipped into a bucket of some white creamy substance, to his horror completely obliterating the decoration he had painstakingly made.

At the time he knew nothing about the technique, and he says somewhere in his writings that he took this to mean that they didn't appreciate his work, and that it was just rubbed out. However, shortly the pots were warmed over a kiln – one imagines a type of portable raku kiln, probably wood or charcoal fired – inserted and fired to raku temperature. After half an hour or so the kiln was opened and the pots drawn out with tongs, red hot. After cooling in the air (no post-reduction was used), the pattern under a shiny glaze reappeared. It must have been a very startling process to him – here were these pots now considerably altered. The colours had changed, he had painted onto a rough, matt, white-slipped clay surface and they were coming out shiny and colourful. But I don't think for a moment that the bowls were highly prized and a bit special, the raku episode was just a recreational aspect of the afternoon.

We haven't very much direct information about what kind of people Bernard was mixing with, except that my father's close association with Yanagi was leading him into a young artist's group that was becoming interested in Western art. Yanagi must have felt it was an occasion on which my father would not only get some insight into the tea ceremony and its Zen associations but also give him an opportunity to meet kindred young Japanese artists.

The experience was completely novel to him and very exciting, and being a person very quickly taken by enthusiasm (then much more than later on in life), he wanted to follow it up immediately. After the tea ceremony, and after this performance he went back to Yanagi, said that he was very attracted by what he had experienced that afternoon, and asked if he could find out more about pottery. Yanagi was instrumental in introducing him to Ogata Kenzan.

Kenzan was a dynastic title passed from teacher to student and this Kenzan was sixth in line of descent and was a raku potter himself. He agreed to accept Bernard as a student for a year. Bernard had already made the acquaintance of Tomimoto who had spent some time in England, and both of them worked together with Kenzan in his pottery. This was 1910–11 and Bernard was about 24. Kenzan and his forebears were known for their raku. It is highly probable therefore that his training would have been in raku technique. Some of our slides and photographs from that period are of raku. Ultimately Kenzan conferred on Bernard the honour of succeeding him as the seventh Kenzan – Bernard being the first non-Japanese ever to receive it. It is thought that Kenzan was highly criticised for making this decision and the title subsequently lost recognition in Japan.

The year with Kenzan ended in 1911 or 1912. Bernard had married my mother in 1910 and I was born in May 1911. In those very early years exchanges with the Japanese were mostly among art students – my father encouraged by Yanagi associated with them, my mother taught some of them English. This was all before any pottery activity. He was getting more and more involved with them and with Yanagi, with a lot of exchanges in thinking and writing. My father wrote his very

Brush decorated raku tray from the collection of Bernard Leach attributed by him to the first Kenzan, 20.5 × 12.5 × 2.5 cm. By kind permission of David Leach.

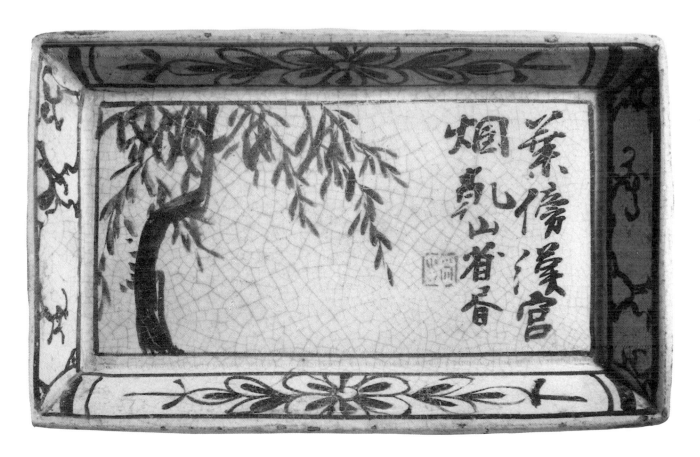

early reminiscences *An English Artist in Japan* in 1912–14.

My brother Michael was born in 1913, but by 1914–15 we had moved to China as a family and my sister Eleanor was born in 1915 in Peking. In China he had an association with a Dr Westharp, a German art philosopher, rather theoretic and very Germanic, whose writings Yanagi had read, forming his own conclusions about Westharp. Due to Yanagi's advice and his own disillusionment with Dr Westharp, Bernard decided to go back to Japan and to pottery. Yanagi had offered him a place on his own estate. So, around 1916–17 he was back in Japan starting up a pottery making stoneware. He must have made some degree of technical study and had some help from others.

I believe Hamada first appeared at one of my father's exhibitions about 1918. It's very likely that my father had an exhibition in Tokyo following one or two firings in the new pottery around 1917. Hamada as a student, encouraged by Yanagi, was very taken with Bernard's work and wanted to meet him and come to England. One must remember that Hamada was eight years younger. He was, I gather, a very promising student at one of the Tokyo technical schools of pottery. Hamada eventually came to England with Bernard and his family to start up the Leach pottery. They had a few raku firings there together from 1920–23 and some of the first firings of stoneware pottery, before Hamada went back to Japan in 1923.

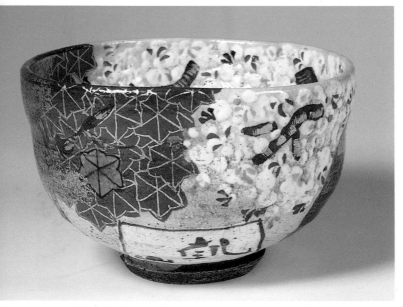

Raku bowl.
Courtesy of Bonhams.

Raku sessions at St Ives

Five years after setting up the pottery in 1920, funds were beginning to dry up and little had yet been done towards its marketing. Hamada and my father began to realise the tourist value of St Ives in the summer, and felt that raku might be the thing to draw visitors to the pottery for one afternoon a week. They decided to use an existing kiln and firing – a slipware firing started in the early morning by George Dunn. He was the general factotum at the pottery, not a potter himself but a general assistant. He would start the firing at 7 or 8 am and by 2 pm, the temperature would reach 800°C (raku temperature). Leaflets were sent to the tourist hotels and boarding houses, and Abraham Curnow, the town crier, helped on the morning of the demonstration by parading up and down St Ives with his sandwich board and bell shouting:

> Oyez! Oyez! Leach Pottery demonstration this afternoon at two o'clock. All visitors invited. Paint your own pots. Take them away at the end of the day. Teas a shilling.

This was a new experiment in St Ives. Expecting between 20 and 30 visitors, we had to organise some suitable biscuit-fired pieces in readiness. I remember making batches of pots to be used for these afternoons, little shallow dishes, ashtrays and bowls, little bottle vases. They were priced and displayed on shelves for the visitors to choose from. The workshop itself was arranged with banding wheels, pigments and brushes on tables at which a person could sit and decorate his chosen piece.

My father initiated the helpers in colours and thicknesses, and the use of brushes, so we were at least a lap ahead of the visitors. None of us was really expert at all. The pigments were about four or five in number, some of which were prepared from recipes my father had first obtained from Japan. The simple glaze used for dipping the pots after decoration was a composition of mostly China clay, with lead and probably some silica (flint). The raku glaze recipes used now probably had their origins at that time.

The visitors were coming for an experience that probably none of them had had before. Guidance would be given for decoration, how to use the brush, the colours that could be expected from the pigments, density of application. Eventually they

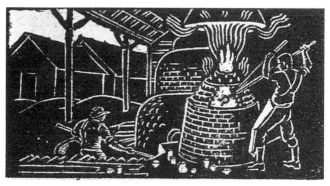

Print by Bernard Leach showing raku firing at St Ives. Copies of the print – taken possibly from a lino cut – were sent out as Christmas cards to family and friends and date from around 1930. Bernard Leach is shown extracting the hot ware from the top of the kiln with long-handled tongs whilst George Dunn stokes the firebox with wood. Finished pots can be seen cooling by the kiln.
Courtesy of Mrs. M. Leach. Photograph by Peter Harper.

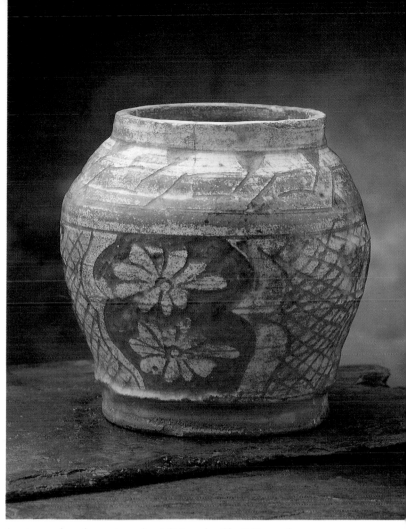

A very early raku pot made at St Ives by Shoji Hamada around 1922. Around 7" high, the pot was thrown from St Erth red clay mixed with sand. It was then brushed with a light ball clay slip and the decoration scratched through. When bisque fired, a white-lead glaze was applied and the pot was then rakued and cooled in the air. This was one of the first raku pots ever to be made in the West.
Collection of David Leach. Photograph by Peter Harper.

would succeed in putting something on their pots and quite surprise themselves. When enough decorated pots had been accumulated they were taken to the kiln where my father would be waiting. The pots were dipped in a big bucket of white opaque glaze, completely covering the decoration, and then dried-off on top of the kiln.

The main body of the kiln was filled with slip-ware (eventually to be heated to a temperature of about 1050° C). A chamber had been left at the top to hold the raku pots. It was a domed updraught kiln, with flames running out through the top. Two or three bricks were removable for access. Firing time would be about 20 minutes to half an hour for each batch, just long enough for the

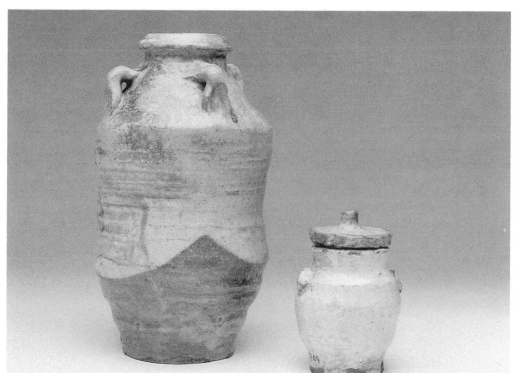

Both items red earthenware clay, cream slip under milky glaze. Impressed with Japanese character for Shoji Hamada. Made at St Ives 1921. Paper label on large jar reads:
    Bernard Leach
    1st Baking
    B. 320. Hamada
    Oct. 11, 1921
The Bergen Collection,
City Museum and Art Gallery,
Stoke-on-Trent.

15

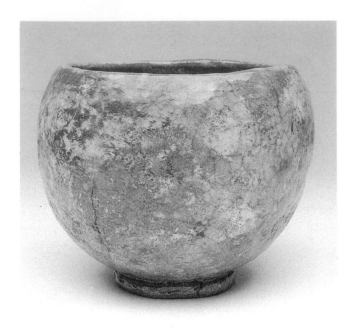

Tea bowl by Dr Henry Bergen, 1920s.
Raku bowl with orange and white surface made at the St Ives Pottery.
The Bergen Collection, City Museum and Art Gallery, Stoke-on-Trent.

visitors to go off and have their tea, provided by my mother in the pottery showroom. Tea was quite substantial, considering it was only a shilling, and included saffron buns from Mrs Penburthy down at the Stennack, rock buns baked the previous morning, splits and cream.

After tea, the pots were taken out of the kiln red hot and put into open saggars on the ground to cool. This was the exciting part. As the pots cooled, the decoration revealed itself through the now transparent outer glaze. Meanwhile another batch would be coming through from the next group. This process would be repeated three to six times throughout the afternoon. In these early days of raku-firing, the pots, when drawn from the oxidising kiln, were left to cool in an oxidising atmosphere. Sometimes to bring out the crackle, umber mixed with oil on a rag was rubbed on to the cooling pot. The practice of putting the red-hot pot into a dustbin of leaves or combustible sawdust was not introduced by my father and Hamada. The introduction to England of reduction came much later from the influence of Paul Soldner and others in the mid-1950s from America.

The new raku experience at the pottery stimulated people to return the following week, sometimes bringing their own designs to try out. It was just as exciting for the potters. At the end of each day we would decorate a few ourselves to use as examples for the following week. I don't think there was any great financial return on these sessions. Twenty to 25 participants generated sales of not more than £20–£30. I doubt whether the takings amounted to more than £40 in a day, although in 1925 that was quite a lot.

My father's activity always centred around the kiln, and his concentration was very much taken up by it. Dipping and warming the pots, loading them into the kiln, putting in rods to test whether reflections showed the glaze had melted, checking whether the glaze was mature enough. Sometimes he would take them out, find they were not to his satisfaction, and put them back again. It was a fairly hot occupation standing over a kiln with flames coming out. I remember him getting very sweaty and hot. I should imagine that the moment the pots were in the kiln and the bricks put back, he would dash off for a cup of water, and probably a little bit of washing to get the sweat and soot off his face.

As it was wood-fired, the stoking was mostly done by George Dunn, and sometimes by me. The firing was helped by a paraffin drip, which assisted the continuity of the flames and maintained a steady heat level. The raku period of the firing required a constant heat of 800° C for two to three hours, without a rising temperature. This was monitored by eye, and with the help of a ceramic cone which melts at the right temperature – pyrometers were hardly thought of in those days. Some students around at that time included Michael Cardew, Nora Braden, Katherine Pleydell-Bouverie (Beano) and Sylvia Fox Strangeways.

Early UK Raku

Raku firings at the Leach Pottery ceased around the mid-1930s and there then appears to be a gap of nearly 20 years before any further activity took place in Britain. Harry Horlock Stringer writes about John Bew, a man with 'ceramically sensitive nostrils', who, in 1952 demonstrated the technique in a department store in Kingston on Thames, Surrey, pulling pots out of an electric kiln 'like rabbits out of a hat, to the delight of onlookers who had previously decorated bisqued pots'.

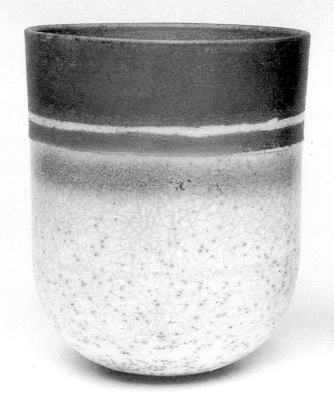

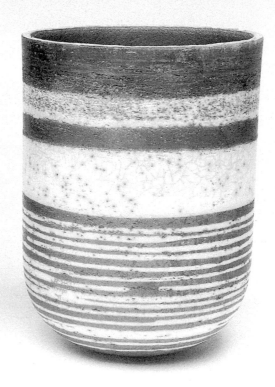

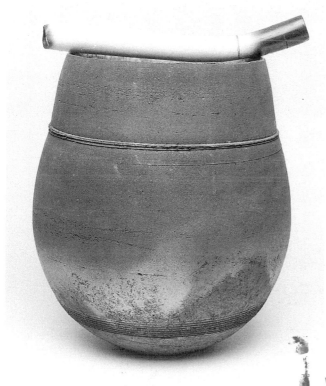

Two jars by Robin Welch, Stradbroke, Suffolk, 1979.
Raku, white glazes with shaded blue line on taller one.
City Museum and Art Gallery, Stoke-on-Trent.

The mid- to late-1950s saw Murray Fieldhouse and David Lane experiment for the first time at Pendley along with Arthur Griffiths at Loughborough College and Harry Stringer in London. All the raku at this time was fully oxidised and it was not until John Reeves came to England from Canada in 1964 that post-firing reduction was introduced. Reeves' influence was felt when he joined Farnham art college where John Chalke first became involved. John Chalke was one of the few potters who began to take raku seriously at that time. Experimenting with a modified domestic copper boiler in his kitchen, a bemused neighbour couldn't understand why the party wall was becoming so hot and cracked!

The late 1960s slowly saw a spreading interest in Britain with potters such as Walter Keeler and Rosemary Wren leading the way and preparing the ground for the rush of young talent which was to come.

Vessel by Ian Pirie, Aberdeen, 1984.
Raku with porcelain tube, interior glaze white and pale green.
City Museum and Art Gallery, Stoke-on-Trent.

17

Early Raku in the USA

In America it is thought that Warren Gilbertson was the first potter to make raku. Having worked for two years in Japan, in 1940 he returned to the US and was invited to stage an exhibition in Chicago. It seems likely that some of his raku pieces would have been shown there. Gilbertson also presented a paper in 1942 describing the raku technique to the American Ceramic Society but, rather like Bernard Leach, he did not take the method too seriously and treated it more as a novelty to interest amateurs. Sadly, he died in a car accident in 1954.

The years between 1940 and 1960 are not well-documented regarding raku. Certainly some activity was taking place, it would seem mostly in teaching environments. Using Leach's *A Potter's Book*, which was published in 1940, small groups of potters began to experiment. Hal Riegger in California was making traditional tea-ware in the late 1940s, and at roughly the same time Jean Griffith and others were firing and indeed smoking raku at Washington University and Calton Ball was also trying out the process in Oakland. These potters and no doubt some others preceded and overlapped the activities of Paul Soldner (although he was unaware of them at the time) and so we should not ignore their contribution to rise of US raku.

Paul Soldner and the advent of American-style Raku

The genesis of American-style raku as we know it today arguably began with Paul Soldner in 1960. I say arguably because it cannot be separated from the wider context of art and ceramics at that time. The postwar era saw the American economy booming, and with it came a self-confidence in home-produced art – Europe no longer provided the benchmark against which all art was to be judged. Standards which had been adhered to for decades were being questioned by an empowered youth culture which, for the first time, became a major influence in society.

Painting was in the vanguard of the arts. In particular, abstract expressionism was achieving respect and recognition from mainstream institutions and influential bodies. Jackson Pollock

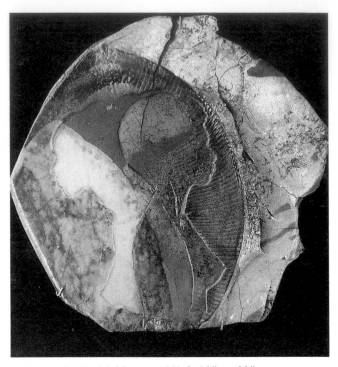

Wall piece by Paul Soldner, c. 1969, h. 23", w. 20".
Bas relief figure, 'Black is Beautiful', low-fired, smoked raku, slips, stains and glaze.

was one of the early initiators of the style which drew, interestingly, on the Zen Buddhist tenet of personal enlightenment achieved through spontaneous impulse. The notion of art as a performance was born.

New and dynamic literature too was emerging from the pens of mould-breaking writers such as J.D. Salinger (*The Catcher in the Rye*). In music, Elvis Presley and others were already leading the rock-and-roll explosion – the Beatles were still to come – again the performers themselves taking on as important a rôle as their music.

In ceramics, Peter Voulkos was a rising star of the US. His appointment in 1954 to head the graduate programme at the Los Angeles County Art Institute had far-reaching consequences. Voulkos was given a free hand to establish and build the programme from scratch. A dynamic figure, he insisted that the department should be kept open 24 hours a day, creating an innovative environment for potters who were encouraged to take chances and to explore uncharted waters.

The first of these trail-blazing students was Paul Soldner. Already 33, and a few years older than Voulkos, Soldner began by fitting out the studio, seeking out materials and building wheels etc. – out of this eventually arose the establishment of his successful equipment company.

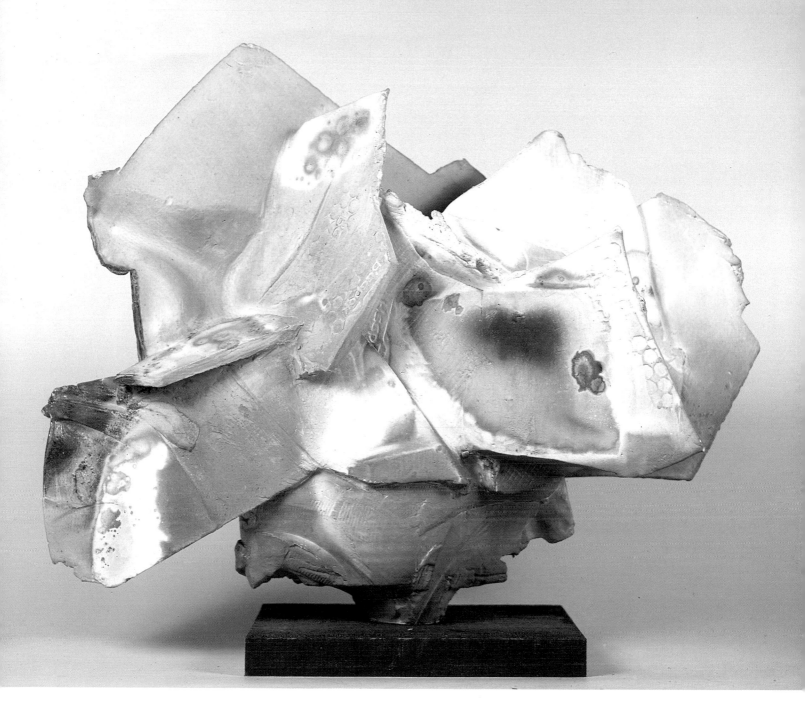

Pedestal piece by Paul Soldner, 27" × 30" × 11".
Thrown and altered with slips and low temperature salt.
Maier Collection, Scripps College, Claremont, California.

The pervading influence of sculptural abstraction and its promotion by Voulkos, coupled with the contemporary interest in the Zen principles of spontaneous expression, encouraged students to produce asymmetric freely-made forms. Soldner to an extent in his early work, bucked the trend and followed his own direction, choosing to make thrown, brush-decorated stoneware vases. Gradually becoming more inventive and intuitive, the pieces became larger and more imposing, culminating in a series of man-sized floor pots which made up his final MFA exhibition. After graduation Soldner took up a temporary appointment at Scripps College in Claremont.

The story of the first raku firings is now well-known and has entered the annals of American ceramic history. In the words of Paul Soldner:

I had read Bernard Leach's description and was intrigued by the subtlety of the raku teabowls that Leach spoke of and what seemed to be an exciting way to fire pots. This interest coincided with several other events which contributed to my first attempts at raku. Firstly I had begun to exhaust my interest in the large formal stoneware I had been making prior to 1960 and was looking around subconsciously for another direction. The other event was the necessity to demonstrate publicly some form of pottery entertainment. In previous years Scripps College would participate in the local Arts Festival in Claremont usually demonstrating throwing. The audiences loved it but we potters became bored. With only Leach's book as a guide I decided to try to make raku.

Building a small, portable gas kiln, the demonstration was a great success. Soldner delighted the audience as hot, glowing pots were pulled out of the kiln and the potters ran through the crowd finally dunking the ware into a fish pond.

> Unfortunately I misinterpreted some of the ideas about raku even jumping to the conclusion that the pots should be cooled in water. On subsequent visits to Japan I discovered that the Japanese never cool their pots in this way.

The first results were disappointing to Soldner. Many pots cracked and the colours appeared gaudy and unpleasant. Acting on a what he describes as a 'serendipitous hunch', he rolled the hot pots around in some leaves of a nearby pepper tree before fast cooling them. The effect was to modify some of the garishness with more muted colours and hints of oxide reduction. 'I was hooked because all of a sudden there was quality available.'

Extensive experimentation followed to mix-up a clay body which would survive the thermal shock and to find alternative glazes to the lead-based formulas in Leach's book. Many potters have benefited from this initial study and Soldner's standard glaze 80 per cent Gerstley borate and 20 per cent nephaline syenite has proved an excellent jumping off point for would-be rakuists.

Enjoying the freedom that raku offered, Soldner's work began to take a new direction, becoming smaller and more spontaneous. He became interested in the Japanese aesthetic and particularly that of asymmetrical balance. A visit from the Japanese potter Kanashinga also profoundly influenced Soldner who began to use clay in a more expressive and organic manner. Exploration of the vessel form, however, remained central to his thinking. In earlier years Voulkos had called

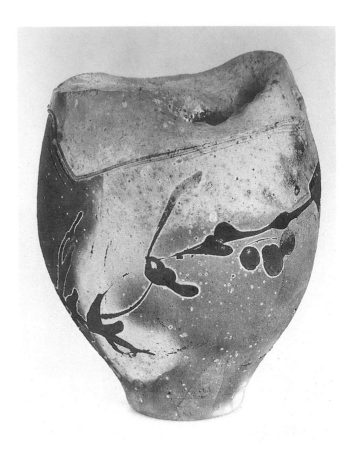

Vessel by Paul Soldner, c. 1970, h. 12". Black and white, unglazed.

into question the rôle of the vessel as a functional object and this idea was continued in Soldner's raku work. Thrown forms were increasingly distorted, trodden on, pulled apart and reconstructed often so that they at first glance no longer bore any resemblance to the original container.

Throughout the 1960s and 1970s his raku work continued to develop, gaining recognition in a ceramic world that for many years had been largely dominated by stoneware. A natural teacher, Soldner was in great demand to lecture about and demonstrate his 'go for it' techniques to others. His teaching programmes at Scripps College, and later at Aspen, Colorado and many places across the US and abroad, inspired a new generation of artists and established raku as a legitimate form of ceramic art.

Along with raku, Paul Soldner has investigated diverse low-fired techniques, many of which have involved salt. His recent work is more sculptural in character and has moved away from smoked raku – to explore the sensuous oranges, yellows, pinks and beiges achieved by bisque-firing the pieces in the presence of salt and fugitive copper in the kiln.

A few years ago occurred a memorable visit to Soldner's studio by David Leach. Paul Soldner explains:

… Accidentally David backed into one of my large, unfired sculures and it fell over and broke considerably. He was very upset at the time and I tried to assure him that it was no problem and that I could easily make a new one or change that one. As it turned out I did change it, modifying it from a vertical to a horizontal piece. When I fired it, it became the most beautiful pink of almost all the pieces I've done. It is now owned by a woman in Miami and it also travelled around the United States in my retrospective exhibition. That piece that David made is one of the best I ever made!

Paul Soldner's impact on American and world ceramics is hard to overstate and I do not have the space here to do more than scratch the surface of his contribution. In the practical field he has revolutionised pottery technology, designing and introducing new and innovative equipment. His development of raku and other techniques has opened up a fertile new territory in which potters can indulge their passion. He has challenged conventions and pushed back boundaries but without imposing his own dogma. He has taught much to many, instilling confidence and a spirit of curiosity. But perhaps his greatest contribution is his contagious energy and enthusiasm which he has shared generously for more than 40 years.

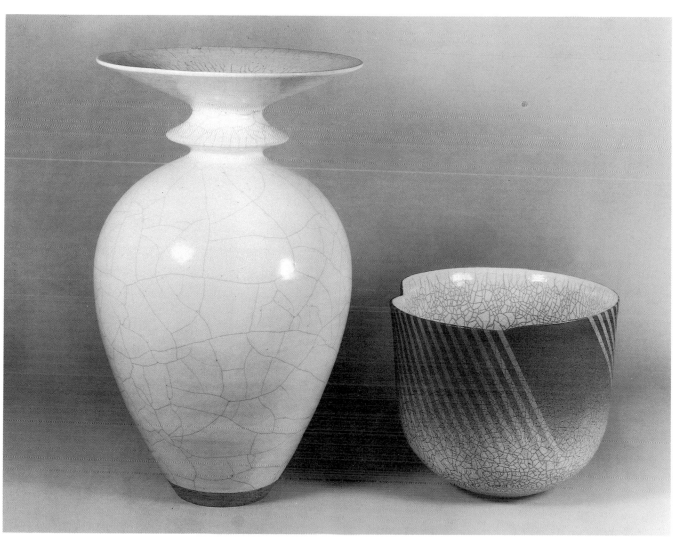

Large crackle glazed raku vase and deep bowl with linear decoration by David Roberts.

MATERIALS
AND TECHNIQUES

Raku clay

There is a popular myth that raku-fired pots inevitably have to be thick and heavy and made of highly grogged clay. This is not true! A quick perusal of the potters featured in this book will show a plethora of different clay bodies used by makers from around the world. Anything from earthenware to porcelain bodies can work, and it is really a matter of finding the clay which will serve your own needs and your own style of work.

Of course, some clays will withstand the shock of rapid heating and cooling better than others and generally these tend to have an open structure achieved by the addition of grog or sand, and are porous after both the bisque and the glaze firings. There are many prepared bodies sold as 'raku' clay but these are just bodies which will perform reasonably well under raku conditions – other clays (particularly stoneware bodies) will do equally well and may suit your own work better.

When choosing a clay, survivability is not the only criterion. The working properties, plasticity, texture etc., as well as colour after firing, are also important considerations. A sandy refractory body may be fine for handbuilding but not plastic enough for throwing, and a rich, dark clay may not be right for taking brightly coloured underglaze decoration or achieving a contrast with the smoke. It's a matter of personal choice.

Bisque firing (biscuit firing)

When trying out or mixing your own clay, it is important to consider the bisque firing. In many cases the glaze firing temperature will be lower than the bisque, so, ideally you need a clay which will be hard enough at bisque temperature to give the pot some finished strength, but porous enough to withstand the fast expansion and contraction of the process. Many potters find that a relatively high bisque-temperature of 1050°C or thereabouts is satisfactory – much higher than that and the clay is not 'soft' enough to take the heat shock.

(See profile of Wayne Higby on page 135.)

Losses

All potters expect to lose a proportion of their work and have to find an acceptable balance of losses against desired results. For some, sheer economics forces the use of a more tolerant clay. For instance to choose a porcelain clay body for very wide, shallow forms is asking for trouble. Others, however, accept a greater rate of failures in order to achieve the occasional gems only possible with a particular clay recipe.

To an extent, working practices can be adapted to minimise the risks of the pots cracking when raku-firing. This is often done anyway with particularly large or difficult pieces. A slower rise in kiln temperature and cooling in the reduction chamber may be all that is needed. Martin Mindermann, the German potter, leaves his giant pots overnight to cool in a covered, sawdust-filled hole in the ground. I have found that some disasters can be caused by the wrong use of tongs (grabbing vulnerable parts of a piece of work in the heat of the moment!) and I often now lift pots out of the kiln with gloved hands and a damp scarf covering what's left of my hair!

(A cautionary note – in the interests of safety I would advocate the use of tongs if at all possible together with the wearing of a proper fireproof body suit and helmet!)

Some popular clay bodies

T-material

Many potters in the UK and Europe are now using a clay body known as T-material. Particularly suitable for raku, it is a good handbuilding and throw-

keting is deceptive, and many potters become extremely frustrated at the difficulties they encounter. Crawling, pinholing and shelling of the glaze are some common problems. It is true that unless you are a purist it is hardly worth trying to make up your own recipes from scratch, but you may have to adapt some colours to overcome any troubles and to suit your own needs. Also, shop around and try colours from various suppliers – they are not all the same. I do not propose to itemise or explain in detail the various merits of different colours here. There is really no substitute for individual testing. There are, however, one or two general points which are worth a mention.

First of all, a good application technique is crucial to success. Colours can be mixed up with water but the product *Universal Medium* is generally favoured. Most colours contain some clay and consequently work best when brushed on to the raw pot and then bisque-fired. Make sure that the pot is free of greasy fingerprints (the use of handcream can cause crawling). Judging the correct thickness of application is very tricky. The thinner the better as a rule but avoid streaky brush marks as these may show up later. The majority of colours will tolerate firing temperatures up to 1080°C but a few (such as some of the lilacs) tend to disappear if over-fired. You will have to test for a range of colours to suit your normal kiln temperature.

If you do have problems with peeling or shelling, try mixing a little of your raku glaze with the colour, and brush it onto the pot after the bisque-firing.

Onglaze lustres and enamels

These commercially-produced colours may be applied to raku work which has been pre-fired but not reduced; lustres and enamels need a firing temperature of around 700–750°C which would burn off any carbonation present.

Also, at this temperature the raku base glaze begins to soften and this may cause some alteration of the materials. Glazed surfaces must be spotlessly clean for the application of enamels and lustres. Lustres may also be applied directly onto unglazed burnished clay, but will require several coats as it soaks into the porous body.

If post-firing reduction is desired, remember that the enamel temperature may not be hot enough to produce heavy smoking.

Warning – *The prepared metal lustres come suspended in a highly toxic medium and must only be used in well-ventilated areas. The fumes produced during the firing are also toxic.*

Soluble salts

These are a range of chemicals – usually metal chlorides and nitrates – which produce lustrous surfaces when used in combination with a raku firing and post-firing reduction. Silver, gold and mother-of-pearl iridescence are some of a number of effects which can be achieved in a variety of ways. The following are some of the most common techniques:

1. Metal salts in glazes

Silver nitrate and/or bismuth subnitrate is commonly mixed into raku glazes together with soda ash which forms the metals into a thin layer on the surface of the glaze, producing lustrous gold, silver and iridescent blue colours under heavy reduction. Fortunately, only small quantities of these expensive chemicals are necessary (try additions of 1% of each material for tests). Silver nitrate is light sensitive (being the raw material for photography) so it should be added to a dry batch glaze just before use. Store any unused glaze out of the light in a sealed, opaque container.

2. Washes and sprays

Metal salts can also be applied as a wash or spray to the glazed surface before firing. Mix a few grams (5 or so) in a cup of hot water and apply shortly before heating (making sure that the pot has dried out thoroughly first). Chemicals such as stannous chloride (which is sensitive to the air and damp conditions), sulphates of barium, copper and iron, as well as silver and bismuth nitrates may be used for this.

3. Fuming

Perhaps the most dramatic technique is that of fuming. This is where metal salts are sprayed onto the molten glaze of a red-hot raku pot straight from the kiln. Extra control is the main advantage. Lustres may be applied to specific parts of the piece, areas can be cooled with a spray of water to arrest colour development, targeted reduction is also possible with the use of handfuls of sawdust or oil-soaked rags etc. Tin, iron and silver chlorides are other additives to try (they can be mixed up in solution as above).

4. Vapour fuming

Fuming may also be achieved by introducing the chemicals directly into the kiln during firing. The dry crystals of salts are simply placed near the pots with a spoon wired to a rod: larger quantities can be poured in using a piece of angle-iron as a chute. The chemicals will vary and experimentation is necessary to determine the right amounts to use. I would not recommend this method of fuming in an electric kiln as the elements will go into a terminal decline!

Warning – *These are nasty chemicals and can do you damage!*

Great care must be taken with the above techniques. All of the chemicals are poisonous to you and are corrosive to metals. Vapours, from the kiln and from hot-spraying the pots, are also poisonous. Always wear rubber gloves when handling solutions. Always wear a respirator, gloves and protective clothing when fuming and make sure that the chemicals are well labelled and stored out of harms way. Metal parts of spray guns etc. which come into contact with the solutions will be corroded so use a cheap garden sprayer or a painter's fixative spray with a compressor, and wash all equipment straight after use.

Copper matt

This technique is referred to in several of the featured potters sections (see also the jacket photograph). It is really a reversal of a standard raku glaze recipe. Instead of a base glaze with additions of colouring oxides, the oxide is the main ingredient here, and the frit is present purely to stick the metal onto the pot. Dramatic colour effects can be achieved by employing post-firing reduction and oxidation combinations, but even the most experienced practitioners regard the technique as somewhat hit-and-miss.

Eighty to 90 per cent copper oxide or copper carbonate to 10 to 20 per cent high-alkaline frit is the most common recipe. Colour development can be further advanced by additions of small percentages of red iron oxide, cobalt carbonate or manganese dioxide. Application to bisque-fired ware is best achieved by spraying (normal precautions should be taken for this), although pots may be dipped or brushed. It is important not to touch the surface after spraying as fingermarks will invariably show after firing.

The pots are heated to around 1000° C to mature the frit. Assessing the correct temperature is difficult with such a matt glaze so a pyrometer or another raku-glazed pot are helpful guides. A variety of post-firing techniques are favoured by potters. If the pots are drawn from the kiln and immediately reduced they will turn an all-over copper red colour. If the reduction bin is re-opened – partially re-oxidising the pots – a variation of colours is achieved: the degree of flashing is dependent on timing and temperature. This flashing of the copper seems to take place down to around 700°C, so another method is to shut down the burners and leave the pots in the kiln for a while to cool before moving them to the reduction chamber when they are no longer glowing. Consistency with these techniques is elusive – most potters are just grateful when it works well! Further alteration of the surface colour can be made by blasting the surface with a blow torch but the results often look contrived and there is quite a risk that the uneven heating will shatter the pot.

Some tips on reduction materials

Most of the usual combustibles work for reducing copper matt glazes but remember that you don't have a nice, shiny surface to clean off, so carbonation marks tend to be more permanent. One solution is to stand the hot pot on a thick bed of folded newspapers. Strategically placed sheets of newspaper can then be arranged around the pot to encourage flashing. Another idea is to construct a wire mesh cage to sit inside the reduction bin. Combustible material is put in the gap between the bin and the cage protecting the pot – which is placed in the middle. Glossy magazines contain chemicals which can also enhance colour development.

Kilns and firing

Thumb through any collection of pottery suppliers' catalogues and you will be besieged by pages of photographs of gleaming new kilns that would look more at home in orbit around the earth than in the average potter's studio. Amongst them is usually a small section under the heading 'raku kilns'. These are normally very small, round objects akin to silver-painted school wastepaper baskets. For the occasional enthusiast, or for sunny day fun activity, or as a test kiln, they are ideal; but the more serious practitioner – unless his work is extremely small – will often find them inadequate.

This is not to say that the potters featured in the following pages all have expensive, large, purpose-built kilns. Many of us are quite happy to recycle used oil-drums or dustbins, or throw a few bricks together to make a temporary structure. Indeed, any kiln which will fire up to the desired temperature reasonably quickly and will allow easy access to the red-hot ware will be suitable for raku. Cheap secondhand stoneware kilns can be ideal and may be given a second lease of life when only fired to the lower temperatures needed for raku.

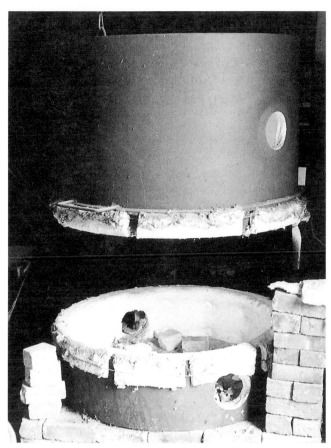

Fibre kiln with suspended chamber. Photograph from David Roberts.

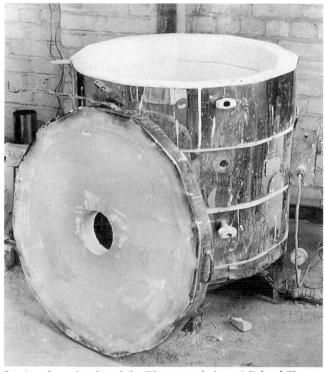

Sectional top-loading kiln. Photograph from Michael Flynn.

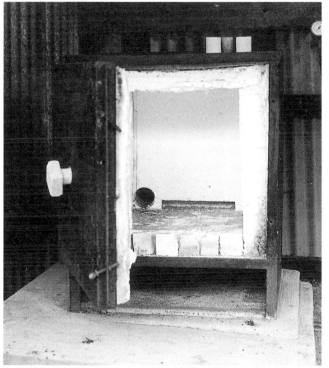

Small simple 'box' kiln – gas fired. Photograph from Anna Noël.

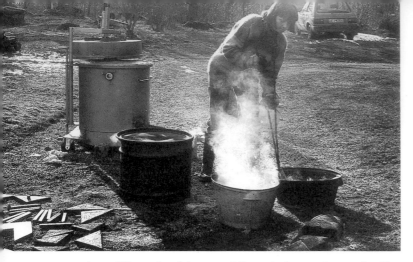

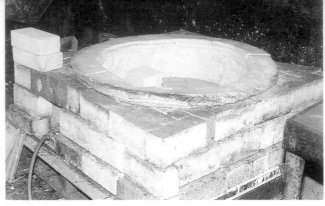

Jennie Hale and Andrew Osborne's raku kiln base – made from HTI bricks with ceramic fibre blanket lining.

Anna Eilert raku-firing a mobile variation on the top-loading fibre kiln. *Photograph by Astrid Eilert.*

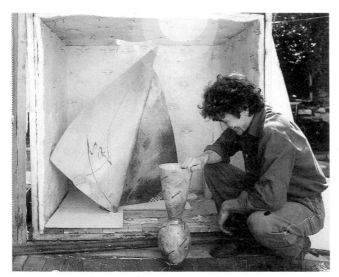

Large kiln, fibrefrax constructed, propane fired, used for bisque firing and occasionally for large raku work. Photograph from Chris Thompson.

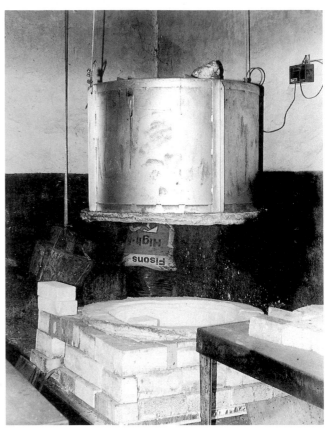

Jennie Hale and Andrew Osborne's kiln – a counterbalanced pulley system allows for easy access to the pots.

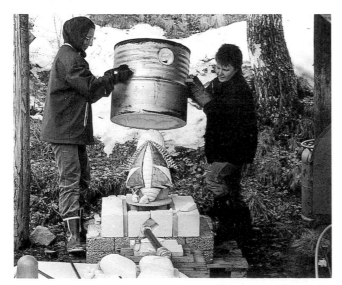

Lena Andersson loading her 'top hat' fibre kiln. *Photograph by Stig Andersson.*

Most kinds of fuels and burners may be used for firing. Oil, electricity, coal and charcoal are all acceptable. My own first pots were fired successfully in a baby electric test kiln. Electricity of course produces a very clean, oxidised firing without the possibility of atmospheric reduction unless you throw caution to the wind and introduce a few moth balls or other unpleasant substances, which tend rapidly to destroy expensive kiln elements. Wood-firing is traditional, economical if you have a cheap supply of wood, but relatively slow and labour intensive. It is favoured by many – especially raku purists – but gas, either

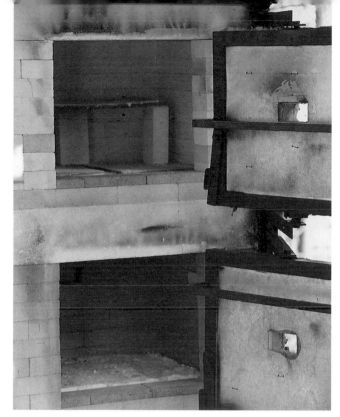

Two-chamber, sprung arch(es), updraft kiln – Penlands, North Carolina.

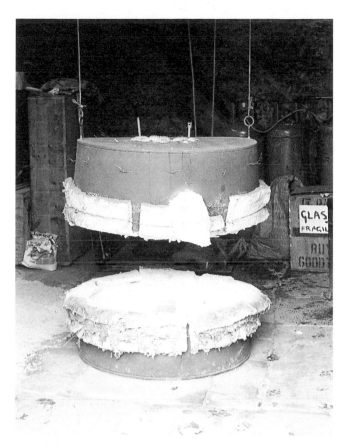

Fibre kiln with suspended lid for flat ware. Photograph from Dave Roberts.

propane or natural, is possibly the most widely used means of heating, being quick and easy – and also portable (in the case of bottled gas). For the full-time raku potter it is almost certainly the best option.

Having said that any kiln and any fuel will do, one of the joys and frustrations of the potter's life is the discovery that all kilns are different, will fire differently and produce different results. Your choice of kiln and the way you fire it therefore, will partly depend on the work you intend to make. There are no hard-and-fast rules to follow but some guidance may be found in the technical information sections of individual potters. In the end, with raku there is no substitute for trial, error and experience.

In this chapter on kilns I have not included lots of construction plans and methods of self-building various types of kilns. There are many extremely good 'how-to-do-it' books which give more information than I have space for here (see Bibliography, page 159).

The other kilns featured are mostly a selection of different types in use by artists across the world. Some designs are simple, some sophisticated. All serve the potters well and, very often, become 'cherished friends' in a partnership often of great disaster as well as triumph.

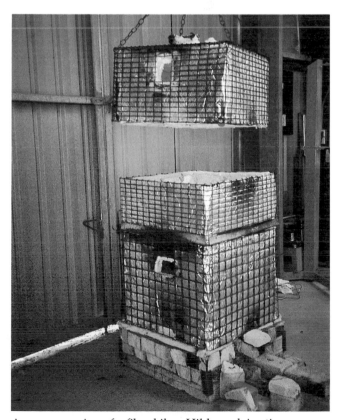

A square version of a fibre kiln – Hildegard Anstice.

Bruce Chivers' small fibre kiln was inspired by a visit from a refractories' company representative. Amongst the products for heavy industry, he spotted a cylindrical section of vacuum-formed ceramic fibre.

In Australia, fibre has been used for years instead of bricks but, until now, always in blanket form. This was new, rigid and dust-free – if painted with alumina wash.

A prototype was constructed and successfully tested over a long period under extreme reduction conditions. Initially intended just for his own use, Bruce soon realised that the kiln would appeal to potters generally: 'It's easy to construct, lightweight, and able to reach 1000°C in twenty minutes. Almost every potter who saw it demonstrated wanted one.'

The fibre sections have since been further developed using a higher alumina content. This enables the kilns to reach a temperature of 1430°C or 1300°C continuously, opening the obvious possibilities of stoneware temperature glazes.

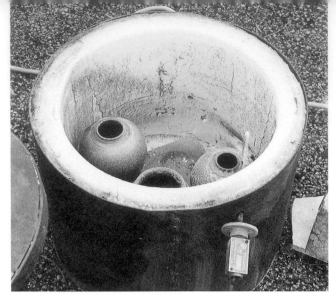

3. Pots are placed in the kiln – another small hole allows the use of a pyrometer.

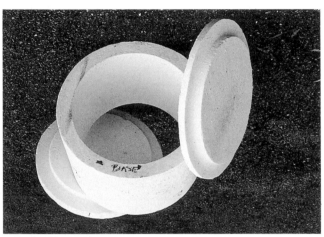

1. The base, lid and 'ring' of vacuum-formed ceramic fibre – other sections may be added to accommodate larger pieces.

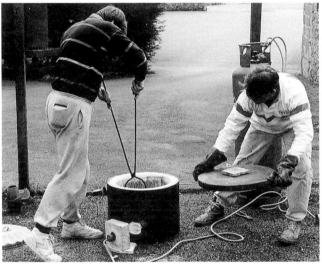

4. The kiln is fired to 1000°C with propane gas in only 15 minutes.

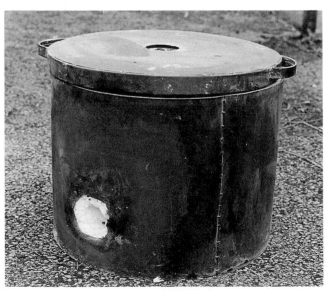

2. A sheet-metal case contains the fibre sections and a hole made as a burner port.

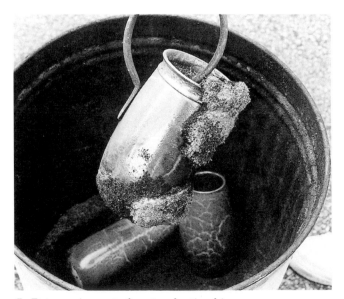

5. Pots coming out of post-reduction bin.

32

Firing techniques

Many of these are described in the second half of this book but here are just a few guidelines to successful firing.

1. Before you start, check the kiln – burners, fuel, pipework etc. (there may be a gas leak). If the kiln hasn't been fired for some time make sure that no animal has made a nest in it, and then warm it up (the kiln) to drive off any moisture which may have been absorbed by the fibre or soft brick.

2. Check safety equipment. Always have a bucket of water (except around an electric kiln) and a fire extinguisher to hand, along with your own gloves, mask etc. Keep the kiln area tidy and unobstructed and have a mental plan of action should the worst happen!

3. Prepare any reduction pit/chamber, making sure that you have a good supply of combustibles. Be ready with other post-firing treatments – for example, fuming chemicals.

4. Make sure that all pots are thoroughly dry before firing. It is quite a good idea to warm them on the kiln, prior to packing. Try not to glaze and fire the same day.

5. When packing the kiln remember to allow enough room for easy access to lift each pot with a pair of tongs. I have lost or damaged more pieces through knocking them over than for almost any other reason. Also, plan how you are going to remove the work, in what order, and exactly where the tongs will grip the pieces. Panic decisions of this nature, in (literally) the heat of the moment often lead to disaster.

6. Putting a large piece of work into a hot kiln is risky. Allow the temperature to drop to a more tolerable level before packing and stand the pot on a new, cool kiln shelf or brick, to avoid the base heating up rapidly.

7. Many potters fast-cool their work by dunking it into cold water. I do not subscribe to this method at all and have never understood the practice. If the idea is just to produce a result more rapidly, then I say have a little more patience. If, as I have been told, the water 'freezes the reduction and prevents reoxidation' then in my experience this is largely a myth. It is true that a fine spray of water can alter the surface of a piece whilst post-reduction fuming is taking place, or enhance the crackle effect of the glaze, but many many artists achieve perfectly good and lasting reduction without a drop of H_2O. To me, at least, it is not worth the risk.

8. Lastly, if you are in charge of a group, make sure that everyone knows what is happening, avoid too much rushing around with hot pots, and be firmly in control of the situation at all times.

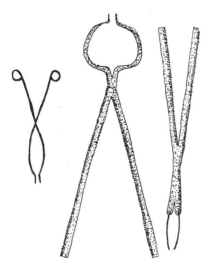

A selection of raku tongs.

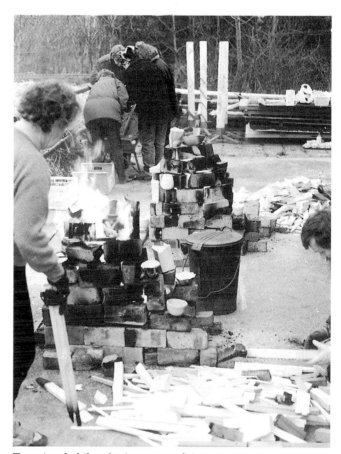

Two simple kilns during group firing.

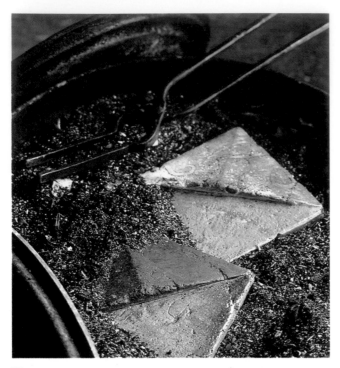

Pieces in sawdust. *Photograph by Anders Qwarnstrom.*

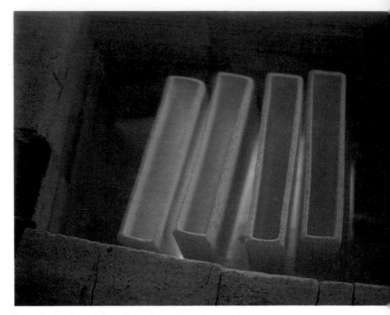

Pots firing in a kiln – Monique Bourbonnais.

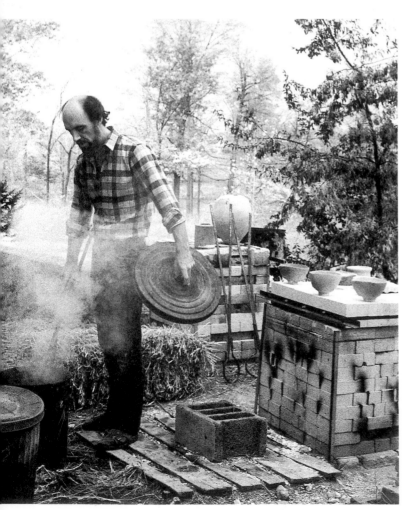

Robert Piepenburg firing his brick-built kilns.

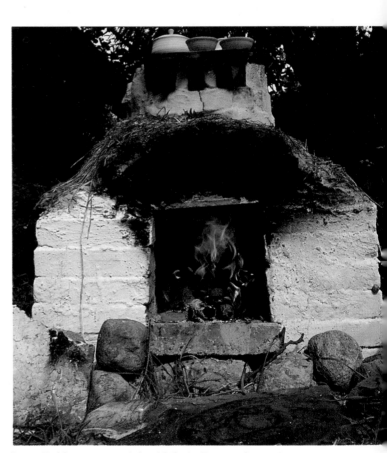

Inger Rokkjaer's wood-fired kiln in Denmark.

Health and safety in raku

I have already mentioned some aspects of safety in other parts of this book but I cannot over-emphasise the importance of taking basic commonsense precautions when handling materials and firing kilns. Many of these precautions are not exclusive to the raku technique but this section gives me the chance to reiterate some of them.

First of all, keep good order in the studio and especially around the kiln site. Regular mopping of the floor will keep dust levels down. Don't stir up the dust by dry sweeping.

Keep all glaze materials in well-labelled containers. Some of the raku glaze additives – e.g. metal salts and oxides – are extremely poisonous. Protect your skin and wear a mask if appropriate.

If any spraying is to be done, glazes, slips, oxides etc., a protective mask is necessary and ideally a spray booth with an extractor should be used.

The raku kiln and the firing itself are potentially very hazardous. Check over the equipment before each firing session and have an extinguisher handy just in case! Check also the weather conditions – windy days can be tricky as burners may blow out and smoke waft where it's not wanted!

Protective clothing of some kind is a must. Long-sleeved Kevlar gloves (not asbestos) without holes are a minimum requirement. I often put them over a pair of gardening gloves for extra protection. Headgear is advisable to protect your eyes and hair and there is growing concern about the effects of the smoke so a respirator is a good idea.

As I write, more and more potters are becoming concerned about the use of ceramic fibre in kilns. Being light, easy to work with and an excellent insulator, the material is ideally suited for raku kilns. But it also quickly becomes worn and ragged giving off a dust which I suspect may soon be found to be rather nasty. In fact, the use of fibre has already been banned in some colleges so I would caution against too much close contact with it without using a mask.

Lastly, panic and excitement can cause accidents particularly in a group situation and when moving hot pots from kiln to reduction chamber. Keep a tight control over the proceedings and rehearse each action before going ahead.

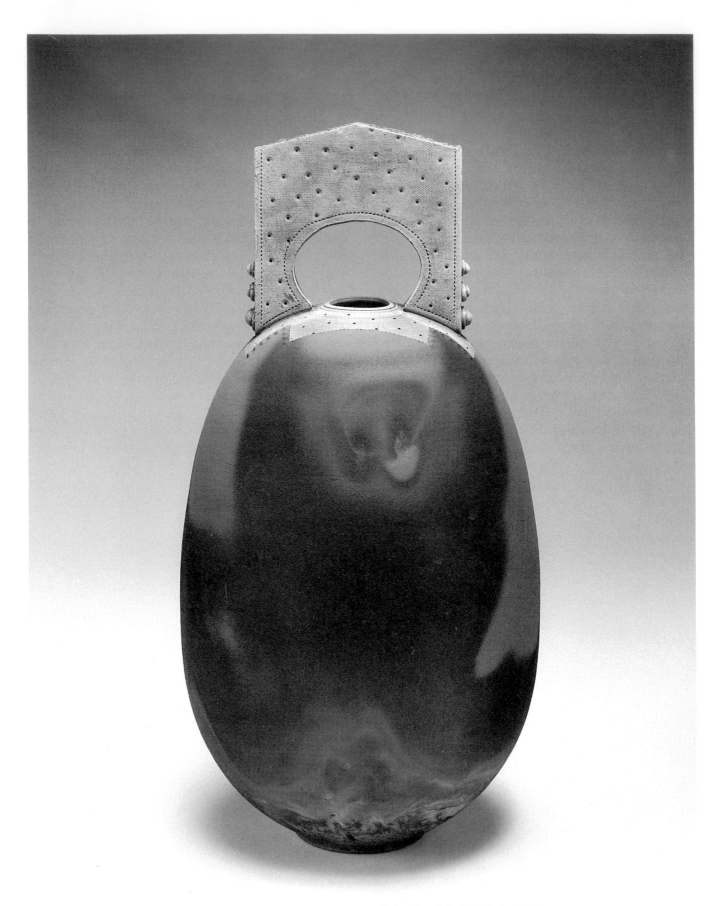

'Raku Vessel' by Rick Foris, h. 21".

CONTEMPORARY APPROACHES

Since the dawning of American-style raku in 1960, potters have quickly become addicted to the process of controlled conflagration which occurs in and around a raku kiln. This lust for the technique and its endless permutations has spread like 'wild-fire' across the Western world and beyond. On a visit to Russia a few years ago, Paul Soldner even discovered a book written in Hungarian entitled, *Raku for Children*.

The major part of this book is dedicated to a selection of raku potters from around the world. They represent only a small sample of countless thousands of smitten firemongers, many of whom produce work of extraordinary skill and originality. As I write this piece I am conscious of whispering voices in my ear saying, 'You should have included so and so' or 'How could you leave out what's-his-name?' But very early on it became apparent that it would be impossible in this section to try to include a really comprehensive choice of work. Instead I have opted for a mix of potters – some well-known, others not – who manifest a range of approaches, styles, techniques and philosophies.

To aid digestion and add a little gentle literary structure, I have divided this portion of the book up into six chapters. Obviously this is not intended to be a definitive categorisation of the work as most, if not all, potters would easily fit into more than one chapter. However, many artists find themselves drawn towards particular aspects of raku – colour, glazes, surface treatment and so on – which makes their work distinctive, so I have tentatively gathered them into half a dozen of these large interlocking areas.

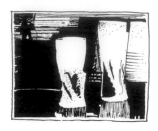

FORM

Most potters would I think say that the pursuit of good form was the first priority in their work. Certainly I could easily have included myself in this section as one of my initial reasons for returning to raku was a growing feeling that the forms that I was making were just vehicles for slick and forgiving stoneware glazes and some neat brushwork. For me, the freedom of raku and the ease with which a lot of very bad pots can be made, forces a self-discipline and a desire to think more seriously about the work, questioning motives and seeking a greater personal integrity. It's a bit like free-will – you have to be very careful what you do with it!

Of course the clay itself has none of these hang-ups. It is innately confident of its unique qualities which so many potters revel in. The bowls of Heike van Zadelhoff could almost have made themselves, their soft undulating forms glorying in a truly plastic mudness. In contrast, Daphne Corregan's more angular pieces and the giant strength of Martin Mindermann's well-defined forms display the purposeful intervention of the human hand.

Dave Roberts's striking and powerful pots reveal an intimate understanding of the materials and the subtle forms that he creates with them. And the flowing, graceful lines of James Lawton's skilfully constructed teapots raise an admiring smile. The pieces of Inger Rokkjaer emerge out of her own Danish-dug clay and Keiko Hasegawa also listens to the desires of her clay and glazes when considering how to make her tea ware.

Rounding off this clay-dominated section is George Timock whose raw volcanic vessel sculptures reflect the harsh beauty of untamed nature.

James Lawton – USA

The graceful vessels of James Lawton are both structurally architectural and anthropomorphic. Contorted teapots, bottles and jars strike engaging poses which mimic human gestures or the flamboyant posturing of fashion models on a catwalk. Certainly a link with fashion is not coincidental as James describes his approach to making pots as like that of a tailor:

I am fascinated by cloth and its ability to be both structural and fluid, taut as well as furling; perceiving the qualities in clay and fibre to be inherently similar.

This fluidity has been a mark of James's stylish pieces for more than 15 years. His raku work of the 1980s examined the contours and volumes of teapots, drinking vessels and boxes – all of which were usually sitting on trivet-like bases. Playing with space and dimension, James adorned his pieces with decorative images of household objects – tables, chairs, pottery and other domestic

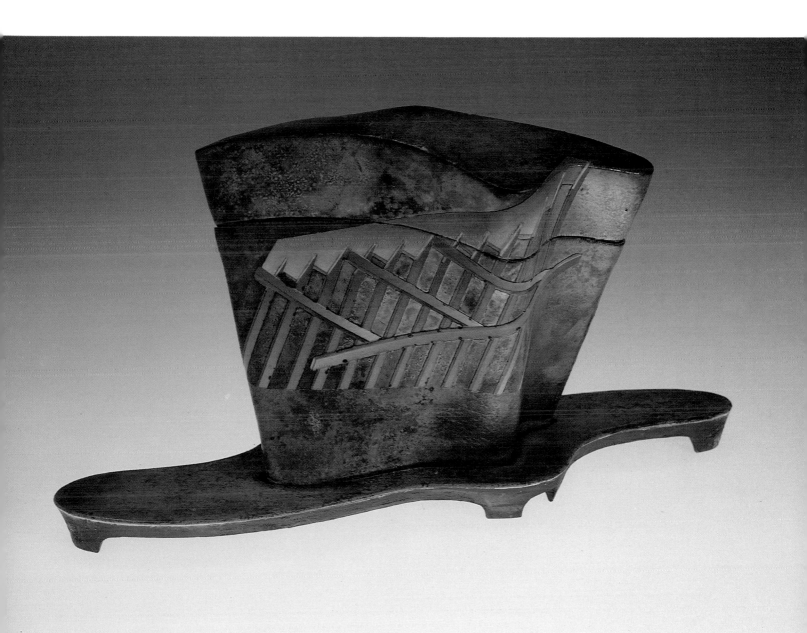

'Furling Box with Stairs' by James Lawton, 8.5" × 15" × 7", 1987. Raku.

icons – which he painted on. Items of clothing were a particular favourite, appearing to float or hover above the pot's surfaces suggesting movement and a human presence. The images eslished an interaction between themselves and physical pieces on which they were painted.

> The use of garments as imagery began not as a direct analogy to the manner of construction, but with the notion of envelopment – covering the body as the glaze clothes the bare bisque. It doesn't seem incongruent to me that physiological and ceramic bodies share certain elemental as well as symbolic connections: pottery possessing the ability to describe the human phenomenon simultaneously while participating in it.

James does not consider himself a 'raku' artist but rather an artist employing particular techniques in order to realise his ideas. Indeed, in recent years, he has moved away from straightforward raku-firing, choosing instead to saggar-fire many of his pieces. Treating the surfaces with terra sigillata, he exposes the pots to various combustibles including banana skins and cow manure to achieve surface textures and residues in the enclosed atmosphere of the saggar.

The forms themselves have developed over the years. The preoccupation with the teapot is still apparent but the shapes have become more elegant and slender, often segmented by bands or lines. Influenced by Keith Murray, a designer for Wedgwood, the lines allude to points of articulation in the human body – shoulders, feet, neck etc. The trivet bases, whilst still present, are now sometimes integrated into the whole piece or have developed into pierced low fences or barriers which enclose the pots tightly in a well-defined space. A marked change in the decoration is also evident in more recent work.

> The glaze imagery has evolved into a type of handwriting, drawn across and inscribing the pot's surface like a topographic map. The decorative intent has shifted away from painting shapes that appear volumetric and separate from the form it was placed on, towards a more accordant gesture. I remain interested in decoration capable of effecting the form, but venture into this via marks that are elastic and indelible, like tattoos knitted into the skin.

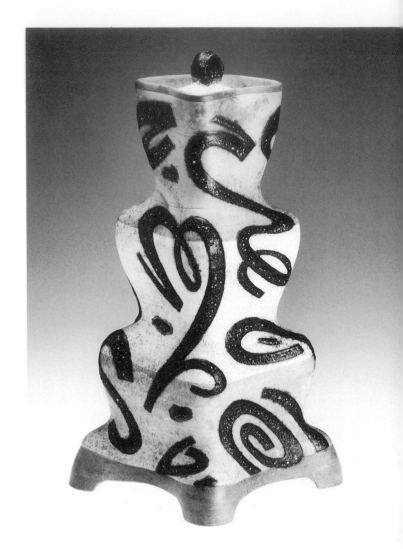

Stepped Jar by James Lawton, 15" × 10" × 8", 1991.
Saggar-fired earthenware.

These calligraphic marks made with glaze, reflect a fascination he has always had with handwriting. Some marks are recognisable letters, some are inventions. James's interest in the Greek, Roman and Hebrew alphabets has provided him with an array of graphics which are carefully arranged around the pot's surfaces pulling the observer into the form. One commentator described them as '. . . playing on the angles and curves of the pots and acting as a kind of tour guide'.

James Lawton's pots have developed in a compelling way not by huge leaps into tangential activity, but steadily and thoughtfully combining and integrating form and surface, decoration and mode of firing. The results bring together painter and potter in an original and expressive way.

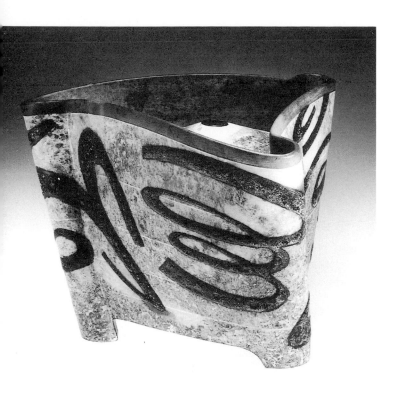

Firing

The raku kiln is a basic fibre envelope design that lifts off the firebox and shelves to give easy access to the ware. It is fired with propane or natural gas with a natural draught burner (venturi). A converted refrigerator, stripped of compressor and all plastic components, serves as reduction chamber. Lying it on its back, James lines the bottom with house bricks. This gives a super-insulated, relatively airtight chamber that produces a reduction atmosphere without an immense dosage of combustible material. It also prolongs the cooling, thus cutting the mortality rate on the work.

Dry hay or straw mixed with sawdust is used for reduction and the pots are usually re-oxidised whilst still glowing red inside. This seems to favour the orange colours James looks for in the copper/lithium glaze.

Triangular covered dish by James Lawton, 8" × 11" × 11", 1991. Saggar-fired earthenware.

Technical observations

Most pieces are thrown and altered. A diligent maker, James is an advocate of 'slipping and scoring' believing that good joins help to cut down the failure rate. After bisque firing the decoration is applied by means of an underglaze slip, beginning with a ground colour (usually yellow or gold) the decoration is airbrushed with other underglaze colours (the same base with various commercial stains added from 5% to 20%). Details are rendered with a small '000' brush with concentrations of the ceramic stains, and highlights put in by scratching through the colours to the base. A clear glaze is then applied over the entire image. The glaze is one which only crackles minimally and it is also used as a base for 'bright liner' glaze colours being tinted with 5–20% of various stains.

After decoration and glazing, each image is covered with a liquid wax emulsion and set to dry. The edges are cleaned up, leaving a raised outline. Lastly, the exterior glaze which surrounds the decorated pane is applied. It is a lithium-based formula which is very sensitive to the raku process.

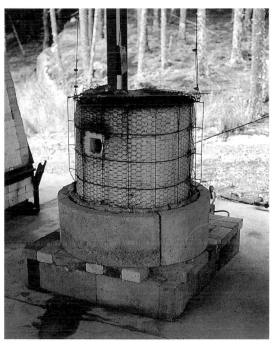

Fibre envelope kiln with cast firebox –
James Lawton, Haystack Mountain School,
Maine.

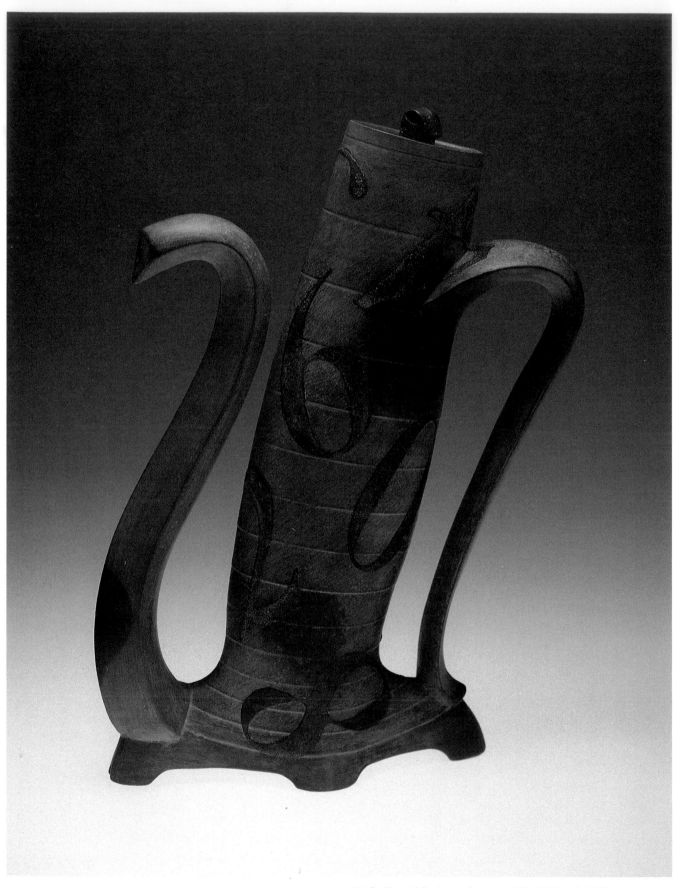

'Italic Teapot' by James Lawton, 15" × 11" × 4", 1991.
Raku.

Keiko Hasegawa – Japan

There is a saying: 'Man without idea – clay with ideal.' And, in fact, according to the clay it should be decided how to form, glaze and fire the clay. 'There is only one matching style for a specific novel . . .', I was once told by a writer. Similarly there is only one sort of clay out of a countless variety, which fits for a certain form and certain pattern.

In a nutshell: somebody who does not penetrate the character of the clay is not entitled to be a true potter. If one does not understand the character of the clay exactly and uses it with the wrong form or colour, its integrity will be damaged and finally die out. The clay of a good pot has a strong character, one might say.

(Quoted from: Kato Tokuro, *Yakimono no Zuihitsu; Tokkan Shoten*, p.110, 1967)

To the Western eye the work of Keiko Hasegawa appears very Japanese in character. She makes traditional tea bowls, water containers, caddies and vases. In Japan, however, her work is considered to be influenced by the West especially in the colour of the glazes and the shapes. She herself is not conscious of potting in any particular style, but is obviously influenced by, as she is steeped in, the Japanese folk-craft tradition (*mingei*).

One famous and ancient kiln site in Japan was Seto. It was here, in the 13th century that some of the very first tea wares were made – copies of simple Tang Dynasty tea vessels used by Chinese Zen monks to enhance their meditation within temples. It was in Seto that the formalised Japanese tea ceremony (*Cha-no-yu*) began to take shape.

In an ancient saying, it is said that the Seto potters regarded the process of firing to be most important, next the choice of clay and materials, and finally the execution of throwing and decoration. Keiko holds to much of this philosophy. The raku-firing technique she has chosen is a creative stimulus in itself. It is not so different from her early experience in her father's iron foundry surrounded by furnaces and molten metal. Keiko still likes to experiment with iron and bronze work occasionally. '. . . I would definitely like to continue using fire for all my creative activity.'

Born in Yamagata, Japan, Keiko studied design in Tokyo, moving on to a promising position in an animation-movie company. Feeling artistically stifled she went back home to work in her father's cast-iron and bronze factory which made the well-

Raku tea bowl by Keiko Hasegawa.
Turquoise and black glaze.

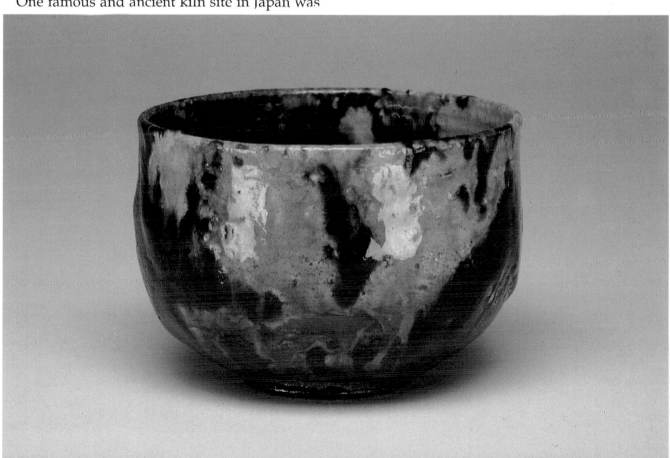

known tea kettles. She found again that it was not for her and decided to pursue a career in ceramics following her instinctive liking for the subject.

Following traditional apprenticeship experience in craft kilns at Mashiko and Hirashimizu she came to England and decided to stay and make pots in Devon. She worked for a short spell with Michael Leach but then, feeling the need for independence, took the opportunity of an invitation to visit Norway. The trip to Oslo introduced her to the raku-firing technique and proved decisive in setting her on course for the establishment of her present workshop.

Clay is very important to Keiko. 'I am not particularly keen on decorative work among Japanese ceramics but I like anything which makes most use of the clay.'

Using a Japanese-type kick wheel for thrown work, the pots are generally made with soft clay which encourages subtle, yielding shapes. She tries to capture the character of the material, allowing it to display its qualities through her work. Irregularities may be accepted and indeed welcomed if they add to the life of the pot. It is an approach which is not always appreciated in the West where perfection is very often perceived in terms of regularity of form, slick glazes and controlled decoration.

Many of the potters featured in this book turned to the raku method partly as a way to find a new life and spontaneity in their work, excited at the possibility of chance happenings which might bring something extra and special to a piece. To Keiko Hasegawa, however, raku offers a more controlled firing technique than the traditional, many-chambered Japanese wood-fired climbing kilns (*noborigama*), which are fired over a period of several days. In these massive kilns the artistic creations of the craftsmen are entirely at the mercy of, and dominated by, the play of elements: fire, air, earth, water – and ash.

In a modern purpose-built gas raku kiln, Keiko finds the ease of control of a truncated firing cycle makes possible the supervision of a single piece of work. Her work features the use of molten glazes, the ebbing and flowing of which can be observed through the spyhole and quickly arrested when the desired effect is achieved.

Traditional Japanese raku pots are allowed to cool in the air when removed from the kiln, producing a bright oxidised finish which is later stained with tea or pigment rubbed into the crazed glaze. Keiko chooses to smoke her pieces in the Western manner using sawdust or grass in a reduction chamber. She finds this enhances the tension between fire and earth emphasising the crackling and giving a depth to the glaze.

Keiko's pots stem from a centuries-old tradition of folk art in her native Japan but she is unafraid to employ space age materials and modern methods to develop her own style. The resulting work combines elements of Eastern and Western tradition and technology to produce work very much a reflection of herself.

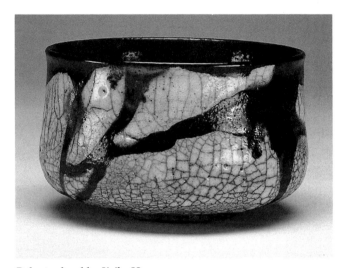

Raku tea bowl by Keiko Hasegawa.
Black over white glaze.

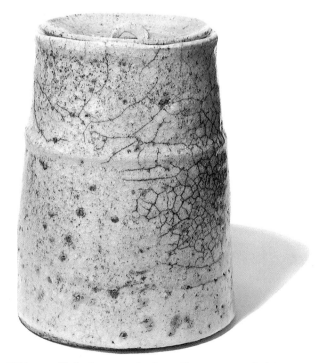

White crackled raku water jug by Keiko Hasegawa, h. 22.5 cm.

Inger Rokkjaer – Denmark

For centuries Danish clay has been used for earthenware: Jutland pottery, confinement crocks (for carrying food to new mothers), commonplace red clay flower pots, and much more.

> When I work with this clay and put it through a raku process, it is essentially a cultural encounter – a confrontation between the simple Jutlandish and the refined Japanese. I try to take only the technique from raku, but must of course acknowledge that the strong Japanese form and style traditions are hard to avoid.

Remaining faithful to the Danish style, Inger digs and composes her own clay. Having dried it thoroughly, she removes any obvious stones and other impurities, renders it down to a slip and sieves it, before laying it out to dry to a workable state.

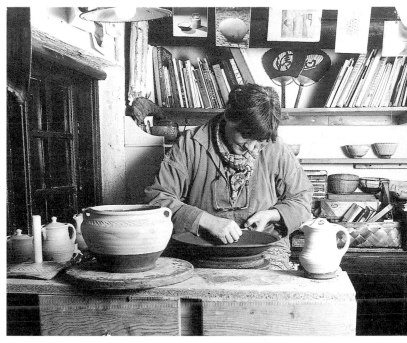

Inger working in her studio.

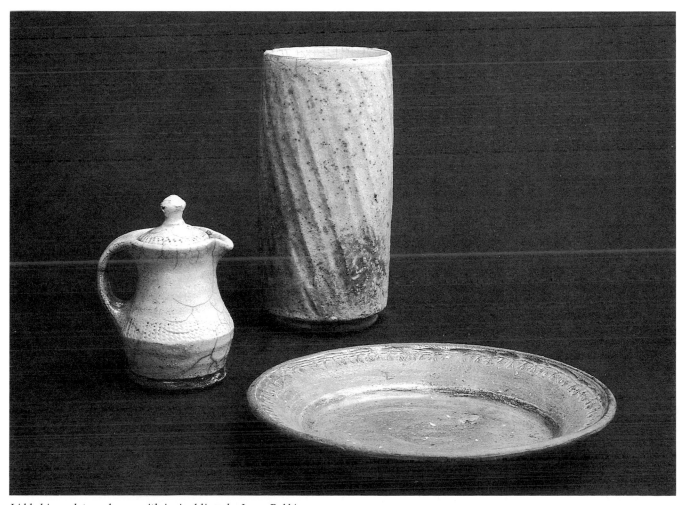

Lidded jug, plate and vase with incised lines by Inger Rokkjaer.
Inger's wood-fired raku pots have a mediaeval feel about them.

This entire elementary process is very meaningful to me. It is, in the most literal sense, the groundwork. Moreover, I strive both in form, glazing and decoration for the greatest possible simplicity, seeking thereby to reach a balance where the fascinating raku technique is fully made use of, but the characteristic expression remains Danish.

Inger was one of the first potters in Denmark to explore the nuances of raku. Since 1969 she has worked in various 'ranges' and themes. In the words of critic, William Hull:

> The pieces vary from architectonic forms of 20th-century Danish design, to an amazing affinity with mediaeval ceramics. But the latter wares are not mediaeval clones. They are works of the present that suggest the past – they speak of where we are and where we have been.

'What I love in a work of art is not its perfection, which is deceptive, but its pulsating life.'
(Paul la Cour in *Fragments of a Diary*)

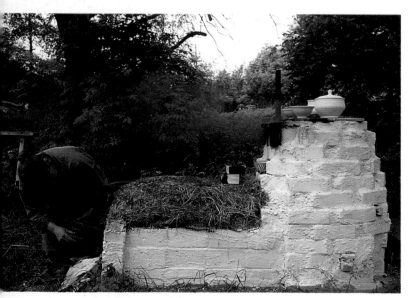

Inger Rokkjaer stoking the wood kiln

George Timock – USA

George Timock has been a full-time professor of art at Kansas City Art Institute since 1973. In spite of this and other teaching commitments, he has found time to develop a unique style of work and has gained a national reputation. His work has been acquired for many permanent collections in the US and he has achieved an impressive list of exhibitions and awards dating back nearly 30 years.

His dramatic sculptures use the vessel as their basic reference point, and certainly he acknowledges the importance of the ritualistic use of vessels through the ages. But unlike many artists' work, his pieces are not consciously derived from historical functional pottery, but are an exploration of the vessel in abstraction; involving a direct and personal response to the elemental forces of nature.

> Probably the greatest impact I've ever experienced is the lava flows in Hawaii. When I saw the serrated edge of the cone at Kilauea, and the miles and miles of lava flows to the sea, I was at a loss for words. It was a discovery of the exterior and interior of my work in nature.

Each piece of work begins from a single solid lump of clay. Working with the pieces upside down, George carves the exterior shape. A plaster cast is made of this – clay then being pressed into the cast, the flat 'top' becoming the base of the piece. The sculptures have a double wall and so the whole process has to be repeated and the interior shape inserted into the exterior one. The edges of the two walls are then joined to complete the piece.

Before the pots are raku-fired, glazes and colours are built-up through a series of oxidation firings in an electric kiln. As many as a dozen firings may be necessary to achieve the desired combination of pastel blushes, hues of blue and red, and iridescent flashes of gold contrasted with matt black and grey. A miniature sandblasting tool is also brought into play to etch the surfaces of the pieces – softening edges, creating subtle textures and revealing and integrating the strata of colours which have been deposited. The final raku-firing then deals its own random hand of flame and smoke in the contrasting hues of oxidation and reduction.

For the past twenty-five years my artwork has been centered within the context of the clay vessel. My continued passion to create vessel forms that embrace an uneasy balance of volume and evoke tension of parts within the vessel, are issues that I find personally and visually challenging and intriguing. My language and visual concerns have been rooted in formal abstractions within the anatomy of the vessel. Hence, within the context of descriptive line, textured variations, juxtaposition of mass and volume and colour hue variations ... these abstract tools are central to my creative instincts ... and are necessary and integral to the ultimate visual impact of my art. The technical processes involved in creating the clay vessels are extremely complex and time-consuming, but are a necessary and vital ingredient to the final statement.

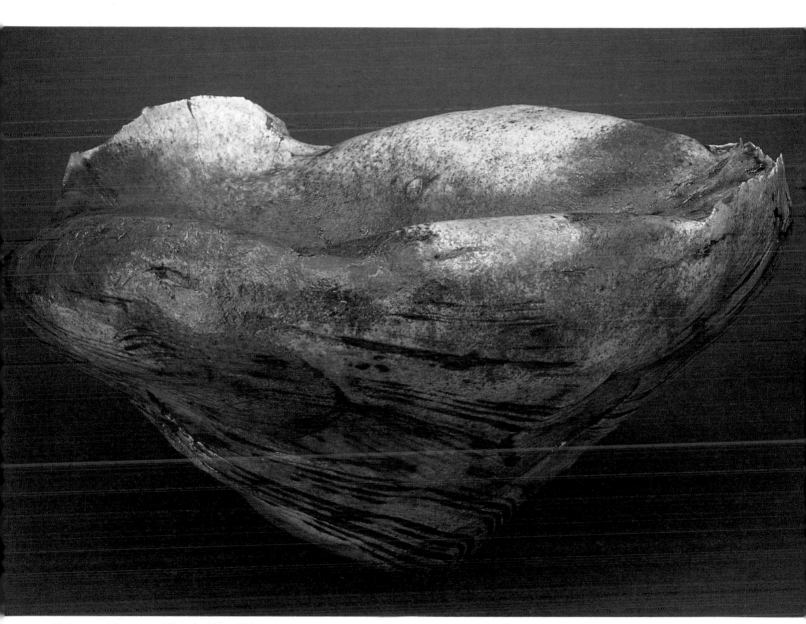

Raku vessel by George Timock, 13" × 23".

David Roberts – UK

Dave Roberts will often be found rummaging through an old shoebox. It is a pandora's box of cuttings, gleanings from magazines and papers, and notes and scribbles of his own. A rich source of material for new ideas.

He is a methodical man. A thinking potter who is not troubled by apparently insoluble technical or aesthetic problems. His workshop is simple and uncluttered – almost spartan. It contains a couple of kilns, a table, chair and banding wheel, a few tools and a gas heater.

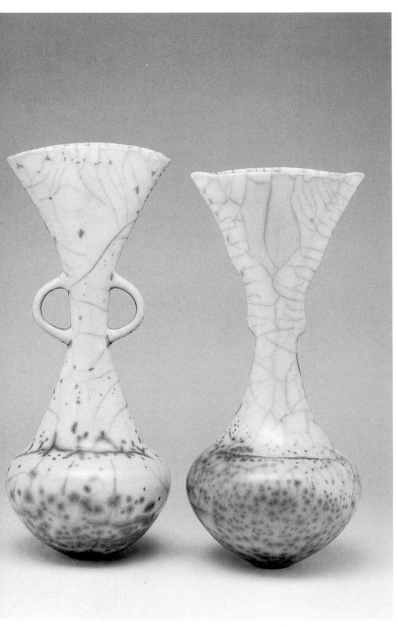

Two coil-built bottles by David Roberts, tallest 46 cm. Burnished raku.

I first encountered Dave Roberts's work in 1980. His obvious mastery of technique was coupled with well-resolved form and sympathetic glaze treatment. Surface decoration in those days consisted of hard-edged patterns made by using masking tape as a resist resulting in positive and negative glazed lines moving across the pot's contours.

The intervening years have seen Dave Roberts's reputation grow and he is now recognised as perhaps the leading exponent of raku in the UK. His work has continued to attract much interest and admiration from collectors and fellow potters alike. Recent work has reached new heights of excellence. Form and decoration have developed a new integration, a partnership of themes drawing inspiration from many cultures. Bronze Age Cypriot art was the basis of one series of tall basket forms. Slender handles sweep up from the narrow opening of a bulbous swollen pot which has the taut, bulging lines of a leather water carrier. Another source is ethnic American art, particularly from the Pueblo Indian and Mimbres ware of New Mexico which is known for its linear geometric designs painted in slip.

> Having been making more complex forms, I wanted to return to simpler shapes either just with burnished slip or with drawn lines and patterns. I had become dissatisfied with the limitations of the tape-resist technique and so developed a more sensitive linear quality with incised patterns drawn through outer glaze and slip layers. The increasingly complex linear and circular designs are derived from 'sacred circles' found in many cultures, from prehistoric remains, Celtic patterns, North American Indian ceramic decoration (e.g. Mimbres), and Japanese 19th-century lacquer and textile decoration.

Born in Sheffield in 1947, Dave Roberts had abandoned a potential career in engineering by the time he was 20, and started a course at Bretton Hall, a teacher-training college in Yorkshire. The course was divided between art and general education. His aspirations to become a painter were tempered by a more down-to-earth expectation that he would probably become a teacher. 'Pop art' and abstract expressionism was in its heyday in the mid-1960s. Dave had come from a traditional academic background based largely on representative art and at first he found the free-and-easy art college scene confusing.

Whilst at college Dave saw an exhibition of pots by Hans Coper and textiles by Peter Collingwood. Coper's work struck a chord with Roberts. He could see a man at ease with his materials – someone whose pots were pieces of abstract sculpture and yet had an accessibility that he had not found in most two-dimensional works of the time.

Although his work is very different, Coper's example and approach to ceramics has had a profound influence on my work: when developing an interest in pottery in the late 1960s, Coper provided an alternative to the prevalent orientalism of the Leach school of potters. Although his sources of inspiration were different from mine, he at least legitimised alternatives to Japan and China.

I am a minimalist by temperament and enjoy working within a restricted range of processes and forms, and have been influenced by Coper's modernist approach to ceramics reflecting the reductivist (less is more) aesthetic drawn from modernist sculptors such as Brancusi. I am also aware of the indirect influence of Japan and Zen Buddhism via modernist theories of the early 20th century.

Hans Coper's deceptively simple pots consist of subtle and complex formal relationships which the multi-layered dry glaze surfaces intensify and support. Using different processes, especially the heavy carbonisation involved in raku, I try to achieve in depth of surface a similar enhancement to my own forms.

Coper's ideas on the position of the potter in the late 20th century has provided a useful rôle model, i.e. that pots on their own terms can aspire to be an autonomous art form in the same way as painting or sculpture. At the same time, the rôle of potter as studio artist has also been useful to me at least.

Bretton Hall college also offered ceramics as a subsidiary subject and, with the encouragement of Tony Reeve, the tutor, Dave Roberts began tentatively to explore the possibilities of clay.

Early work was thrown but Dave eventually settled on coil-built pots as a favoured technique.

He has a great love of handbuilt, circular forms which express a sense of enclosure, containment and volume and has experienced and enjoyed these qualities in vessels from pre-Columbian, North and Central American, West African and early Mediterranean ceramics.

I coil build my pots as the formal qualities of containment are a natural result of this chosen building process, i.e. a circular form, swelling from a tiny, narrow base giving a tense, inflated quality to the pot – similar to a balloon full of air where inner space is tangible and reflected in the 'stretched' skin of the pot's contours.

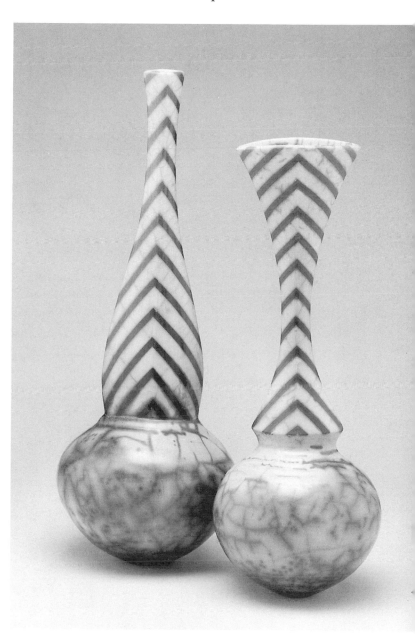

Two coil-built bottles by David Roberts, tallest 48 cm. Burnished raku.

49

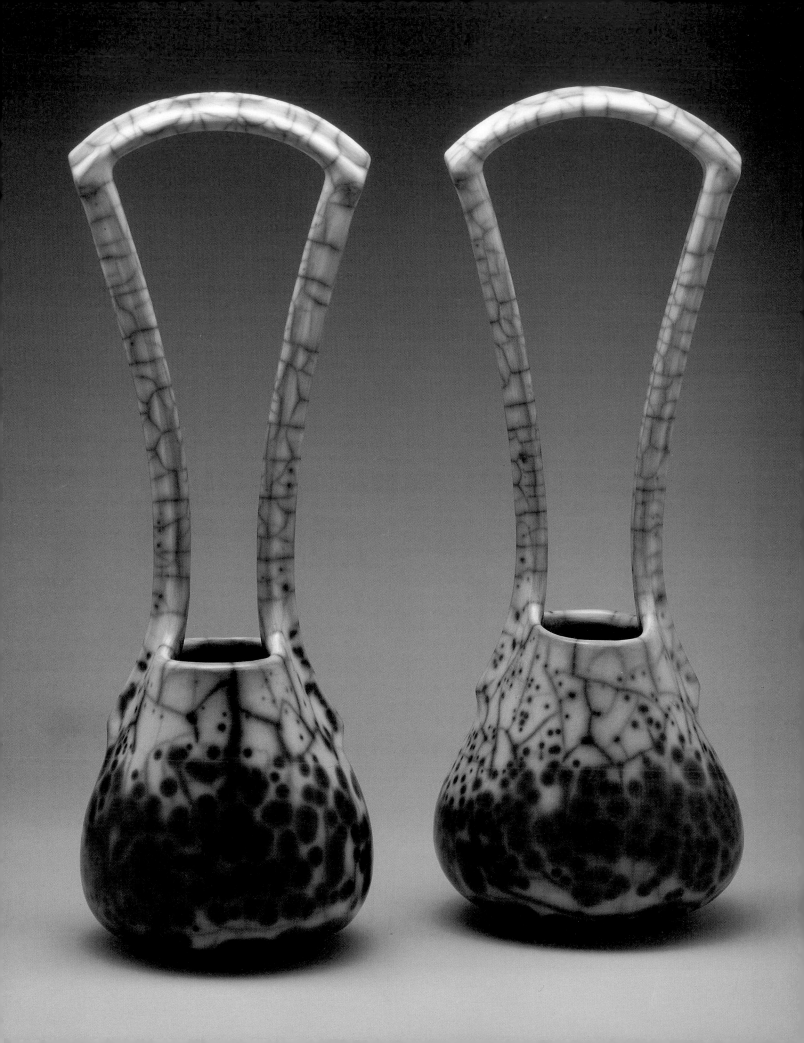

Although at first glance symmetrical, my pots exhibit a slight asymmetry inherent in the handbuilding process. This, I believe, gives the pot's form movement and 'life' and just escapes the static quality of mathematical accuracy.

On leaving college, Dave taught for a while in the south of England. In 1973 he moved back to Yorkshire where he met Jim Robison, an American potter living in the UK. Jim showed him slides of American raku by Paul Soldner and others, which were a revelation. Until then the only raku Dave had seen had been small Japanese tea bowls.

Now he became aware of the range of possibilities that the technique could offer and which could satisfy his desire to work on a bigger scale. In 1975 technical information was hard to come by but an American article about an oil-drum kiln provided the answer. Dave contacted a refractories manufacturer in Stoke-on-Trent and obtained some of the then revolutionary insulation blanket to line the oil drum. A year later he built a larger version which has subsequently been copied by many potters around the world. It provided Dave with a large firing chamber, quickly and easily heated with a couple of propane burners. The counterbalanced, hoisted chamber was perfect for allowing unhindered access to large hot pots by one person. This meant that Dave could give the necessary attention to each individual piece that he fired – a very different situation from the production potter filling every last crevice in a capacity-packed kiln.

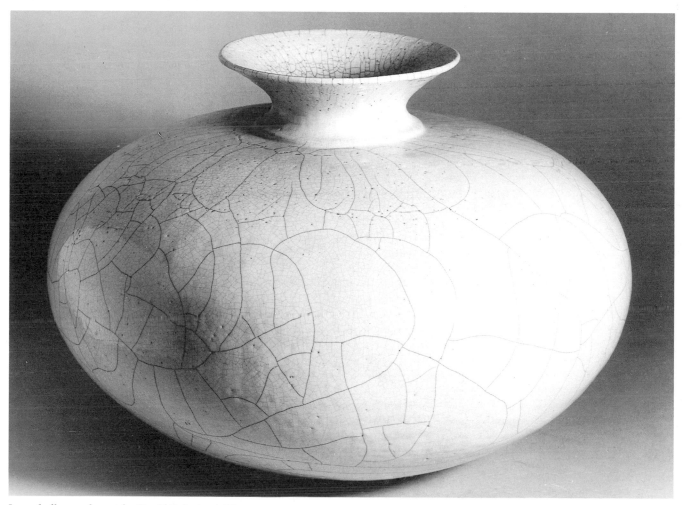

Large bulbous raku pot by David Roberts, d. 50 cm.
White crackle glaze.

Opposite
Two coil-built baskets by David Roberts, h. 50 cm.
Burnished raku.

Technical information

Dave uses a white St Thomas's stoneware body. A fairly coarse (20s to dust) grog is added in a pugmill to open the clay. The body has a low coefficient of expansion to help prevent cracking. All the pots (including the giant plates) are coil-built. A simple wall-mounted extruder is used to make the $\frac{1}{4}$ in. thick coils. A higher speed of construction and a more even wall thickness is achieved by this method.

Nowadays he works on one pot at a time using a blow torch to speed up the drying. The clay is used fairly stiff, and the form is built up with the coils and smoothed with a flexible metal scraper. After a blast with the blowlamp to harden the base a little, more coils are added and compressed, always working from the inside pushing out. In this way a large piece can be built up quite quickly.

When finished and dried leatherhard, the pots are brushed with a ball-clay slip sometimes containing some added commercial stains to give a hint of green or blue.

Using the back of a spoon, the pots are then laboriously burnished and then dried. An electric kiln is used nowadays for biscuit-firing to a little over 1000°C.

Various glaze treatments are employed: some pots are glazed directly – either by pouring or spraying; others are decorated using masking tape as a resist. Many of the most recent pots are coated with a thick layer ($\frac{1}{8}$ in. or so) of a refractory slip which is sprayed on and allowed to dry thoroughly. On top of this is sprayed a high-alkaline raku glaze. Toxic lead glazes are avoided entirely. When fired and removed from the kiln to the reduction chamber the molten glaze cools rapidly. The resulting crazing allows smoke to penetrate through the refractory slip to the surface of the pot. Glaze and slip then fall away leaving the effects of the smoke on the burnished pot surface.

When a batch of work has been accumulated, a concentrated period of firing is embarked on. Only one pot is fired at a time in the kiln, but the rapid heating and cooling of the top-hat design means a number of pieces may be fired in one day. A small amount of residual heat is usually present in the kiln and most pots reach their required temperature in about three-quarters of an hour. A digital pyrometer is used for an accurate temperature reading and a range of 850–950°C is usual, depending on the glazes.

The kiln is slowly cooled to around 850°C to 'soak' the glaze and the pot is removed to stand for 10 to 20 seconds before being placed in a reduction chamber, covered with fresh sawdust, usually softwood, and allowed to cool for an hour or two until it can be handled with gloves.

When cool, the pots are removed and cleaned off – most of the slip and glaze falls off or is brushed away. The pots are cleaned up with a cloth and polished with a non-silicon wax.

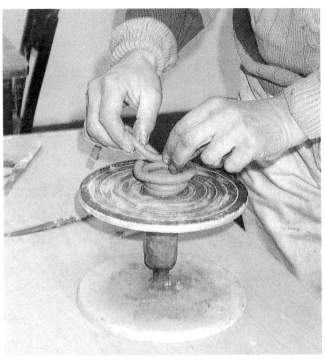

1. The first coils are assembled.

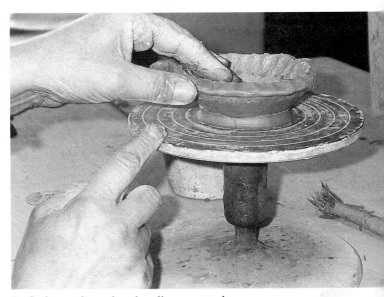

2. Coils are slipped and well compacted.

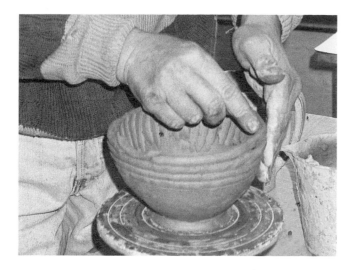

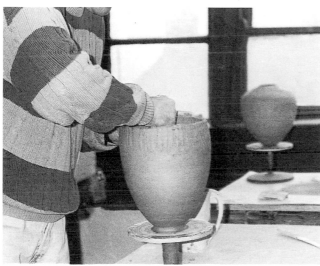

3. 4. Further coils are added and the form scraped and refined with a metal kidney.

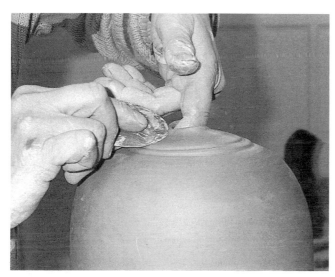

5. Refining the rim and lip using a rubber kidney to press grog back into the body creating a smooth surface suitable to receive a burnishing slip.

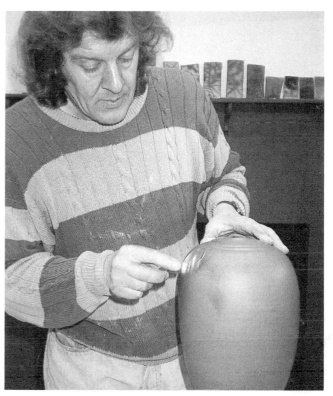

6. Applying and burnishing the first layer of slip.

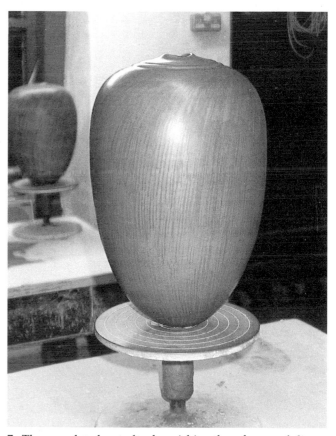

7. The completed pot after burnishing three layers of slip.

The work of Dave Roberts is unique. His pots represent very human values and his thoroughly unpretentious approach has delighted many and has brought honesty and clarity to a craft increasingly in danger of becoming lost in a tide of over-pretentious 'fine-art' criticism.

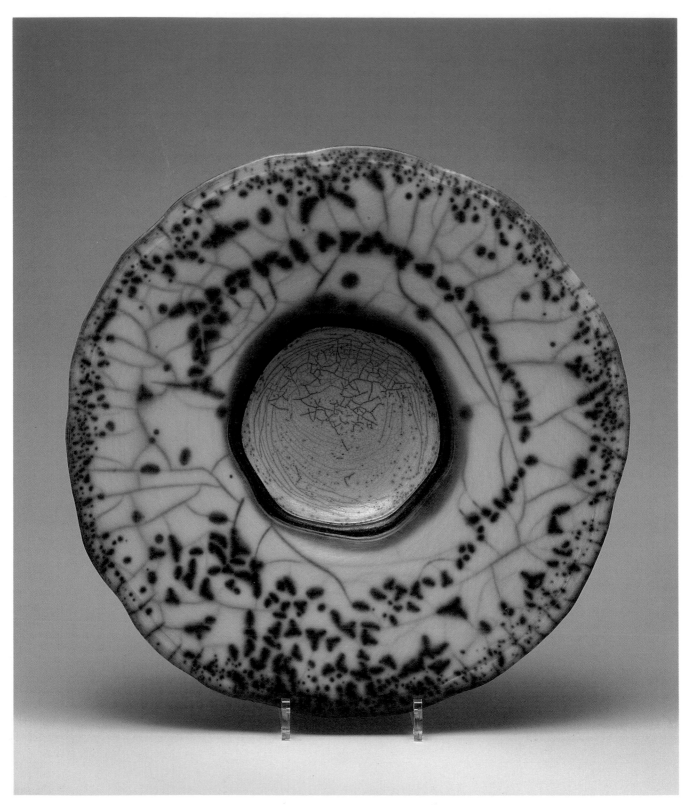

Bowl by David Roberts, d. 45 cm.
Coil-built, burnished and glazed.

Martin Mindermann – Germany

There is a common English expression used to express the higher than expected cost of something (for instance a car repair bill): 'Think of a number and then double it.' Well, think of the largest raku pot you can imagine possible, and then double it. You may then be somewhere near assessing the scale of the work of German potter, Martin Mindermann. His monumental forms – up to two feet in diameter and three feet tall – exercise the imagination of the first time observer. Their impact demands a mental adjustment to cope with something which has the presence more of a piece of furniture than a decorative pot.

Raku form by Martin Mindermann, 56 cm × 62 cm. Crackle glaze and gold lines.

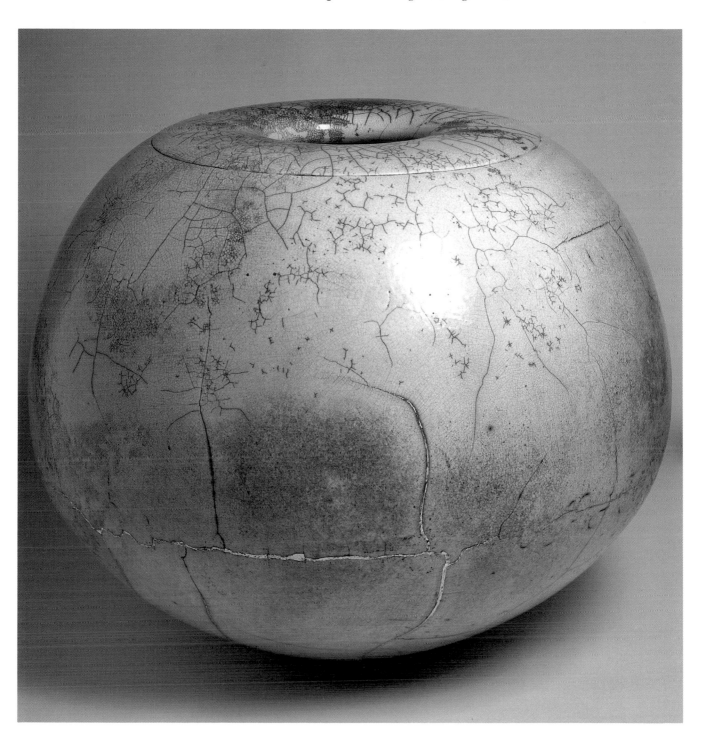

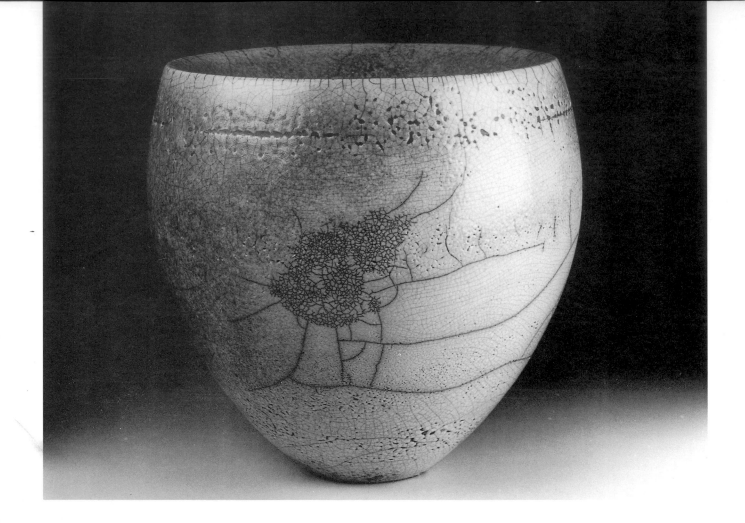

Form by Martin Mindermann, d. 48 cm, h. 36 cm.

Vessels of the early Bronze Age have been the models for Martin's exploration. The pots themselves are uncomplicated: many of them based on variations of squashed or elongated spheres, sometimes in the shape of a jar with a lid or a deep bowl with a flattened shoulder, constricting to a small central opening. Almost all are bulbous, with tight outer curves rising up from a narrow base and ending in a voluptuous rolling rim which entices the eye into a voluminous dark internal void.

The glazes on these massive pots seem to hug the forms and reveal qualities not seen on smaller pieces. The large expanse of surface area visible exhibits manifold variations of colour, tone and crackle, offering the beholder an impressive picture. A vivid blue/green glaze is much in evidence.

The same turquoise-blue colour has been widely employed in the Egyptian culture and can often be found in combination with gold.

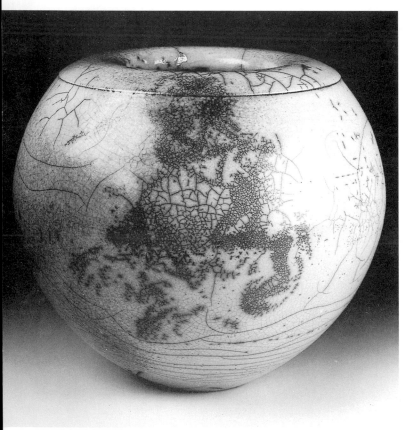

Raku bowl by Martin Mindermann, w. 37.5 cm, h. 47 cm.

56

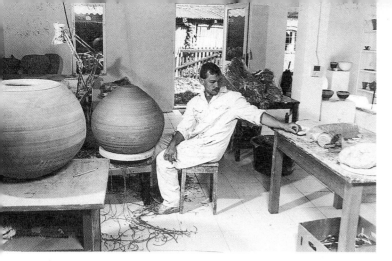

Martin Mindermann in his workshop.
Photograph by Mathisas Wilm.

This metal is important to me as an additional material: with its associations of archaeological excavation and the search for treasure.

Many of Martin's pots have one or two meandering gold lines which follow the crackle pattern of a particular piece. He uses gold much in the way that the ancient Japanese raku potters did – filling cracks in tea vessels with gold lacquer. The 'mended' pots were highly prized in Japan.

Martin's work is technically brilliant. He tests the materials to their limits and brings off spectacular results. Perhaps the reason for his success lies in this personal confession: 'Raku is the cultivated form of pyromania. I like to handle fire, fire as a ceremony.'

Technical information

All the work is thrown, turned and bisque-fired in an electric kiln. Metal chlorides are sprayed on to the pots as an underglaze. This is 'in order to obtain fine colour distribution and transition'. For health reasons, Martin does not use glazes containing lithium or lead. Alkaline-frit glazes are sprayed on to give an even coating.

The kiln is a home-built fibre box, mounted on a table. The top and one side are joined together and can be removed from the rest of the kiln rather like the bonnet of an old-fashioned car. This allows easy access to the large pots within. A gas burner heats the kiln to 1020°C, after which the pots are removed to an earth-hole filled with sawdust and covered completely. They are left there to cool for 24 hours.

Daphné Corregan – France

Daphné Corregan's prize winning sculptural ceramics are widely acclaimed in Europe. Daphné trained in Toulon, Marseille, and first became interested in raku whilst working in the ceramics department of the *Beaux Arts* in Aix-en-Provence. American potters Jim Romberg and Paul Soldner were visiting artists to the college, and subsequently Daphné spent six months travelling in the US, visiting university departments and attending another Soldner workshop, which was a further catalyst for her development in raku.

Slab-built vessels of one sort or another form the basis of much of her work. One series of pieces features exaggerated cup and jug forms, sitting on variously shaped and constructed tables, made from smoked ceramic and metal. In another series, Daphné has added strong African references. Tall, narrow, tapering bottle shapes bring to mind elegant images of Nubian women adorned with vibrant headdresses and tiers of colourful neck bands. The sharp lines of a wide, angular-lidded pot zigzag in and out, much in the way that the late Michael Cardew observed in Nigerian vessels, and indeed, adapted to use in his own work.

The American influences of Soldner and others are quite apparent in Daphné's work. She is unhindered by traditions or conventions and is able to experiment freely with form, and particularly surface treatment which is of great interest to her. Raku provides the perfect vehicle to explore the nuances of surface texture and colour. She fully exploits the effects of the smoke directly on the clay, and subtly introduces slips and 'dry' glazes to add colour and tone.

I've always been terribly impressed and influenced by half-torn down buildings, half-deteriorated walls where you can still read the traces of old wallpaper, layers and layers of paint, where there must have been a mirror or painting, a greasy kitchen, or the bathroom with its tiled walls. Using slips and refractory glazes leaves that old, fresco-like surface.

My ideas are always conceived considering the raku process as well as the form. I like the neutrality of the smoked clay. I need the subtlety of the washed-out engobes and I need the light brought to my surfaces by the reoxydation during cooling.

Technical information

Glazes

I use very few glazes. Most of my surfaces are decorated with stains mixed in a slip or a glaze. My slip is either made from the clay I'm using, or four parts kaolin, two parts silica and one part frit (or Gerstley borate). My base glaze is Soldner's 80% Gerstley borate and 20% kaolin, so that the slip and glaze are almost compatible. I enjoy using a Gerstley borate-based glaze because of the way my brushes slide over the clay (wet or fired). I usually decorate on bisque ware but have also decorated before firing, the result is the same – although it is more convenient, of course, on bisque – considering my forms and the size of my work. I have and do use commercial glazes from time to time, but rarely.

Both glaze and slips are brushed on. Daphné colours them with stains – she has no recipes – just adds them directly until she is satisfied with the colour. Occasionally she will use 1%–5% copper carbonate in the glaze and sometimes a bit of titanium oxide.

Finished pots are usually bisque-fired to 1050°C in a gas kiln, then fired to about the same temperature in another fibre kiln Daphné uses for raku. This kiln is a coffin-like box with two gas burners placed at each extremity at the bottom. Raku temperature is reached within two or three hours after which the work is removed to the reduction bin.

Daphné uses hay, newspaper, sawdust or straw to smoke her pots. Normally two or three pieces of newspaper or a handful of sawdust or straw is put in the bottom of an old steel barrel, and one or more pieces of work are put in on top. The chamber is covered and left for a few minutes before the can is opened and the material allowed to re-ignite. More newspaper may be added and the process repeated; or the piece of work may be removed and cooled with a gentle spray of water.

'Boite' by Daphne Corregan, h. 50 cm, w. 50 cm.
Slab built and decorated with stained slips and glazes.

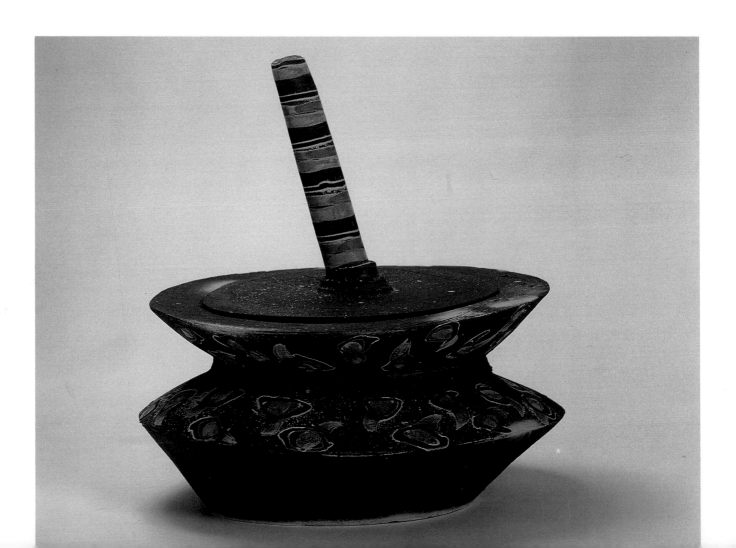

'The rapid cooling tends to accentuate certain colours, particularly oranges, and reduces brittleness in my clay.'

The raku kiln is also used for her smoked firings (*enfumage*).

Once temperature is reached, we close the kiln tightly for another two or three hours while we feed in pieces of rubber inner tube from the burner holes at the bottom. With the kiln almost sealed there is no leakage of unpleasant fumes. It is then allowed to cool with the pots inside, so we are no longer talking raku, really.

I usually prefer not to cover over my clay (which is extremely groggy) with thick glazes. I scratch it, claw it, smooth it and crack it. Smoking the clay is a way of ameliorating the colour without destroying the surfaces.

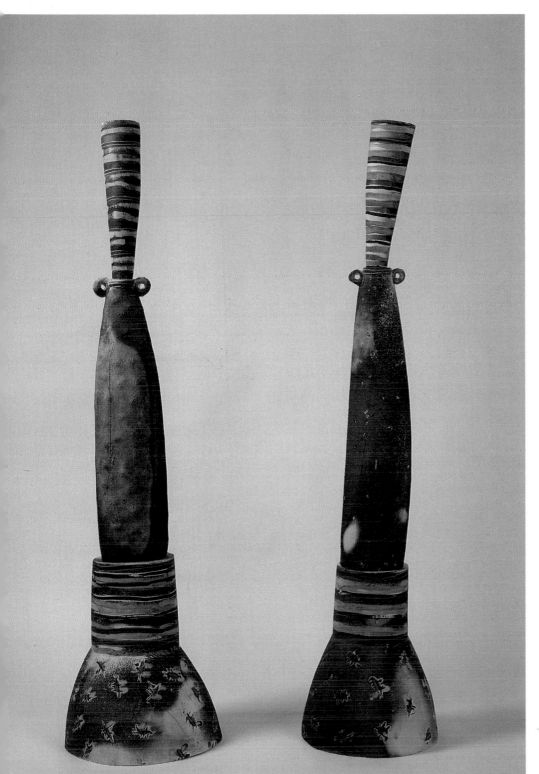

'Les Africaines' by Daphne Corregan, h. 165 cm, w. 40 cm.

Heike van Zadelhoff – Germany

Like an increasing number of potters today, Heike van Zadelhoff bridges several ceramic disciplines. When inspired to a new creation, she feels the technical processes – making and firing – should serve the idea, not dominate it. Most of her work combines two firing techniques: raku, and salt glaze.

She writes:

> For me, raku is a technique that, in certain cases, is necessary to realise a special idea – it is part of the idea. The piece may demand a modified raku approach, or even another method of firing altogether – then I have to take that road.

Heike's work glories in the character of the clay. Her forms, invariably bowls of one sort or another, some up to two feet across, capture the soft sensuous qualities of this unique material, producing almost a living landscape. By pressing, twisting and stretching a lump of clay, her bowl forms take shape. Burst and cracked rims document the working forces in a solidification of movement. The soda-raku creates surfaces of vitality which support and enhance the body.

Technical information

Heike fires in a home-built, gas-fired updraught kiln made of insulating bricks which are protected with Kao-wool ceramic fibre. One side is removable to allow easy access to the hot pots.

Before firing, a solution of copper and cobalt salt is applied to the pots. The ware is not bisque-fired, and so a slow rise of temperature is needed. Each firing takes 9–10 hours to complete. At a temperature of 1060–1080°C the salting process takes place by spraying a soda solution into the kiln. When the pots are judged to be ready, they are removed to holes in the ground for reduction. Leaves are preferred as a combustible, but often a mixture of sawdust, hay, straw etc. is used. The smoking chamber is covered with a metal lid and is left until the pot is cool.

Raw-fired raku bowl by Heike van Zadelhoff, d. 25 cm, h. 12 cm.

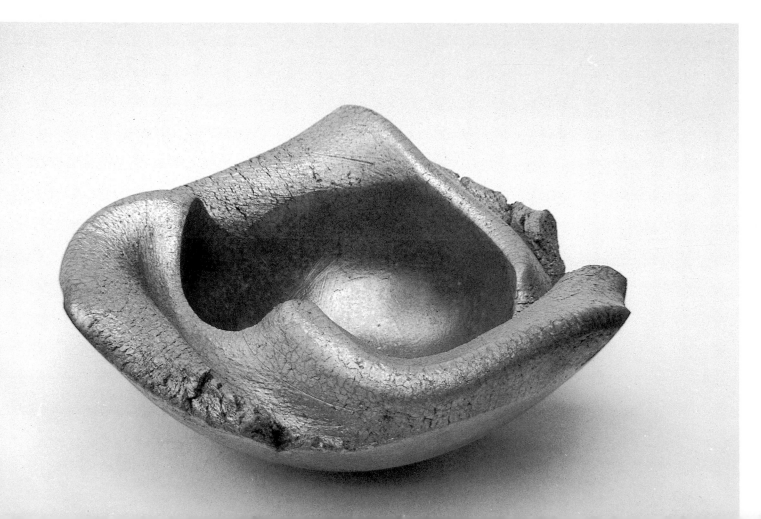

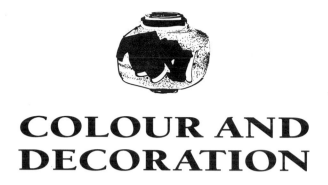

COLOUR AND DECORATION

This chapter looks at some of the potters who emphasise decorative techniques and the use of colour in their work. Raku offers a wide range of decorative options and a huge colour palette from underglazes to post-reduction chemical fuming. The immediacy of the firing method is often reflected in the spontaneous decorative styles chosen. A good example is David Miller whose bright painterly designs perfectly set off the enjoyable quirky pots. Chris Thompson on the other hand employs a more controlled, mathematical approach. His architectural designs create clever spatial conundrums on the surfaces of the pots.

Underglaze colours are used to great effect on the architectural pieces of Andrew Osborne. The vivid colours well match the optically distorted shapes giving them the characteristics of a 'looney toon' cartoon.

Walter Dexter's giant colourful raku wall combines many techniques of decoration and Swedish potter Lena Andersson also uses tiles for her intricate geometric patterns. Gail Bakutis, working in Hawaii, richly decorates her teapots with sponge techniques, slips and glazes and Australia's Ray Taylor has developed a range of coloured glazes which achieve a mixture of textures and lavish colours in a series of sweeping brush strokes. American Bob Smith adds some of his colours at the firing stage, removing the hot pots from the kiln and spraying them with chemicals such as ferric chloride. And post-firing reduction is controlled to achieve the fumed copper effects on the pots of Rick Foris. All these and many other decorative and colour techniques featured in this book make up a vast range of possibilities to try with raku.

Karin Heeman – The Netherlands

Karin Heeman makes pots in both France and The Netherlands. Her father was a graphic designer and her mother a mezzo-soprano. Growing up in an artistic family, Karin initially decided on a career as a professional ballerina. Eventually, the visual arts enticed her away from the footlights and she trained with the Dutch potter Eila Schrameyer, later attending many national and international workshops and seminars given by established makers. One such potter was David Miller who, in 1985, inspired Karin to experiment with raku. His influence is evident in her use of colour and spontaneous brush decoration, but she has acquired her own, less idiosyncratic, style of work; quieter forms which are perhaps influenced more from her other great love: porcelain.

Many of Karin Heeman's pots celebrate the bowl as one of the most elementary ceramic shapes. 'It is a form that generates tension, being sturdy and elegant at the same time, but also modest, deriving its useful function from its contents.' Her own pots are not in themselves functional, but emphasise the bowl as an object to be admired for its own sake. Their fragile thin walls and irregular rims are embellished with carving and impressed surface textures – revelling in swirling colours.

> I like richness and deep, warm colours in my work. For me, a good piece should have all this. Right from the start whilst making a piece I begin blending in body stains. It is more-or-less like working as a painter: *creating*, right from the start – with the great excitement of the firing at the end.

Coloured body stains are mixed into the clay (usually T-material) to produce plain or marbled slabs. These are then pressed in or onto moulds made from plaster, paper or foam rubber. Other stained inlays may be added as the piece is built and modelled. Before bisque-firing, more oxides and stains are painted on, building up a depth of rich colour. Glazes and pigments are applied after the bisque-firing either with fluent sweeping brush strokes or by spraying. Some areas are masked to provide a dark smoked backdrop to the theatre of riotous colour.

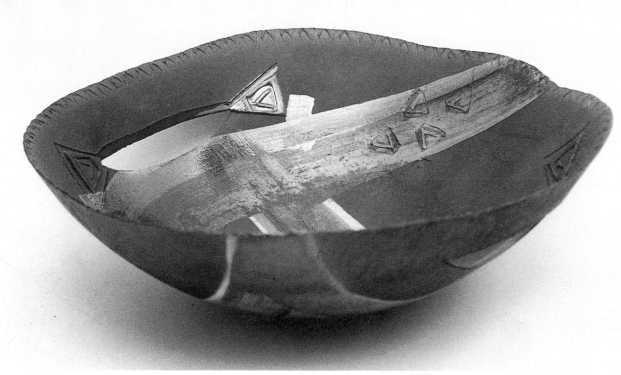

'Turn Around' raku bowl by Karin Heeman, d. 46 cm.

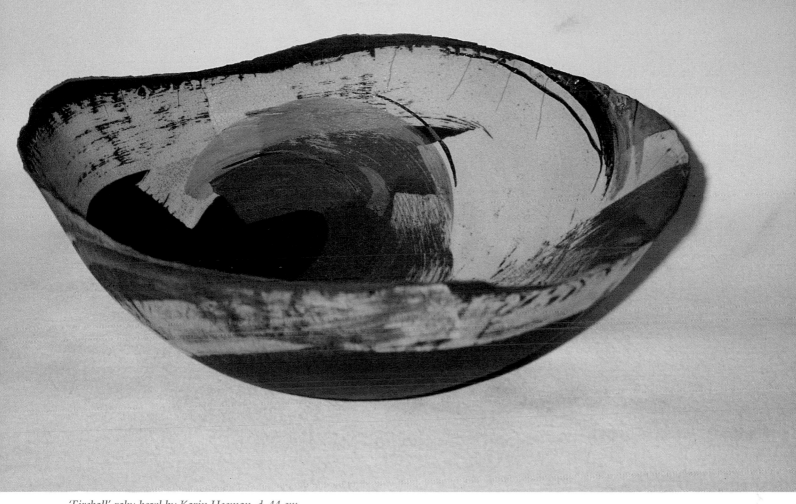

'Fireball' raku bowl by Karin Heeman, d. 44 cm.

I love painting on my pieces, and there are so many – almost endless – possibilities in combining, at once, creativity, form and firing. It is, for me, the way to make a piece with body and soul!

Much of her inspiration is derived from the Art Deco period, combined with the architecture of as diverse styles as early Greek and Roman, and the American architect Frank Lloyd Wright, who is a particular favourite.

Technical information

The kiln

The kiln is a purpose-built three-storey gas kiln (55 cm diameter and 78 cm high) which means large or small pieces may be fired with the addition or removal of one or two rings. It has a single burner and will reach 1000°C in about an hour. A digital pyrometer is used to monitor the temperature.

Smoking a piece of work

I use sawdust in a fairly large trunk. I prefer sawdust of oak – not always easy to get. Pieces are smoked for about an hour underneath a layer of cardboard or a thin layer of sawdust, sometimes a combination of the two. They are cleaned very thoroughly with steel-wool or sand. Never with washing-up liquid, I find that can leave terrible marks.

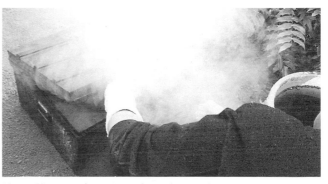

Karin Heeman fuming and smoking raku work.

Christopher Thompson – Canada

One thing that I have noticed about potters in general and about raku potters in particular is that we have a tendency to push ourselves, our making and firing techniques, and our materials, to their absolute limits. It might seem to some to make no sense at all, for instance, to spend ages constructing a very large slab-built piece of work, blast it for an hour or so in a homemade kiln, then remove it to a dustbin full of sawdust hoping that it won't fall to pieces in the process!

But Chris Thompson from Toronto, Canada, does just that. Twenty years of experience, trial and error and stubborn dogged determination, however, has seen him succeed where others have failed. His work – much of it on a massive scale for raku – is well-known in Canada and further afield, and admired for its technical as well as its aesthetic merits. Large plates, vessel forms and wall pieces feature amongst the variety of work that Chris produces. Some of them have reassuringly familiar elements. Large shallow bowls are softly altered and decorated emphasising their expansive surface areas. Elongated vessels hint of a Greek past, but then elegantly take a different road of their own. The tall organic forms have tight lines and constrictions in their long necks as if tied off with garden twine.

The strong connection running through all Chris's work is an interest in surface decoration. Pattern, texture, tone and colour are lavished on his pieces. Much labour is involved with glazing and decorating. Stains and underglaze colours are used along with wax-resist patterns, metal oxide washes and lustres.

A recent theme in his work is the use of architectural and spatial designs. These came about after a trip to Italy and Spain: the piazza-inspired stepped motifs set up visual puzzles for the viewer in an interesting play on space and dimension. The juxtaposition of the 'finite' simplicity of the vessel, and the intriguing 'infinite' graphic design, which leads the eye continuously around the pot, creates work with depth and substance.

The late Angus Suttie wrote:

> What I especially like in Thompson's work is his obvious enjoyment in taking risks. He hasn't succumbed to raku's inordinate power to 'Zenify'. There is nothing more inherently philosophical about raku than any other

technique. 'I raku, therefore, I think' is mystification. Chris Thompson uses the raku process with refreshing vigour.

Like many raku potters, Chris's early influences were from artists such as Paul Soldner and Wayne Higby in the USA, and, more recently UK potter, Dave Roberts. Now, however, most inspiration comes from travel and historical ceramics, such as those from Etruscan and Mediterranean cultures, although, as he says, 'his is a very changing area and hard to explain.'

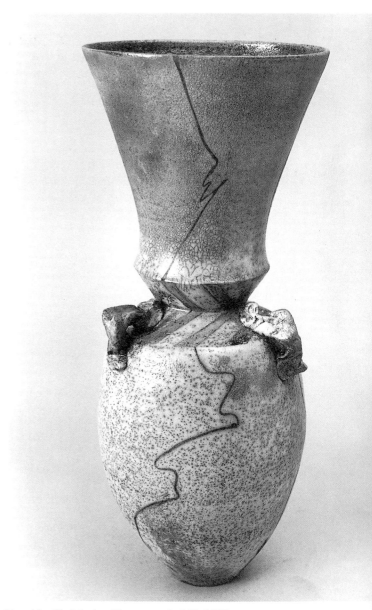

Vessel by Christopher Thompson, h. 16", 1982. Wheel-thrown.

Working in this medium is a continual challenge. There is a constant need to observe and learn from the fire itself, it is hard and dirty work, but fulfilling and strangely satisfying. I love the quality of the surface, the crackling of the glaze, the timelessness of the smoked clay as well as the immediacy and excitement of the firing process. Like nature itself, capricious and wilful, you are forced to accept that no matter how careful and sure of your work or yourself you are: at times you will fail. It is tempering and sometimes downright awful, but the times things work out more than make up for the disappointments. I like the process but it is certainly not for everyone.

Chris, like many others, combines making with some teaching. He is an instructor and head of department at the Koffler Gallery School of Visual Art and also conducts various workshops for both adults and children. He has exhibited widely in Canada as well as in London, Helsinki and New York.

Technical information

All of my work is first biscuit-fired to red heat 1600–1700°F. Glazing is built up with stains, commercial underglazes and wax-resist patterns. Then varying thicknesses of transparent glaze are sprayed on depending on the desired surface (matt or glossy), and then any sulphates are sprayed on top. If more intense lustres are required then washes of copper or iron oxides are used.

When the pieces have reached temperature they are removed from the kiln with gloves (there is less breakage this way) and put into a pit in the ground and covered with a mixture of sawdust and sand. The soil controls the amount of flame and helps slow down heat loss to prevent thermal cracking. For very large bowls or slab pieces he covers the pit during reduction with fibrefrax thermal blanket. The work is allowed to cool naturally and is sometimes sprayed with a very fine mist of water in order to 'freeze' particular lustrous effects.

Chris Thompson's clay body:

Bell Dark ball clay	3
Hawthorne clay	3
Kentucky ball clay	1
STP sagger ball clay	1
Talc	0.5
Wollastonite	0.5
30s mesh grog	2.5

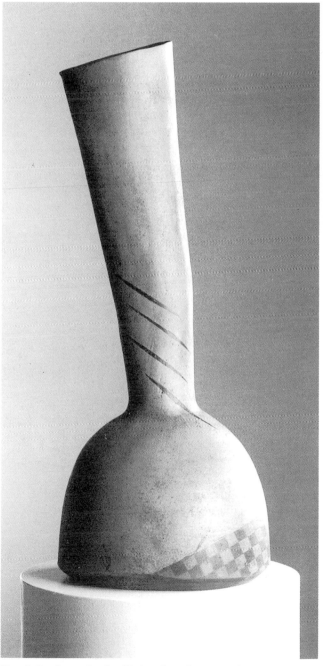

Vessel, Garden series, by Christopher Thompson, h. 68 cm, 1990.

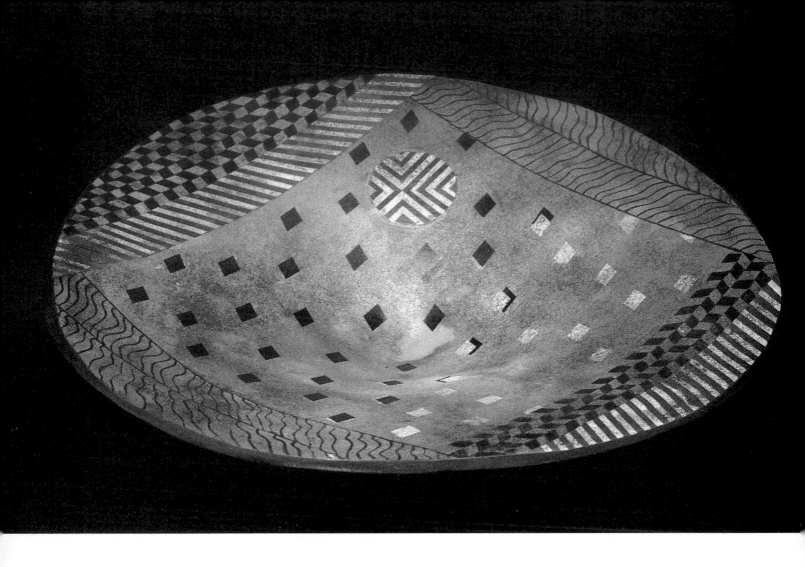

Above
Bowl, Sienna series, by
Christopher Thompson, d. 68 cm.
Raku, decorated with stains,
underglazes and wax resist
patterns and smoked in a pit
in the ground.

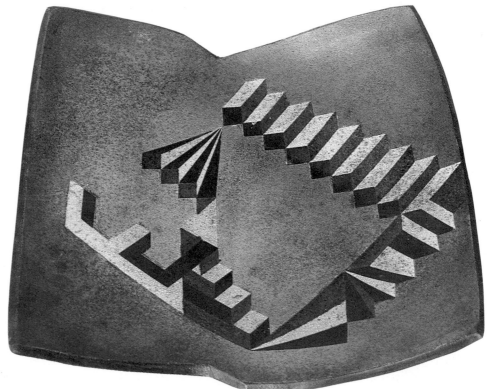

Plate, Labyrinth series, by
Christopher Thompson,
36 cm × 42 cm.
Raku.

David Miller – France

David Miller is a British potter who, for the past few years, has been living and working in France. He has been influential in both countries encouraging many to work with clay, low-fired salt and particularly raku.

At first glance, David's quirky imagery may seem frivolous. He produces absurd lampoons of teapots with extravagant spouts and 'sausage' handles, giant bowls and beakers, and strange sculptural objects which wouldn't look out of place in a clown's prop basket. Certainly his pots are parodies and poke fun at sacred institutions such as tea drinking, but fundamentally they are 'good-natured' and comfortable – combining a free style of colourful decoration with a lively and imaginative use of the clay.

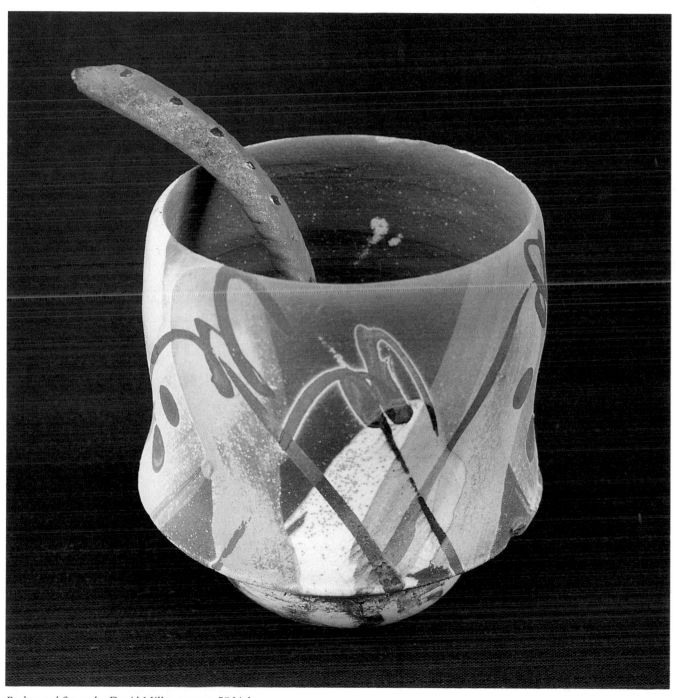

Beaker and Spoon by David Miller, approx. 5" high.

For all his humour, David Miller is admired by many for his mastery of technique and his professionalism. Most of his work is asymmetrical, but carefully balanced with the use of exaggerated coiled handles, spouts, or the flourish of a brush stroke. David's pots have many of the qualities of a drawing, such as spontaneity and freedom of the hand. Drawing itself is indeed important to him: 'I draw to liberate ideas through the simplicity of contact between head and heart, brush and paper.' As his ideas evolve and develop, drawing helps him to resolve any aesthetic or practical problems which arise. David studied Fine Art in the 1960s, specialising in sculpture, and followed on with a postgraduate course in printmaking at Brighton College of Art. Since 1970 he has been a part-time lecturer at a number of colleges.

Like many of the potters featured in this book, David divides his time between his one-off raku (which at present only provides around 15 per cent of sales), a range of decorated slipware, and some lecturing/demonstrating.

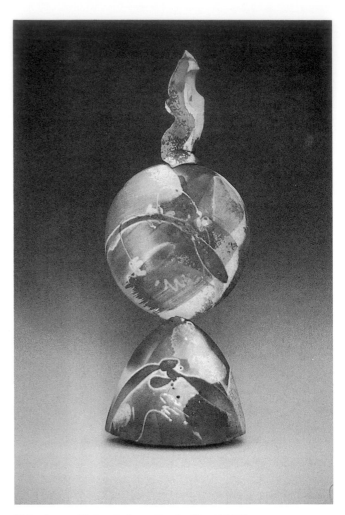

Raku form with brush decoration by David Miller.

Technical information

The pieces are mainly thrown, and re-formed in clay moulds. Feet and other attachments are modelled by squashing or rolling small pieces of clay. These are joined at the leatherhard stage or, occasionally, very delicate attachments may be glued on after firing. Other textured surfaces are moulded or modelled by hand.

A thin base slip is applied to all pieces before biscuit-firing. This provides a suitable surface for decorating with various colour stains. Decoration is brushed on using stains mixed with slip or glaze. Sometimes a thin layer of a transparent glaze is brushed poured or trailed over the decorated areas to limit local reduction, keeping the colours bright.

The high-temperature colour stains have to be modified by mixing with 25 per cent alkaline frit. This is important, for otherwise the colours do not adhere to the surface of the pot.

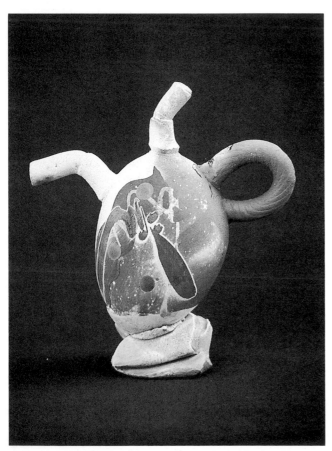

Teapot by David Miller, h. 10".
Thrown and altered.

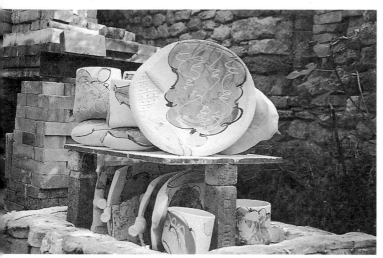

David Miller's tightly packed kiln.

A bisque-firing to 1020°C in an electric kiln is followed by the second firing in an oil-fired top-hat fibre kiln. The pots are packed touching, but not piled up on top of each other. Many pieces of work are fired together. This is possible as the pots are not glazed all over, and so with a little care, shouldn't stick together.

The kiln is warmed up gently (this is particularly necessary for a dense pack) using gas burners, and then quickly fired to just over 1000°C (1–1½ hours). Little control is exercised over the firing but an experienced eye judges the 'right' moment to remove the pots. David looks for the formation of a brilliant halo developing around the iron and copper decoration on the pots.

Post-firing reduction is achieved in circular metal bins with fibre lids. A couple of handfuls of sawdust are placed in each bin and the pots are removed, one or two at a time, and put on the bed of sawdust. Pieces of screwed up newspaper are placed carefully around the pot and the lid closed.

> I try to achieve heavy 'early phase' smoking – with military grey-green smoke – and then repeat the process of introducing paper until there is no colour glow from the pots. At each opening of the bin I allow oxygen to enter – sometimes this is accompanied by violent explosions!

Walter Dexter – Canada

Raku was introduced in Canada in the late 1960s and early 1970s. One of the pioneers was Walter Dexter whose first attempts, as early on as 1957, were less than successful:

> A colleague and myself had read of this technique: unknown in Canada, but historically common in Japan. We purchased a small, second-hand gas-fired dental kiln, and we believed that it would do for a trial run. We were simply experimenting, in total ignorance, for the fun of it. We made and glazed some very minute tea bowls: bowls so small as to be able to fit into a kiln not more than four inches in height and depth. Predictably, we failed. We didn't understand that the pottery had to be dried out by pre-heating before it was fired. All of our glazes bubbled and peeled; the insides of the pots literally foamed up. Defeated, we abandoned the project, and it was not until about twelve years later that I tried it again.

Workshops with the American potter Hal Riegger and later with Paul Soldner set Walter, along with a small group of potters across Canada, firmly on the raku trail again. Riegger taught from a traditional oriental perspective using local clays and ochres, fired in simple wood-burning kilns. By contrast, Soldner brought a new contemporary approach which removed the perceived restrictions of the technique thus making all things seem possible.

Walter Dexter's work has evolved over the years: moving from oriental influences, through a period of 'Greek' amphorae, and '. . . what may be considered classical shapes'. Favouring simplicity, he is concerned more with spiritual or emotional expression than with intellectual, or indeed, practical notions. He is a much respected potter who, for many years, has made his living almost entirely through his studio work – dividing it roughly between stoneware and raku. His innovative work has been widely exhibited and has won international acclaim. Walter has also shared his knowledge and experience with many others through his teaching in various colleges and universities in Canada.

> I find the greatest pleasure in doing the work. The process itself, particularly the glazing and

decorating, enables me to move beyond my surroundings into a concentrated space which is all engrossing. In order to find this space, I have to be able to free my mind from extraneous interruptions and thoughts – particularly those to do with gain or recognition. I found in past years that the mechanical process of throwing sometimes enabled me to reach this state of mind; but I now find the concentration required for the decorating and firing of raku a more stimulating and lively method of reaching the goal towards which I am directed. Here there is endless variety and the unexpected. The subtleties in colour, the richness of surface, and the unpredictability of technique give me great pleasure. The word raku means 'enjoyment': for me, this is the perfect definition.

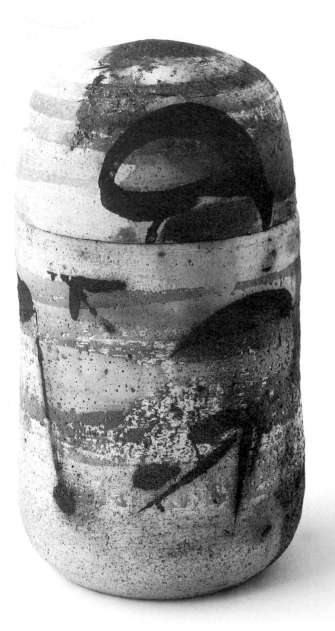

Lidded pot by Walter Dexter.
Raku with coloured vitreous engobes and iron, copper brushwork.

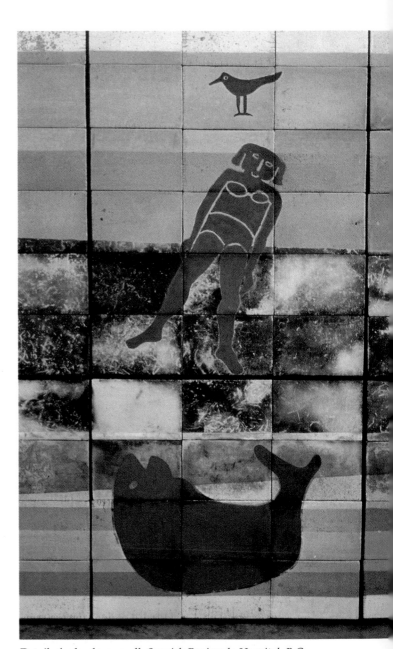

Detail of raku donor wall, Saanich Peninsula Hospital, B.C., 6 × 1.5 m.
Coloured terra sigillata bands decorated with animals and birds and a dry copper glaze.

70

Bob Smith – USA

Artist's Statement

The experience of working with clay for a living – as with most mixed blessings – is a confounding one. Like other professions, pottery requires a necessary dedication: discipline, organisational skills, a continuing education, an opportunity for interdisciplinary learning, and hard work. Unlike most jobs it can provide a sense of independence, a certain amount of recognition, the heady feeling of going against machined mass-production, and the satisfaction of beginning, carrying-through, and completing a project.

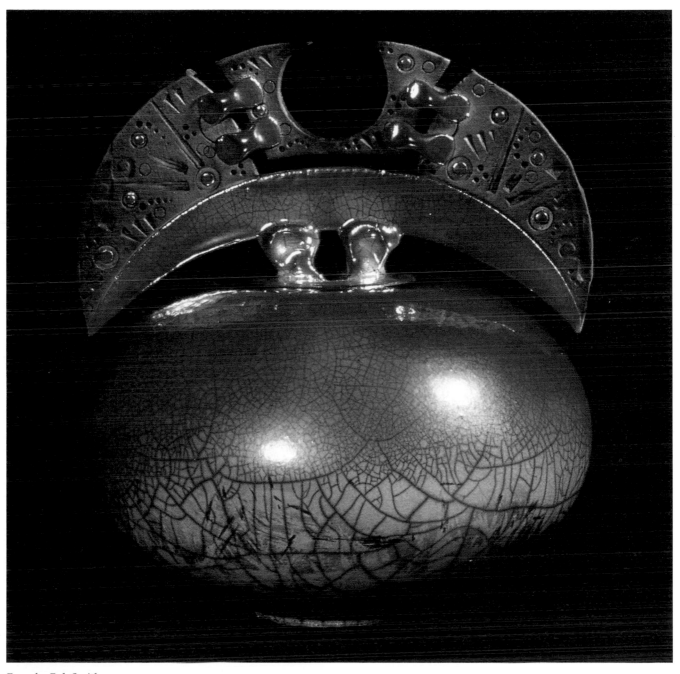

Form by Bob Smith.
Wheel-thrown piece with additional construction, bisqued and glazed in an electric kiln to cone 06, then raku-fired and fumed with chemicals.

... And it also offers deadlines, periodically inferior supplies, over-fired kilns, poor photo processing, work destroyed in shipping, galleries that suddenly fold, dried-up creative juices, the prospect of poverty ...

But it contains the intangible – and herein must lie the reasons one stays with clay. The intangible: of creating 'something' out of 'nothing' – of working at a chosen pace for interested people; of a connection, conscious or otherwise, with a history rich and varied – and so essential and human; of bringing into the world an object that intentionally exists to affect other people; of that rare moment when the pot (or sculpture or object or idea) works – when the sum is greater than the parts, and something wonderful has happened.

Silhouette and form, with a quiet contained presence: have always been my major concerns. My current work reflects this ongoing fascination with form, and an increased exploration of greater depth and subtlety in the surface – with new directions in colour, scale and texture. I continue to use the vessel as my point of departure, enjoying the historical connection. But it is what I do to the piece after it comes from the kiln – air-brushing, specifically applied combustibles, controlled water – and air-quenching – that dominates my thinking.

Bob Smith lives and works in Idledale, Colorado. A history graduate from Stanford University, he has had no formal training in art or ceramics. For more than 20 years however, he has expressed his enchantment with clay and has gained a reputation for low-fired, smoked and raku pottery.

No major influences led me in this direction – I couldn't *not* make pots once I first got my hands dirty. Raku, with its spontaneity, directness and pace followed naturally. I tried functional ware for two years or so, and never discovered the benefits of making multiples. It is, however, what I buy.

My processes have evolved from my needs as a one person studio. Being in charge of virtually all aspects of the potter's trade demands a simplified flow: clay production, kiln construction, firing procedures, marketing, packing and shipping, gallery rapport, etc. – all require patterns of operation that minimise my time and energy. For instance, my firing process requires that just 1–3 pots are fired at a time, but the yard is set up compactly so there are few unnecessary or redundant motions – it is truly a dance when I am firing.

Bob finds that the speed of firing and his ability to fire a single pot at a time allows him to get quick results from experiments and tests. Just as importantly, raku provides frequent small portions of time, which he can profitably use for the fulfilment of family commitments.

Some technical observations

The pots are bisque-fired in an electric kiln to cone 06 (995°C). After glazing (one to two brush coats, plus a pouring or dipping), he refires the pieces in the electric kiln to the same cone 06 temperature. The following day he fires the pots in an oversized oil-drum lined with kaowool (a high refractory kaolin/silica blanket). The fuel is natural gas and the pots need only get hot (possibly 1200°F/650°C) before they are removed for post-firing procedures. Set on a soft brick with tongs, they are oversprayed with chemicals (e.g. ferric chloride), or just with air to create crackle patterns, or put directly into the reduction chamber with specific amounts of straw, sawdust or newspaper to achieve a particular smoking density. The pots are in the reduction atmosphere from 10 seconds to 20 minutes depending on the pot, the glaze, the weather and the desired effects.

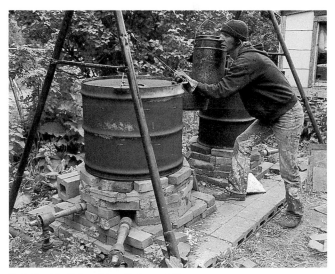

Bob Smith firing his oil-drum kiln.

Ray Taylor – Australia

Ray Taylor is one of Australia's foremost full-time potters. With numerous exhibitions at home and abroad, and an impressive array of awards to his name, his work is in demand across the continent.

Specialising in raku work and ceramic sculpture, the emphasis is very much on glaze decoration. Glazes are applied in a series of sweeping brush strokes which vary both in colour and size, producing an effect similar to an impressionistic painting.

This glazing technique produces a rich uniform colour when viewed from a distance, breaking into many different tonal harmonies on closer observation. The individual brush-strokes vary greatly in glaze thickness, creating areas of relief texture which can produce a jewelled effect, adding a positive textural element to the overall design.

Ray leaves some areas of the pot's surface unglazed, turning them black when smoked. This frames and therefore intensifies the colours of the glaze, similar to the effect of the leading in a stained glass window. The varying colours and thicknesses cause a further illusion of depth, encouraging the eye to linger on the complex pot-pourri of decoration.

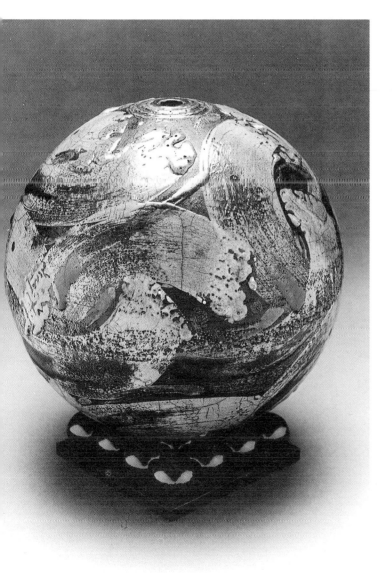

Raku Sphere by Ray Taylor, h. 36 cm.
Yellow, orange and blue glaze decoration.

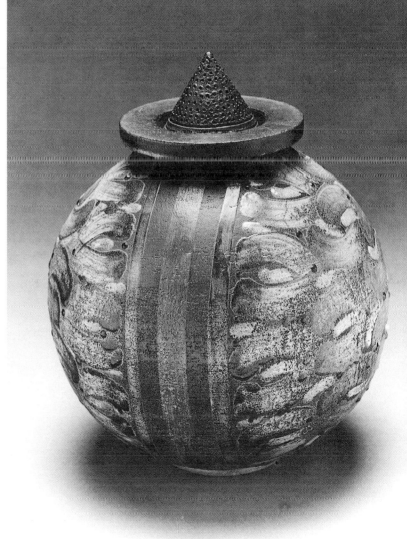

Raku Container by Ray Taylor, h. 37 cm.
Blue brush strokes with pink and green lines.

Technical information

Construction of the pieces is by a combination of throwing, turning, moulding and wrapping techniques. Most of the shapes are based on simple derivations of spheres, cones or cubes.

For convenience he uses only one base glaze:

Frit 3110   98
Bentonite   2

By 'line-blending' common oxides, Ray has developed a palette of over a hundred colours to be used with this glaze.

Firing

The ceramics are fired with liquid petroleum gas (LPG) for approximately one hour in a fibre-lined metal dustbin. The atmosphere in the kiln is controlled for each piece. Full oxidation produces a wide range of bright colours. Reduction softens the colours – generally decreasing the range of hues – but can result in dramatic effects such as vivid copper reds. Ray favours a mixed atmosphere and an uneven kiln temperature which encourages localised variations of colour (and indeed texture, when the glaze melt is affected). Each pot is removed, when ready, to a newspaper – lined drum. Initial ignition of the paper is snuffed out with a lid and the piece is left to smoke for only 10–15 minutes before being removed, doused with water and cleaned.

Raku Box by Ray Taylor, h. 32 cm.

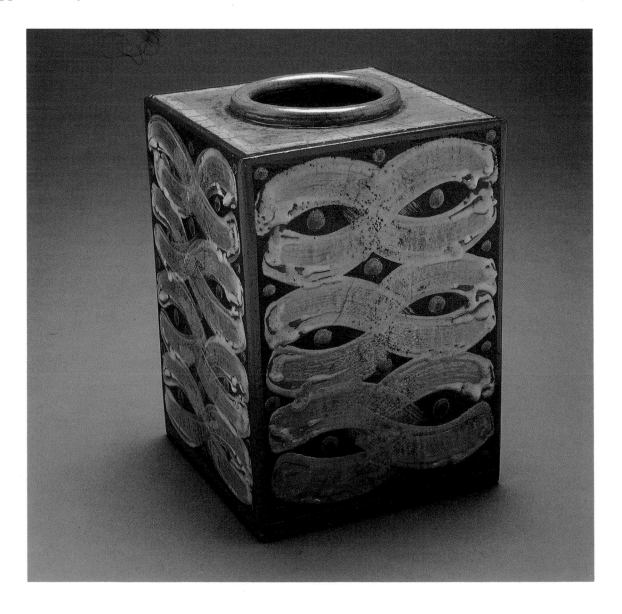

Gail Bakutis – USA

Gail Bakutis lives and works on the Hawaiian Island of Oahu and her work is strongly influenced by the beautiful and dramatic surroundings thrown up by ancient volcanic activity. The continual process of creation which is this elemental theatre of rock, fire, sea and wind, is reflected in the natural forces she harnesses to fire and smoke her work. Her semi-organic pieces display the colours and textures of lichen, the salt spray of the sea or the burnt sulphurous qualities of prehistoric lava flows.

Temples, pyramids and ruins also impress her greatly. Many of her pieces exhibit Mayan or Japanese or Indonesian features. Made for ornament, they also allude strongly to function – teapots being a particular favourite.

Self-taught in ceramics, Gail has been involved with raku for nearly 20 years but also fires to earthenware and stoneware temperatures as well as pit-firing. Her potting was preceded and overlapped by her other main interest, the theatre. Training and working in the USA, Greece, Paris and Hawaii, she has been an actress, drama teacher, theatre director and critic. Now she exhibits with a cooperative art gallery in Honolulu in addition to a schedule of local and mainland US shows. She also teaches adult classes at the Academy of Arts.

Samurai Tea Series by Gail Bakutis, 12" × 7" × 3".
Raku-fired with slips and glazes.

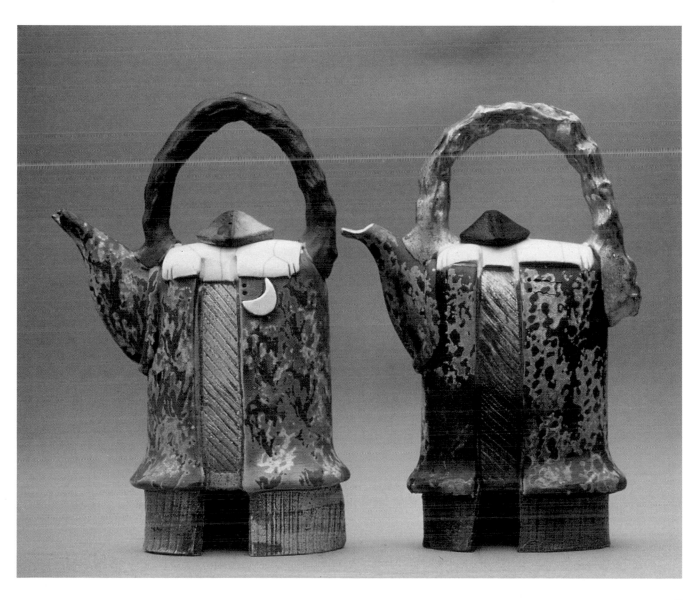

Technical information

All Gail's work is handbuilt using her own heavily grogged and sanded porcelain body for large pieces (some up to three and a half feet tall) and a commercial porcelain for smaller work. The clay is rolled into slabs which are assembled into box shapes. These are covered with old clay and vinegar water and 'whacked into shape with a koa paddle'. The rough blanks can then be turned into teapots, temple boxes or whatever she has in mind. Decoration is often by sponge application and consists of an assortment of slips, slip glazes and raku glazes with various stains and colours which Gail has formulated.

Firing

A gas-fired stacking sectional fibre kiln is used (up to five sections) which will accommodate the largest pieces. The kiln has no base and can be lifted clear of each pot when the firing is finished. A large rolling reduction chamber is then pushed around the piece which is left in place on two pads of ceramic fibre. The door is closed and reduction materials such as banana leaves are added and a lid put on. While the pot is left to cool, new fibre pads are then laid out and the kiln set up for another firing. In this way there is no need to move very large and heavy hot pots and so there is less chance of breakage.

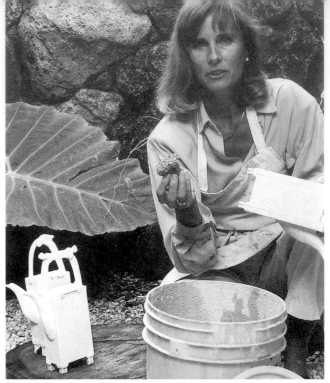

Gail Bakutis slip glazing/sponging bisque ware for raku firing, 1989.
Courtesy of Studio Potter. Photograph by Gerry Williams.

Some observations on safety:

I always wear a surgical mask for smoke and a specialised fire-suit made for airport fire fighters, with a hood, jacket and trousers. I also use cotton gloves inside my raku 'mittens' for lifting hot ware. Always safety – safety – safety in raku!

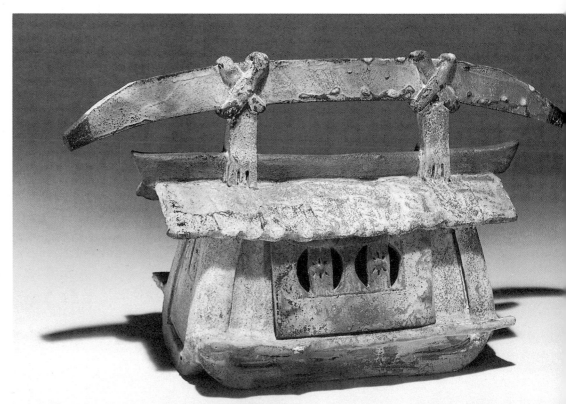

Palanquin (vessel) with sliding doors and lid by Gail Bakutis, 16" × 24" × 9".
Photograph by Paul Kodama.

Lena Andersson – Sweden

Interest in raku amongst Swedish potters has grown considerably in recent years. Influenced largely from the USA, many ceramists are making raku either exclusively or together with the more traditional Swedish ware of pale colours and perfect finish.

Lena Andersson first tried out the technique at a seminar held at *Blas and Knada (Blow and Knead)*, a cooperative owned and managed by some 35 professional potters and studio glass artists, all of whom run their own workshops in Sweden. She set up her own kiln at her house in the Halsingland countryside where she and fellow potter Gertrud Båge fire their work a few times a year.

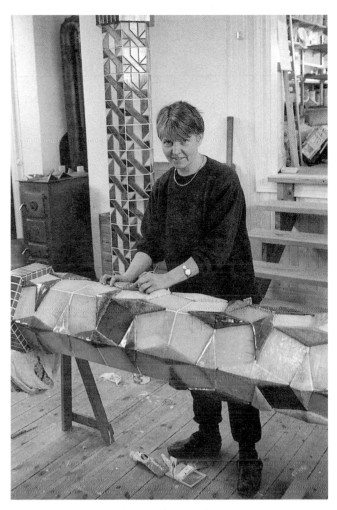

Lena Andersson working in her studio.

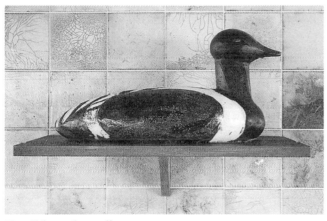

Detail from the wall.

A wall at Landstingsforbundets Hus in Stockholm by Lena Andersson.

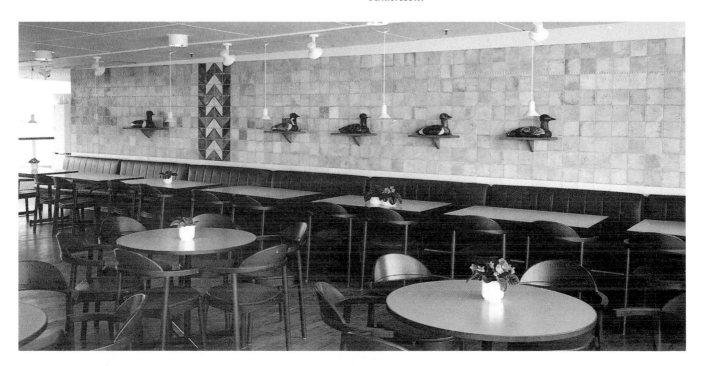

Lena's work is varied. The making and firing of tiles takes up a sizeable part of her time. She has completed several large public commissions for walls and columns, often involving large numbers of tiles put together in complicated geometric patterns. Together with – and sometimes integrated into – these often monumental sculptures, are smaller pieces: half spheres, shell-like structures, and stylised forms derived from earlier insect shapes. Lena's insects, and beetles in particular, are of special interest to her. Many of the iridescent colours found naturally on the feathers of birds or the wings and bodies of insects, are mirrored in her use of raku glazes and engobes. Terra sigillata is a favourite technique, having been brought to Sweden from the USA by Karin Nordling, another member of the cooperative.

Firing procedure

Firing the pre-bisqued pots in an oil-drum kiln, the larger pieces often have to be supported. The average temperature for Lena's work is around 900°C – this takes about one and a half hours to achieve. Each piece may be fired two or three times until a satisfactory result is obtained. A day's rest to allow the piece to dry out is taken between firings but a second or third heating is more likely to crack the pot. Post-firing reduction takes place in a metal drum containing fluffed-up newsprint. The pieces are then quenched in a water-bath and, weather permitting, cleaned off in the snow.

Lena Andersson cleaning off a pot in the snow. *Photograph by Stig Andersson.*

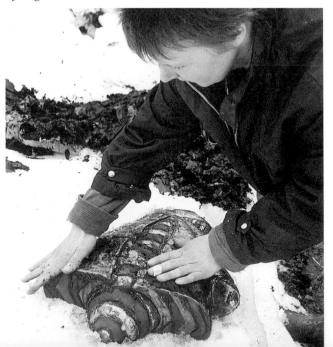

Rick Foris – USA

It's not unusual for me to fire a pot a dozen or more times before it is acceptable. Time, temperature, amount and type of combustibles, volume and shape of the pot relative to the smoking chamber, even barometric pressure are all factors in determining the eventual outcome of the pot.

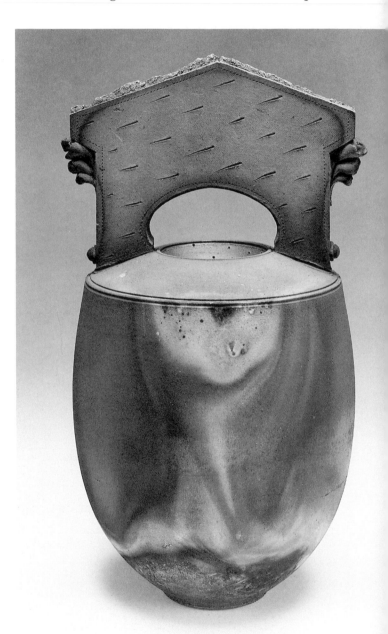

Vessel by Rick Foris, h. 16".
Raku with matt lustre glaze.

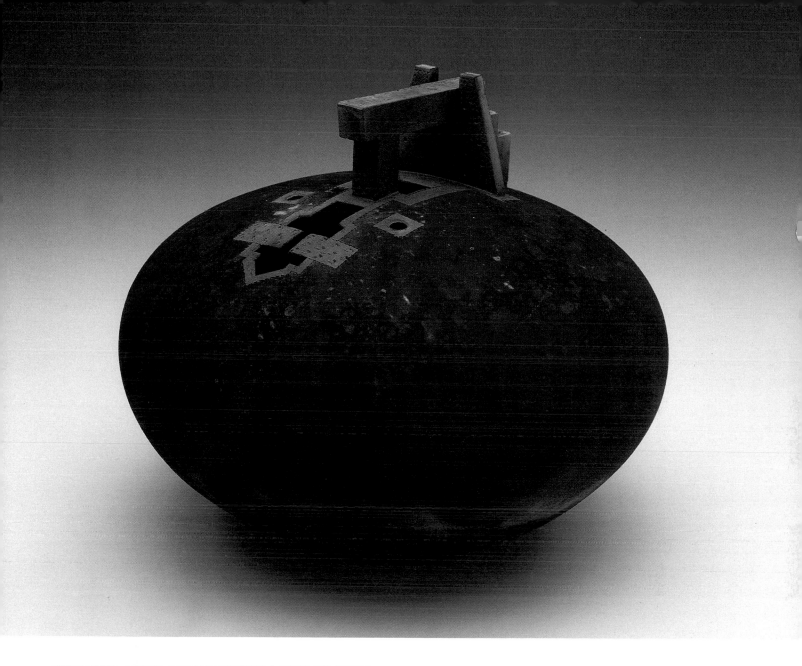

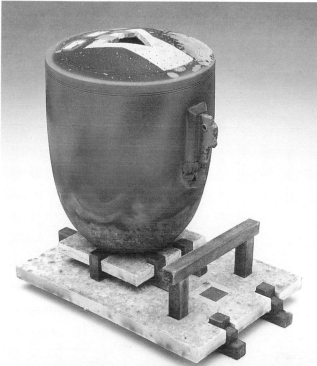

Above
Raku vessel by Rick Foris, 9" × 12".
Thrown and cut slab construction. Sprayed copper matt
lustre glaze.

Raku vessel and pedestal by Rick Foris, h. 16".
Thrown and slab construction with matt copper and iron
lustre glaze. The pot was bisque-fired to cone 08 before raku
firing with propane in a converted electric kiln and then
smoking in a dustbin with a small amount of sawdust and
straw.

79

Andrew Osborne – UK

Andrew Osborne's raku pieces display a confidence of line and perspective which betrays his architectural training. Ships, trains and cars are frozen in an optical distortion like moments from a 1950s movie. Cock-eyed rows of terraced houses twist and lean precariously as if made from the brightly coloured rubber of childhood toys. A 'cartoon' palette of underglaze colours adds a further humourous dimension to the pieces – the jazzy shading enlivening and enriching the surfaces.

Andrew's seed bed of ideas is his sketchbook. Working largely from memory, transport and building themes are explored in detail on paper. For more complicated shapes some research is necessary, but the idea is not to reproduce accurate facsimiles but to play around with familiar images and the contortion of perspective. To achieve this in three dimensions, the sketches are translated to clay and reworked and refined until resolved. Progress is very slow and new ideas take a long time to come to fruition. With the added pressure of orders and exhibitions only a dozen or so new designs are completed each year.

The influences that have come to bear are quite varied. Obviously, architecture and the way objects are constructed and perceived is of primary interest. The brightly decorated Art Deco pots of Clarice Cliff, and the saltglazed wares of Walter Keeler and others are also listed as sources of inspiration. Indeed, for some years, most of Andrew's own work was saltfired. The move to raku was in part governed by the need to speed up one aspect of production as the pots themselves became more complicated. The technique also offered an exciting range of colours which best suited the new pieces.

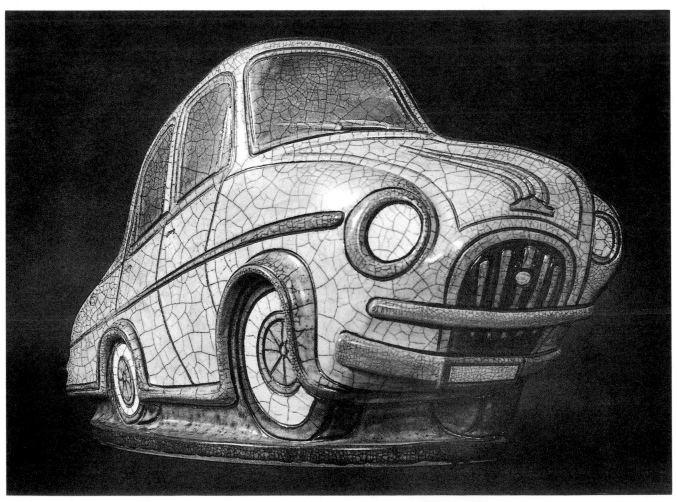

Raku car by Andrew Osborne, 18" long.
Photograph by The Image Company.

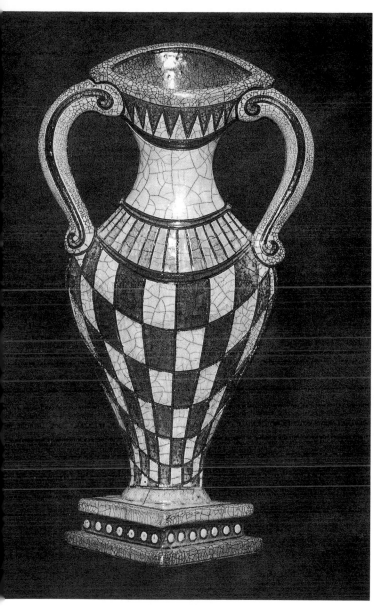

Amphora by Andrew Osborne, h. 24".
Incised pattern with underglaze colours.
Photograph by The Image Company.

Making and firing techniques

Drawings from the sketchbook are transferred to paper or cardboard and cut out as templates. Slabs of clay (T-material) are then rolled out and the shapes cut out. Stiffening up the slabs – usually overnight – he then carefully assembles them, creating a crude 'box' section. Another period of slow drying overnight achieves a uniformly leather-hard piece. This is followed by extra refinement – paddling, adding sections, texturing, scratch-line decoration etc.

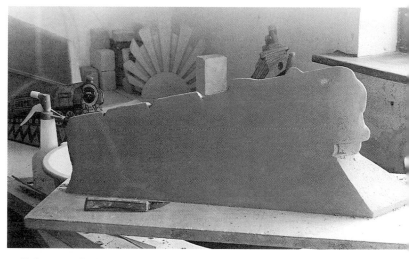

1. Slabs are rolled out, cut using a cardboard template and carefully assembled. The surfaces are smoothed before decoration begins.

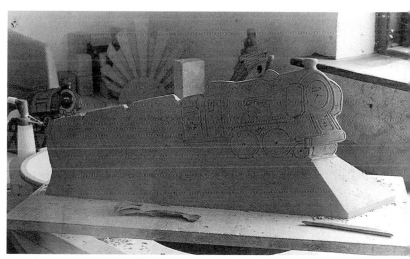

2. Using a wooden tool, lines are carved to provide areas for underglaze application. Most colours are painted onto the dry clay surface before bisque firing.

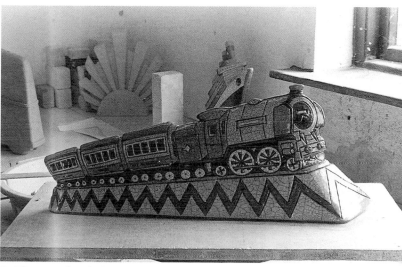

3. The completed piece after firing.

When thoroughly dry, most of the underglaze colours are applied (some colours will only adhere properly if applied to bisque-fired ware), brushing on with 'Universal Medium'.

A very slow bisque firing to 1000°C follows in an electric kiln. The high alkaline glaze is then sprayed on – thickness is crucial and is judged by eye. The pot is left until any absorbed moisture has evaporated before being raku-fired in a top-hat fibre kiln. A temperature of around 900°C is reached in roughly two hours – again the melt is monitored mostly by eye with a pyrometer as a back-up. When ready, the burners are turned off and the pot is allowed to cool for 10–15 minutes in the kiln before being removed to the reduction chamber to be smoked in hardwood sawdust. Timing is crucial, for if the pot is too cool it will not take up enough smoke to develop a sufficiently dark crackle, and if it is too hot it is more likely to shatter. (Large vulnerable pots are treated in this way, small items may be removed from the kiln almost immediately.)

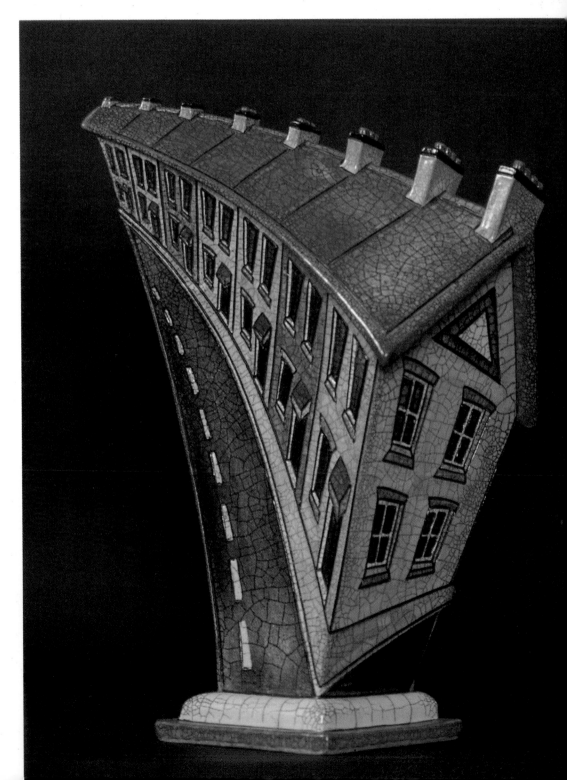

'Terrace' by Andrew Osborne, h. 22", w. 15". Slab construction with underglaze colour decoration. *Photograph by The Image Company.*

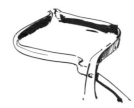

POST-FIRING, BURNISHING, SMOKE AND SAWDUST

Pyromania is endemic in the world of ceramics but perhaps practitioners of raku have a worse case of it than most. I have set aside this chapter for those whose lust for smoke and fire has led them down different but parallel avenues of combustion. Not all the potters here are strictly-speaking raku artists. I have bent the criteria for inclusion slightly to allow in one or two who sawdust fire their work. In my book (literally) they qualify anyway as paid up fellow incendiarists!

The first of these is Antonia Salmon. Her distinctive sculptural pieces are becoming well-recognised in the UK. Their elegant and balanced forms, and burnished, smoked surfaces display qualities of quiet strength and presence. German born Gabriele Koch also sawdust fires her large coiled rotund pots. The flashing of the heat causes dramatic 'halos' and patination.

I have also included my own work in this section which combines 'true' raku techniques with burnishing, lustres and an assortment of other methods. Anne James is another cross-over potter. She skilfully applies resin lustres to great effect on her porcelain raku pots, achieving rich and beautiful surfaces which are enhanced further by smoking. Jason Wason burns an assortment of materials for his post-firing technique, almost destroying his pots to obtain the most dramatic results possible.

Post-firing specialist Biz Littell is a pioneer in fuming techniques. His innovative work in clay and glass has been recognised widely in the USA. A leading light in UK ceramics is Judy Trim. Some of her highly decorative burnished lustreware, meticulously made, is subjected to the rigours of a relatively uncontrolled sawdust firing in an addictive partnership with the fire

Antonia Salmon – UK

Antonia Salmon's sawdust-fired pieces demonstrate many of the qualities of mainstream raku work.

Her main influences come from sculpture rather than ceramics, especially stone carving. Ancient Egyptian and Greek reliefs play a part, along with the 20th-century work of Eric Gill and Epstein. Ethnic decorations and the shapes of tools from South American, Maori and Celtic sources are also apparent:

> ... even small items such as farming implements, combs, stools, mirrors and wristbands whose forms are uniquely related to function and whose craftsmanship is to be cherished for its dignity ...

> ... My main area of exploration is with form. The process of honing the shapes down, burnishing and so on, takes many hours, and is a time of contemplation valuable to the evolution of new shapes. The experience of

placing the objects in the sawdust kiln, exposing them to uncontrolled heat and smoke, is uplifting. The extraordinary drama and subtleties of the smoked surfaces is not something that the human mind could easily contrive. Naturally, the forms I make are based on the knowledge of the firing process, therefore I tend to keep both lines of form and surfaces uncluttered.

Technical information

Making

The pots are generally thrown, and altered or handbuilt using a white stoneware clay, or T-material for larger pieces. 'Because the shapes are fairly pure, any splitting or cracking is unacceptable to me, therefore great care is taken, especially with joints.'

Sawdust fired white stoneware by Antonia Salmon, 15 cm × 21 cm.

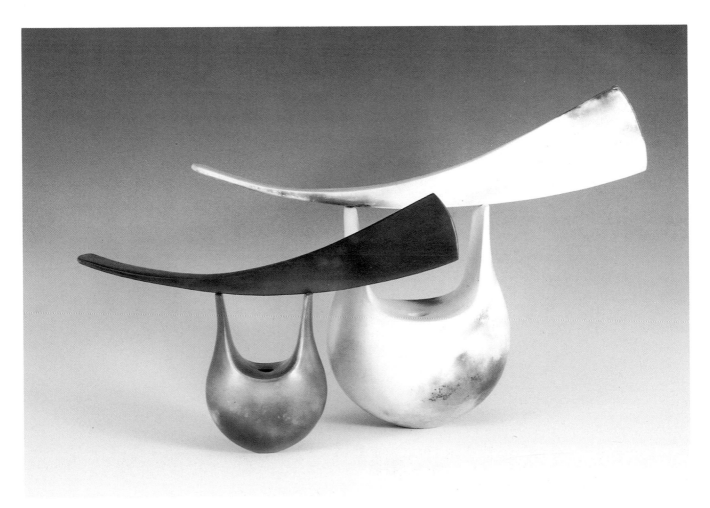

There is occasional use of slips made up from the white stoneware with the addition of coloured stains. These are painted on and burnished. Also some use is made of inlaid oxides (manganese and iron) and carved relief lines and incisions.

Initial bisque-firing to 1060°C burns off the burnish but ensures some vitrification and strength. This is necessary as some of the sculptural work is extremely fine and the larger pots are often used in gardens.

Sawdust firing

The type of sawdust used varies. Loose shavings burn faster and produce more dramatic flashing. Finer dust gives a denser carbonisation. The pots are carefully placed in relation to each other to shield some areas from smoke. The sawdust is lit from the top and allowed to burn down slowly. The work may be fired two or three times until it is satisfactory.

Breakages are inevitable, around 20–50% of any firing. Large flat shapes are especially vulnerable. I've learnt to be philosophical, but when there are deadlines to work against it does raise the blood pressure!

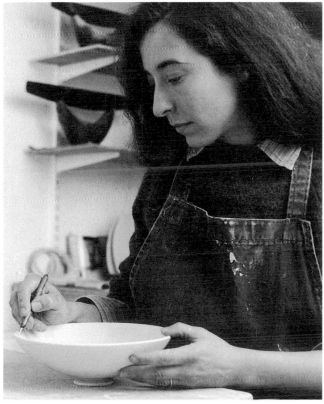

Antonia Salmon in her studio.

Biz Littell – USA

Biz Littell is a technical innovator in clay, glazes and glass. Many of his developed techniques are now used by other artists and craftsmen.

My work in clay is specifically related to a fuming technique I discovered at Alfred University as a graduate student. After glaze firing (cone 4 to 5), Hanovia Gold is airbrushed over the surface of the piece, then fired to cone 17 in an oxidation atmosphere. At approximately 1000°F (538°C), I vapour glaze with barium chloride, strontium nitrate or stannous chloride, for approximately 15 minutes – then remove the piece from the kiln and cool it rapidly in fibre blanket wrapped in various combustibles. I tend to vary this technique, but have developed a high degree of consistency in colour at these temperatures. Slower cooling tends to produce green hues whereas fast cooling with reduction produces hues towards red.

From an exhibition review by Josef Woodard in the *Santa Barbara News*:

For sheer disruption of expectations, Biz Littell's shimmering blend of clay and metal puts forth some of the most intriguing conceptual energy in the show. Aside from the rugged quality of his pottery, you have to marvel at the way he gets metal to behave in a malleable, clay-like way.

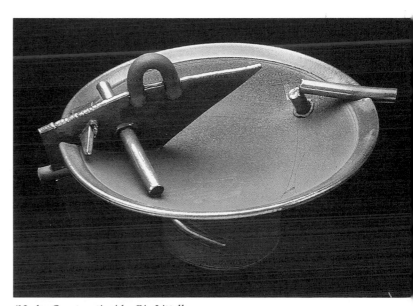

'Under Construction' by Biz Littell.

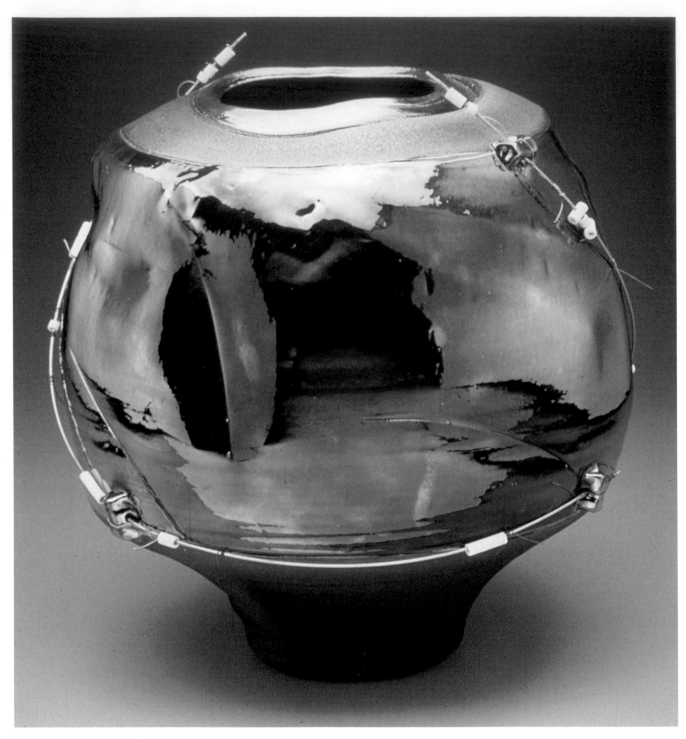

'Oz' by Biz Littell.
Vapour-glazed raku.

Judy Trim – UK

Judy Trim has, for a number of years, been internationally recognised as one of Britain's leading potters. Her work is often exhibited alongside that of such major figures as Dame Lucie Rie and Elizabeth Fritsch – each of whom have had a great influence on her. She is not a true raku potter (by the normally accepted definition) but falls into the category of artists who employ some aspects of the technique, or perhaps more appropriately, to use the words of Paul Soldner: 'display a "rakuness" in their work'.

The pots themselves have evolved along with the maker but generally Judy chooses bottle and bowl forms referring as much to the classical traditions as to more contemporary work. They are not functional or domestic pieces but instead belong to 'a more contemplative tradition' which is to do with feelings and emotions. Here she describes her work and her approach:

> I often muse over John Berger's suggestion that artists are motivated by a deep-seated desire to overcome, and to replace, disappointments from early childhood.
>
> My first eight years of potting were active in the search for the tactile, soft open warm closeness of surface effects (absent Father?). And for sure the arrival of baby altered my work for the next few years. The desire for those qualities inevitably became less urgent and I had a need to retreat somewhat from the domestic, humble, mundane to a world of dreams, contemplation, rich colour, celebration, ceremony and glamour even. Subsequently I produced a body of glittering, unsmoked, decorative lustreware – and yet smoking is never far from my concerns, and currently I make intermittent dashes for the sawdust kiln with my lustreware.
>
> I have always felt tremendously drawn to pots from the past and present primitive cultures which were and are unglazed and low-fired in low-tech kilns. The strongly tactile quality of these soft, warm, open bodies has a formidable appeal to me, and those splendid Chinese, African, pre-Columbian, Greek, Egyptian slipped or burnished pots are a constant source of inspiration.

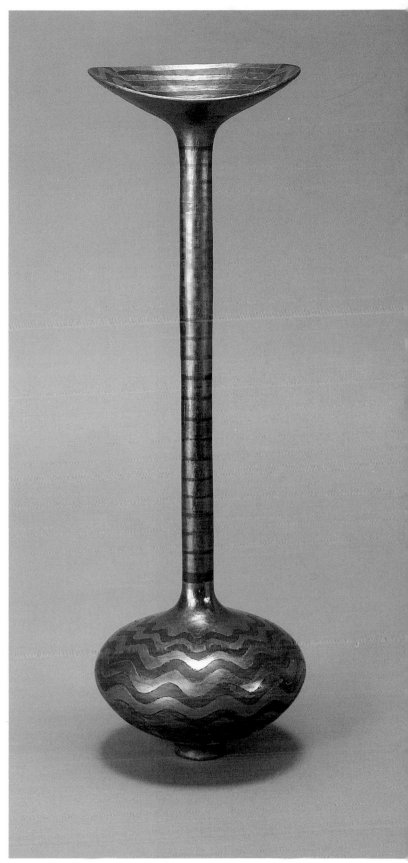

'Tear Jar' by Judy Trim, h. 36cm. Lustred and smoked.

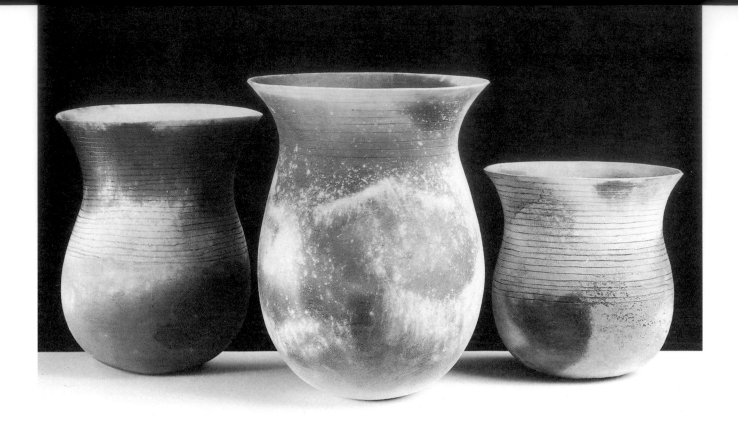

Porcelain forms by Judy Trim, h. 4" -6".
Burnished and coloured with slips before smoking.
Photograph by David Cripps.

I make my pieces painfully slowly, as they are meticulously refined and controlled. Consequently, I love the thrill of surprise from the unknown, and the sense of freedom evoked by the surrender of control, when abandoning my work to the chance smoking of the surfaces. These surfaces (usually slip-painted, sgraffitoed, burnished or lustred) are modulated, enriched and somehow completed by the spontaneity of the smoke, affecting the whole.

Perhaps the above description implies 'unplanned' activities, but, in point of fact, I do carefully orchestrate each firing – i.e. pots upside down; pots half-smoked; use of assorted resists; dustbin lids on; dustbin lids off; use of saggars; use of different sawdusts and so on.

The 'process' of smoking is also addictive. I am a confirmed pyromaniac, and the direct, active, energetic, demanding involvement with smoke and fire, a collaboration with the elements, is irresistible.

And finally, being also a coward, the fact that the surface is always flexible and free, never fixed dead with that hard, unyielding, probably wrong coat of glaze, is of huge appeal, and I have re-smoked my pieces many times in some instances to achieve the end result (smoke can be burnt off around 600°C).

Some technical observations

Each piece is very slowly built up using coils of T-material ('... which gives a slightly grainy white canvas with its bonus of great strength'). Some of the larger pots can have up to 200 coils and, at an average of 20 minutes per coil, may take a week to complete. Burnishing has to be done as the pot dries from the base whilst under construction. Slips with colour stains are applied first (basic slip–50% ball clay, 50% China clay). Recent work also involves the use of lustres – layers are built up like a painting – sometimes upwards of 20 on one piece, each requiring a separate firing.

Careful packing of the pots in sawdust produces semi-controlled variations in the final carbonisation. Occasionally in a frenzied act of raku madness, pieces are removed from the fire at a critical moment to 'freeze' a particular effect.

Gabriele Koch – UK/Germany

German-born potter Gabriele Koch has now made her home in the UK. Her gourd-like bulbous pots have become familiar objects and are exhibited widely in Britain and Europe. She first tried raku at the Camden Institute in London and further exploration of this technique and smoke-firing was made later at Goldsmiths College.

Burnished and unglazed, most of her pots are sawdust-fired; the pre-bisqued pots are packed tightly in sawdust in an oil-drum. There are no holes in the drum but a lid is placed on top leaving a slight gap. The sawdust is set alight with a blow-torch from the top and left to smoulder. Gabriele gives one word of warning: 'Don't use I.C.I-marked oildrums in public places for smoking – you might get the bomb-disposal experts round!'

Some pots are occasionally raku-fired, taken from the kiln hot and plunged into a bed of sawdust or leaves. This produces a more dramatic effect with lustrous flash marking. 'I am fascinated by the elemental qualities of clay and its transformation, and the effect of this very direct contact between fire and earth.'

An extended stay in Spain and repeated visits in the late 1960s and early 1970s proved to be a formative experience, and they have had a profound effect on later work. She writes:

I am very influenced by the open desert-like landscape of central Spain with simple horizon lines and strong earth colours from black to ochre and red; and the experience of a still largely rural, more contemplative, yet also quite dramatic society, and the warm randomness of handmade wood-fired terracotta with its flashing marks.

Burnished, coiled pot by Gabriele Koch, h. 35 cm.

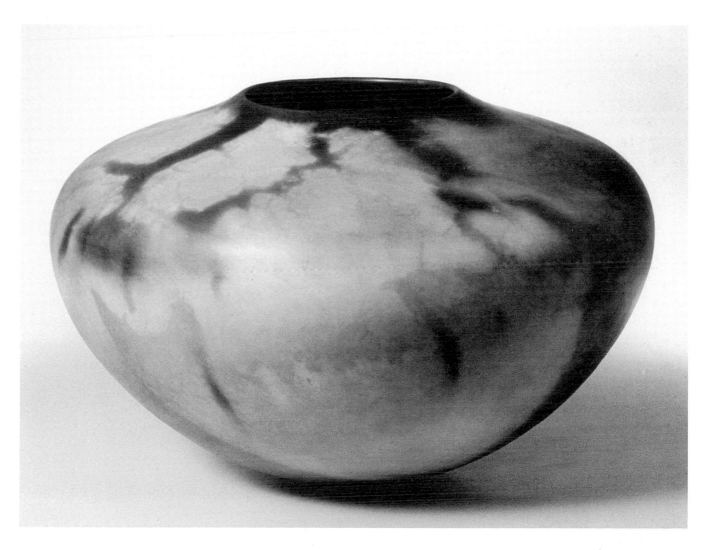

Tim Andrews – UK

A conversation I often have with visitors to the workshop is conducted as follows:

Visitor: 'What kind of pots are these?'
Tim: 'Well, most of them are raku-fired.'
Visitor: 'Ah yes, I've heard of that – how do you do it then?'

At this point I usually find myself struggling for a simple description to sum up raku in one line. The best I can come up with is a quotation from Dave Roberts: 'Raku is drawing pots hot from a kiln and then doing something to them.'

Whilst this may not be a very profound statement, it does describe possibly the only common activity of all raku potters – i.e. extracting a piece of work from a hot kiln. All other related activities I explain – smoking, fuming and additional post-firing high jinks – are particular in one form or another to the individual potter.

After this opening gambit (no doubt spurred on by the sight of me with a steaming wet towel wrapped around my head, a red face and more than a hint of *eau de fumé* about) the smiling visitors enquire whether they can watch the 'fun' of the next pot coming out of the kiln. To me this is a little like asking to peer over the shoulder of a bomb disposal expert at the crucial moment of defusing, but not wishing to dampen their enthusiasm I give them a tour of the kiln site, dropping in at some suitable point the suggestion that the pot will probably not be ready for a while yet!

Opposite
Large round bottle form with fumed copper surface by Tim Andrews, approx. 12" × 12". Photograph by Peter Harper.

Below
Fumed copper raku bowl with glazed interior by Tim Andrews, h. 4". Photograph by Peter Harper.

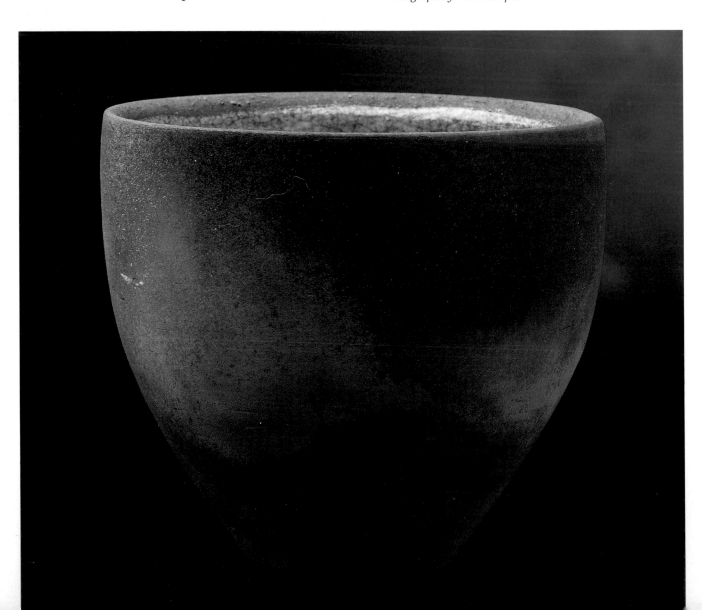

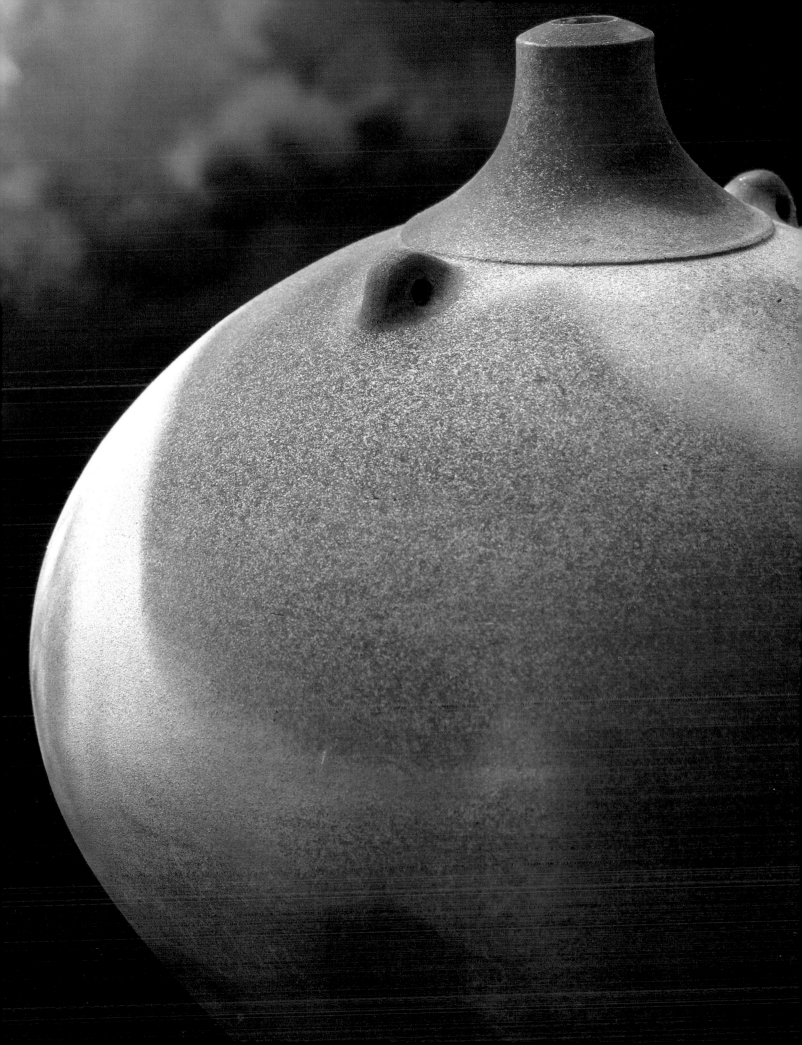

My training was unusual by today's standards. After leaving school, a move to art college was diverted at the last moment by an invitation to work as an apprentice in the studio of David Leach for one year. As any past students of his reading this will know, David ran a tight ship – and an intensive and formative period of practical training and hard work followed. A further two years was spent at the Dartington Pottery training workshop. A grant from the Crafts Council helped to establish my first tiny studio where I made functional stoneware and porcelain selling in a few small shops and galleries. Later, a move to a larger workshop offered the space for more experimentation and the opportunity to organise summer schools. The need to offer a varied teaching programme turned my thoughts again to raku.

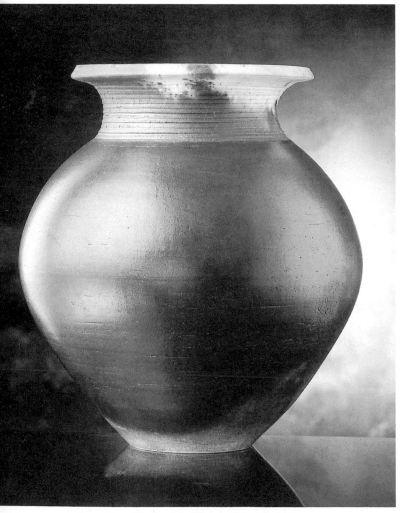

Large burnished pot by Tim Andrews, h. 14".
The white areas have been achieved by allowing the sawdust in the reduction chamber to ignite and burn off some of the carbonation.
Photograph by Peter Harper.

This coincided with a perception that my own work was in need of a new direction. Perhaps an in-built predilection to careful, precise making, encouraged by my training, tended to result in technically slick but artistically stifled work. Raku seemed to me to provide a solution. I had never been taught how to do it and so was not constrained by the 'right technique' and the fact that the nature of the method forces the maker to accept a certain lack of control over the process appealed to me. This, for all its frustrations, offered possibilities of exciting 'happenings' which had been all but ironed out of my previous work.

Returning eventually to share a studio with David Leach, who by then was no longer taking students, I began seriously to concentrate on more individual raku pieces. Adventure beckoned, and with the development of more tolerant materials and better techniques, gradually the pieces grew larger and more dramatic.

In recent times my work has been hybridised by a cross-fertilisation of different methods and ideas. Keeping raku as a core technique i.e. most pots are drawn hot from a kiln and smoked or fumed, aspects of stoneware, earthenware, burnishing and extra lustre firings are now also included.

The thrown and handbuilt pieces made usually from T-material and porcelain, are often covered by a dense red clay burnishing slip, resulting in a leathery sheen which softens the forms with a rich smooth 'chocolate' patina. This surface treatment stems from a love of old wood: Jacobean furniture, cottage doors, carved architraves, even simple roof joists or the stud work of a wattle and daub wall (a wooden construction infilled with 'cob' – a mixture of mud, straw and cow manure). Delapidated brick walls and the textures and colours of crumbling facades also hold a fascination for me.

Pots of inspiration include the burnished black ware made for a brief period in Dorset, England, in Roman times. These unusual pieces were a happy marriage between simple thumb-pot shapes of the primitive indigenous culture with the sophisticated refined forms of the great Roman empire.

Other favourites are Nigerian village pots, handbuilt with great skill; South American, Mexican, and Pueblo Indian work, all made and fired unself-consciously by artists responding in a direct way to their culture and surroundings. Cycladic sculpture which so affected the work of Hans Coper and others, holds a similarly powerful

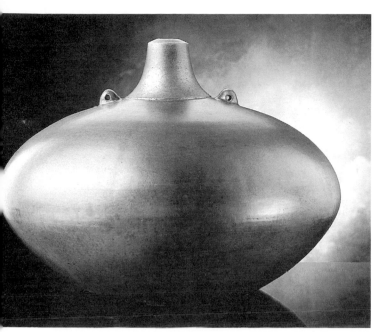

Large elliptical burnished pot by Tim Andrews, d. 17".
The piece was constructed from two thrown bowl shapes which were joined and then thrown as one pot.
Photograph by Peter Harper.

magic for me. The strength and surety of form together with a true elegance tells of the confidence of the makers and is the envy of many an insecure artisan today.

We have become too obsessed with the 'artistic statement', the pursuit of the original, or of technical excellence. Perhaps we overlook the simple: an emotional response to our history and environment. A cynic might say that in this age of market forces, we need to manipulate the system in order to achieve success: shout loud enough and perhaps people will believe that the king is wearing new clothes. Certainly marketing and selling techniques have their effect, but no amount of 'clever' intellectual posturing can replace the genuine and unconscious expression of the life-spirit of the artist. Maybe in too much striving we can lose the very thing we seek. That is for others to judge. For myself, the enjoyment, the challenge, the rewards and even the frustrations that raku brings, keeps the creative fire burning and, hopefully, the spirit alive.

Anne James – UK

It is very hard to say what sparks things off in my work. It has no message in the political or social sense, and is still structured very much as a product of my training. I still enjoy throwing and turning, the structure and restraint that the techniques demand.

Beginning with functional oxidised stoneware, Anne went on to make small porcelain pieces very much based on natural forms and landscape – for instance, seeds and stones.

Then came raku, and I find it almost impossible to say exactly how this came about. It was, as these things tend to be, a confluence of experiences: visits to exhibitions and demonstrations, combined with a growing dissatisfaction with my very small and tight porcelain.

The need to change direction was strong. Anne researched and read up about lustres, traditional paste, in-glaze, dry copper, and raku lustres. Initial tests were encouraging but she determined to press on with raku. A tiny top-loading kiln was forced into service for the first trials.

I ended up doing an odd version of raku. I was using some smoking in the kiln and some post-firing smoking with sawdust. Then I was quenching them as well, to retain good carbon-black on the body. This was a mad method – all the problems you can imagine – talk about 'fools rushing in where angels fear to tread!'.

Deciding to abandon the use of true glazes, she opted instead for burnishing her pots, together with the use of applied resin lustres and post-firing 'raku' carbonisation.

I thought it might be a more predictable process, but of course, if the resin lustres are used freely, mixed, thinned or multi-fired, then they are almost as unpredictable as any other process. So I still don't know how things are going to turn out!

My sources are still very much the materials: the porcelain, coloured slips, the burnished surface, the lustres and the painting, printing, resists and layers. I am still very hooked on textiles: Indian, African, Turkish – worn and battered preferably. Also on other things which have the quality of something very fine which has been worn, broken or weathered, such as worn wood, frescos and buildings. I love surfaces which are soft and warm but structured and yet enigmatic at the same time. I try to achieve surfaces which have structure, but are not complete – revealing themselves a bit uncertainly. There is a little bit of magic and mystery when it works. Colour is also important to me; the slips must feel integrated with the lustres to make up the whole.

Technical information

All the pots are thrown and turned in porcelain clay (David Leach porcelain body with 7% added calbrite). Slips are usually sprayed on. Lots of colours are applied: oxides, body stains etc. An old teaspoon is used to burnish them before bisque-firing to 1000°C.

The resin lustres are applied by various methods: brush, sponge, cut sponge printing, scrunched up paper or plastic printing, and over-resists (using artist's masking fluid). The pots are often fired several times between each application of lustres. At 800°C (lustre temperature) the pieces are drawn from the kiln and smoked in sawdust – some heavily, others just sprinkled. They are then quenched with water to hold the carbon patterning. 'I have to be very choosy about the sawdust. Fine, dry, hardwood such as beech is best. Pine makes nasty tarry marks.'

Health warning

The solvents in resin lustres are highly toxic and should be treated with great care. A good extractor fan and plenty of disposable gloves are necessary.

Bowl by Anne James.
Burnished porcelain raku, decorated with resin lustres.

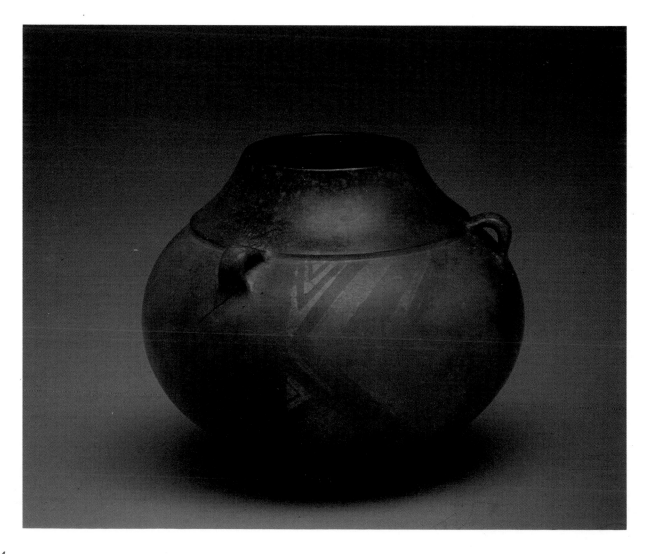

Jason Wason – UK

I live with my family in an isolated farmhouse up on the cliffs at St Just, Penwith, Cornwall. The workshop is in the middle of this ancient rock-strewn landscape. Blasted by winter winds: vegetation is scarce, mainly gorse and bracken. Yet the moors hold the presence of those that came before, for whom only the burial chambers, the megalithic circles, and standing-stones remain to tell the tale. In the mid-1980s, in every firing, I used to throw something extra into the kiln – from old bones, to bits of old bike: just to see what happened. This led to a fascination for surfacing my pots with various metals. The derelict tin mine workings just below me on the cliffs have slag heaps with slabs of molten rock and metal ores, fused through tremendous heat. This highly-textured material burnt an image into my mind, becoming a great source of inspiration for my work.

The metals I play with are mostly red and black iron, manganese, copper, and the metal saturated slurry that pours out of the old mine workings on the cliffs.

My first results with post-firing techniques produced intense violets, peacock greens, scarlets and blues. These astonishing variegated colours were produced by the cooling effects of highly-reduced saturated copper compounds. It was very exciting to sense the heat involved in the firing, which was left on the pot through these marvellous fiery tones. The pots were fired to 1050°C, then, wearing boiler suit and goggles and huge welding gloves, I picked the pots out of the kiln and threw them into a pit of sawdust, leaving them to sinter overnight.

Smoked pot with incised lines by Jason Wason, d. 12".
Collection of Miss C. Halstead. Photograph by Peter Harper.

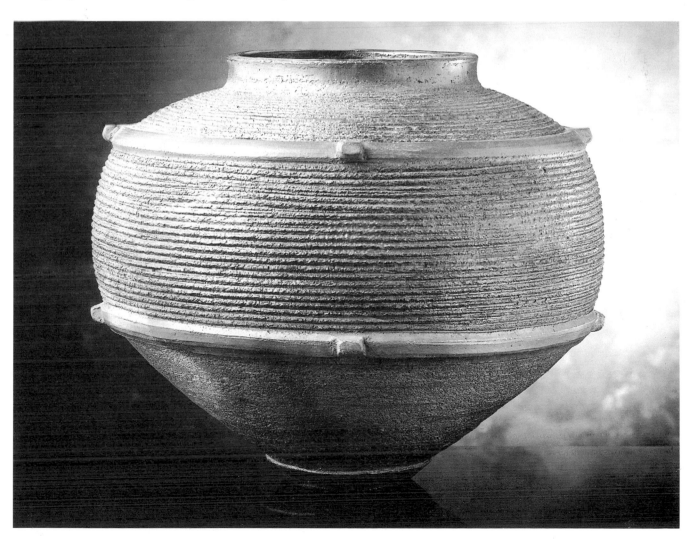

Clay body: I use my old Leach stoneware with 30 per cent grog, in the form of molochite. This is available from J. Doble + Co. on the cliffs at St Agnes.

Glaze: I rarely stick to one recipe but constantly play with ideas, but basically use as much metal, and as little flux as possible – just enough to get the stuff to stick on the pot.

Firing: A bisque-firing is made in a gas kiln, then a raku-firing in a ceramic-fibre oil-drum construction. I used this for two years, then abandoned it on safety grounds. Lifting the lid up and down, and in general use, dust particles from the blanket are released, even after being painted with hardener. Dear potters, do not trust it, despite manufacturers' assurances! Wrap chicken-wire or rendering-scree against the fibre, then secure it with nichrome wire. When it feels solid on the fibre, face up the whole inside of the kiln with fireclay – rather like an Adobe kiln. This then traps the blanket inside, yet still retaining the amazing thermal insulation properties.

Jane Perryman – UK

The pots are handbuilt using a combination of coiling, slabbing and press-moulding techniques. A mixture of T-material and porcelain clays is used, covered with a ball-clay slip. The slip is coloured with oxides and stains. The leatherhard pots are burnished, and after bisque-firing, treated with resist slip, then refired in sawdust. Organic material is often burnt into the pot during bisque-firing. After the sawdust-firing the resist is cleaned away, revealing the gradations of tone caused by penetration of smoke to the body.

The shapes are inspired by organic forms, and African and early Celtic pots. There is a link with primitive coiling and sawdust-firing techniques. I like the juxtaposition of the controlled hard edges of the stripes, with the accidental gradations of tone caused by smoke. After many hours of careful work I enjoy the suspense and risks of relinquishing the pots to the spontaneous effects of the smoke.

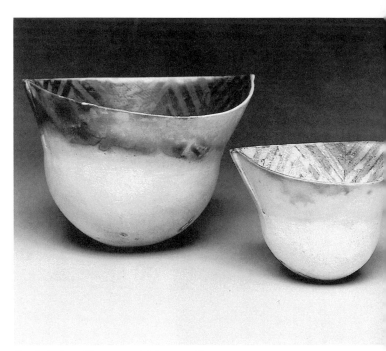

Bowls by Jane Perryman, h.13 cm, w. 9 cm.
Porcelain, handbuilt and smoke-fired.

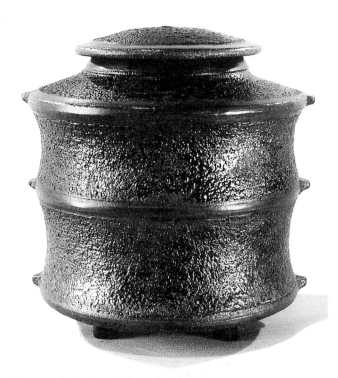

Funerary jar by Jason Wason, height 23 cm.

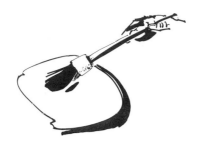

GLAZE AND SURFACE TREATMENT

This chapter contains the largest number of potters which, although the selection has been somewhat random, indicates to a degree the possibilities that the raku technique provides to achieve a range of interesting glazes and surface treatments.

Taking traditional Japanese tea ware as his inspiration for form, the German potter Horst Kerstan has developed a range of raku glazes and colours much more in the Western tradition. A well-known exponent of high temperature wood-firing, he has found a new warmth in the vivid, clean colours of low-fired raku.

From the smooth glazes of Kerstan we move to the earthy colours and textures of Anna Eilert's tiles. A leading Swedish raku potter, her relief panels make up deceptively simple 'patchworks' of harmonious smoky hues. Earth colours of a quite different kind are evident in the work of one of Australia's leading artists, Jeff Mincham. He makes his pieces on a monumental scale, the carbonised surfaces of his giant vessels swirling with deep flowing lines and textures which are emphasised by the blushing dry copper glazes and blazing red-earth colours so characteristic of that continent.

The pots of Christopher Wolff also carry a copper-rich glaze but their shiny metallic surfaces could not be more dissimilar. Bruce Chivers too has evolved a copper glaze which, under the pressure of reduction in his small fibre kiln, pools and separates in a unique patination of the surface.

In another direction the 'naked' and 'candy' raku techniques developed by Eddie Porck of the Netherlands manipulate the smoking of the pots to cause a network of lines and patterns on the surface of the clay. The smoke and fly ash of a wood kiln is the choice of Nesrin During to play on the surfaces of her pots. Something of a kiln expert, Bert Mens also wood-fires some of his pieces, smoking them also with anything from oily rags to potato peelings.

These and the other potters featured here offer just a few examples of the almost infinite number of glaze and surface variations that raku can offer.

Michael Parry – USA

Michael Parry is a potter who has chosen to use one surface treatment almost exclusively on his raku pieces. While teaching ceramics at Metropolitan State College, Denver, Colorado, he became acquainted with the copper matt fuming technique (see page 28). He was immediately attracted by the spontaneity of the process and the interesting colour spectrum which occurred in the post-firing reduction.

Several different making procedures are used: throwing, handbuilding, coiling and press-moulding – all in various combinations. Vessels or vessel-related forms give way to strictly sculptural pieces, some with a touch of whimsy. Common to most is an expanse of surface area, acting as a canvas to the spontaneous mix of colours which develops during post-firing.

His gas-fired kiln is a fibre-lined oil-drum top-hat type – raised and lowered by a pulley system from a large swing set, and counterbalanced with a bucket of concrete. He frequently puts in cones and a pyrometer as temperature indicators, and normally fires to cone 5 (?°C).

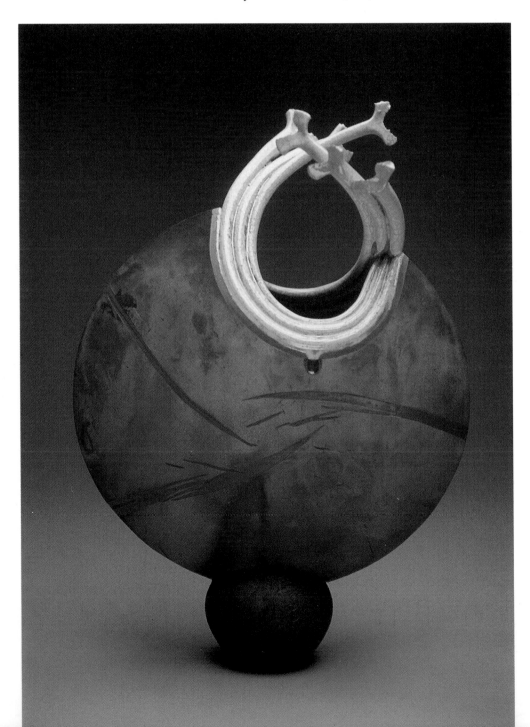

'Single Disk Vessel'
by Michael Parry,
h. 16" × w. 12" × d. 5".

Anna Eilert – Sweden

Now considered one of Sweden's leading raku potters, Anna Eilert was born in 1956, educated at the Swedish School of Arts, and now works from her own studio. Her work falls into two main areas: impressive large geometric raku reliefs often made for public commissions, and smaller handbuilt pyramids, dishes and other sculptures. The common theme is her love of muted, earthy colours – greys, blacks and rusts – which was kindled by her other main interest, archaeology. Anna has taken part in excavations in northern Sweden and has become fascinated with the textures and colours of ancient clay pots and artifacts. Whilst at college she discovered raku which seemed to provide the means to create pieces in her own 'language'.

Her exploration of the subtle palette of colours produced with degrees of reduction, results in a skilful blend of tones and textures. The clay surfaces are scored or carved with an old fruit-knife and sometimes enlivened with a little copper glaze, or occasionally a splash of vivid turquoise as a contrast. The relief sculptures are often designed for schools or other public buildings and so can be on quite a large scale. Some incorporate stone and terracotta elements along with the raku-fired tiles. Her smaller pieces more directly reflect the archaeological theme. Arrowheads and other weapons are suggested in strong angular shapes which are pinched or slab-built in sections – their surfaces appearing distressed and pitted like old iron or copper.

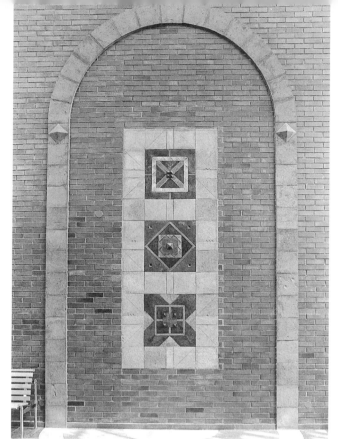

Three raku-fired reliefs surrounded by light by Anna Eilert, 1991–92.
Terracotta tiles and a darker terracotta arch. The limestone floor was designed as part of the commission.

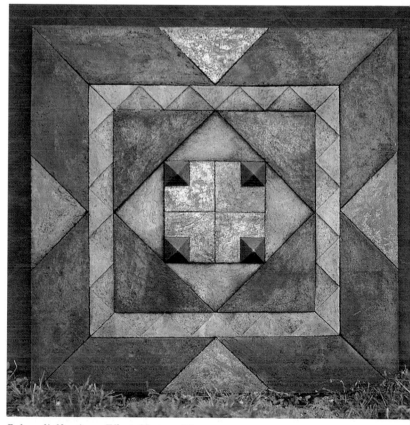

Raku relief by Anna Eilert, 90 cm × 90 cm.
Photograph by Kerstin Eilert.

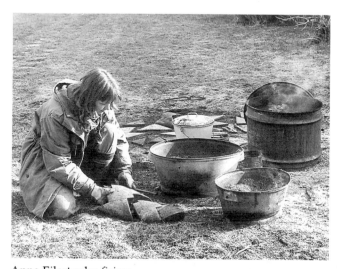

Anna Eilert raku firing.
Photograph by Astrid Eilert.

Eddie Porck – The Netherlands

Driven by curiosity and a restless desire to experiment with new techniques, Dutch potter Eddie Porck freely admits that he is never completely satisfied with his work. The recognition he has received for his past work has had little effect on this self-taught potter's enthusiasm for seeking new techniques.

Before becoming a full-time potter in 1975, Eddie worked for the Royal Dutch Airlines (KLM) until, at the age of 48, he received a back injury which caused a change in his lifestyle. He bought himself a kick-wheel, rebuilt a spare bedroom into a studio, and began his new life as a potter.

In 1978 he saw the work of the American raku potter Paul Soldner in an art museum. Eddie was fascinated by this style of working with clay. So much so, that he wanted to use the same method

for his work. He set to work building his own kiln out of fireproof tiles, heated it with wood, and made his first raku-fired piece. Since then, he has stayed with raku.

In 1981 something unexpected happened in the transporting of a raku-fired piece. During the cooling period, after the firing, a piece of the external glaze chipped off. Apparently while the piece lay smouldering in the sawdust, the smoke had penetrated the hairline cracks in the glaze, forming extraordinarily rich patterns and forms in the unglazed shell under the surface.

He decided to try to repeat this 'accident', but in a more controlled fashion. After several months he succeeded in taming the process, so that the

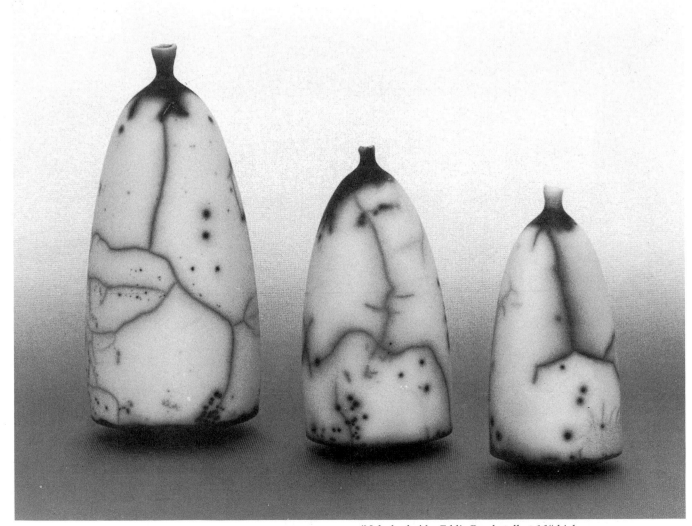

'Naked raku' by Eddie Porck, tallest 16" high.

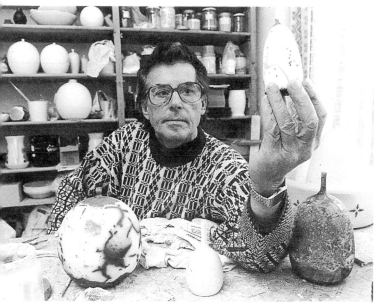

Eddie Porck in his studio.

... Each piece of work is a surprise. Each time that the glaze mantle is stripped away, it is like a new piece is born ...

I never use decoration, and my work is always black and white. New effects are created by changing the process slightly each time. The form of the work must harmonise with the appearance of the outer surface. The simpler designs of my later work create a background contrasting with the sometimes busy patterns which result from the raku firing. For my work, I use a Rodenveld Raku pyramid. For the smaller work, I use my homemade kiln which is very economical in its use of propane gas.

whole glaze shell chipped off. 'I named this new technique **Naked Raku**. It is still in essence, a raku-firing technique, only the pieces have, as I put it, "taken their jackets off".'

The next development came much later in 1986, when he experimented with an intermediate glaze layer. A piece made from Limoge porcelain, biscuit-fired to 1040°C, was given a 2mm shell of clay, sugar and water, mixed together to form a glaze. Finally it was covered with the usual raku glaze. The work was fired in his homemade kiln (a washing tub with the inside covered with insulating ceramic yarn, and fired with propane) to a temperature of 1000°C. It was then placed in a tin filled with sawdust, covered over, and left to smoulder for around eight minutes. Once the piece was removed from the sawdust, it was gently sprayed with water from a pot-plant mister, until the layer of glaze came off by itself. 'Again, the effect was breathtaking. The layer of sugar had burnt crisp black crystalline figures into the surface of the work, each accentuated by a light border. Since then I have produced many objects in this **Candy Raku** style.' Eddie derived the name **Candy Raku** from the sweet aromatic smell that comes from the pieces during the firing process.

In both Naked and Candy Raku, one can of course experiment endlessly. But in order to gain a control and experience with the medium, it is very important to keep a workbook – not only for the numerous new ideas, but for the step-by-step description of each firing.

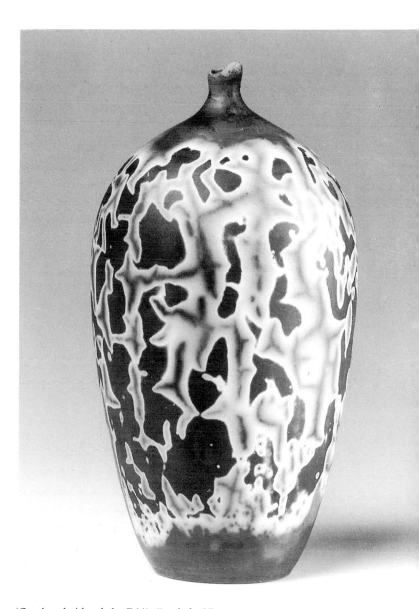

'Candy raku' bottle by Eddie Porck, h. 8".

Horst Kerstan – Germany

Born in Frankfurt in 1941, Horst Kerstan is best known and highly regarded for his accomplished wood-fired stoneware pots. He fires a self-built, two chambered Anagama-type kiln and has studied and assimilated many of the techniques and much of the philosophy of the traditional Japanese potters.

Although much skill and labour is involved with a large wood kiln of this kind, the pots within are – for the most part – at the mercy of the elements. In contrast, raku offers direct involvement and handling of the hot pots during the firing.

> Four years ago I started to use the raku process, and very soon I was impressed by the possibilities of the technique. All my potting life I have fired stoneware at high temperatures. The results have always been a little cool in their colours, so I was delighted to find a new warmth and variety of colour in raku. It seemed to be a completion of my work with glazes and shapes.

Horst has made many trips to Japan where he has become familiar with the Raku Chawans (tea vessels) of Kichizaemon. The 14th and youngest generation of the 'Raku' dynasty works within, and carries forward, the strict discipline of tea ceremony vessels, but, to a mixed reception in Japan, has also added his own blend of characteristics – mostly in the form of a slightly 'Westernised' colour palette.

Much impressed by this work, Horst was spurred on to make raku in his own way. The resulting forms offer strong allusions to the tea ceremony: Mizusashis (water containers), Chaires (tea caddies), chawans (tea bowls) and slab-built trays (for the sweets offered at the tea ceremony) make up the majority of his work.

The glazes, however, are his own creations and hardly in the tradition of, or influenced by, Japanese raku glazes. Translucent, shiny smooth yellows, strawberry pinks, orange, and shades of white all give the softly thrown forms a clean, crisp, glowing radiance which is further enhanced by sporadic jewel-like blooms of vivid colours. These are joyous pots whose quiet forms revel in their blithe glaze treatment and which well express the vitality of their maker.

Raku Chawan (tea bowl) by Horst Kerstan.
Yellow glaze and red 'splash'.
Photograph by M.P. Photography.

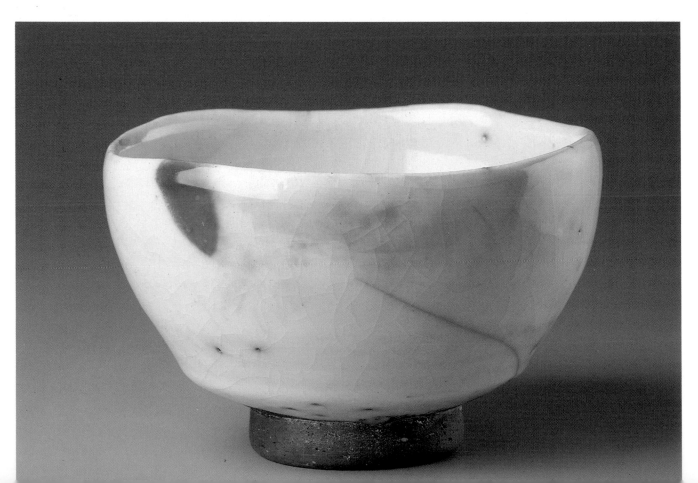

Nesrin During – The Netherlands

Eighty kilometres north of Amsterdam lies the first Frisian island of Texel. Inhabited by thousands of seabirds, it has no heavy industry or high-rise buildings, the economy being largely based on tourism and sheep-farming.

Turkish-born potter Nesrin During and her Dutch furniture-maker husband live and work on the island. A self-taught potter, she originally studied comparative literature, working as a teacher before the pots took over. 'Being 100% auto-didactic in the beginning, has its disadvantages, but it also allows you to be totally free to do your own thing.' Nesrin now makes pots full-time, and lives on a mixed economy of high-fired domestic ware, some 'functional' oxidised raku, and more individual wood-fired raku pieces. She also runs courses in handbuilding, raku-firing, glaze theory and kiln building.

Much of her motivation comes from the wood-firing itself – which is her passion. African, Far Eastern, 'primitive' or sophisticated, old or new: all wood-fired pots are alive to her – she is a true pyromaniac! Her style is uncomplicated: simple deep bowls, pebble-shaped elliptical spheres and bottles, all natural forms which respond well to the licking flames.

In this Western society, people's lives are very uniform – we live in similar houses, wear similar clothes, eat similar food, watch similar TV programmes – all very predictable. I make pots by hand, firing them in a wood-burning kiln, and they come out all very different. Some are beautiful, some not so. They are glossy and matt, oxidised and reduced, crackled and plain. By giving my pots over to the wood fire I'm letting the fire gods decide their fate and transform them for good or for bad.

Pots by Nesrin During.
Wood-fired raku with poured glaze.

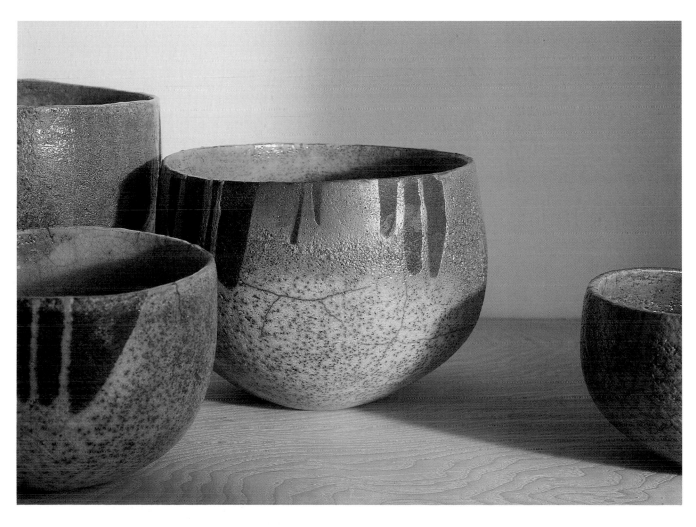

Most of Nesrin's raku pots are coil-built from German Westervald stoneware clay (KW 201) mixed sometimes with fine chamotte. The clay contains oxides, notably iron which responds well to the wood-firing. Some of the pots are scraped with a metal kidney, roughening the surface and causing the glaze to pinhole. Under oxidation, the iron bleeds through producing 'thousands of tiny raised dots'. In a reduction atmosphere, interesting stony-grey tones are created. The same clay with the addition of silver sand, may be smoothed to effect a shiny glaze.

No underglaze or onglaze colours are applied, as she finds enough variation of colour and surface coming from the wood-firing. Just one simple glaze is used:

70% Alkaline frit
30% Kaolin (China clay)

Addition of synthetic iron oxide (Fe_2O_3) (0.5%–3%) gives light pink to pomegranate red in oxidation, or tones of grey in reduction.

Addition of copper carbonate ($CuCO_3$) (2%-3%) gives Granny Smith apple green in oxidation to Bordeaux Red in reduction.

Other combinations such as iron plus copper, or iron plus manganese are also good.

The kiln

Nesrin During's wood-fired raku kiln is very simple, practical and functions extremely well. It is built from 40–50 porous bricks, a kiln shelf, and a grate from an old furnace. Stacking the bricks dry means the kiln can be assembled in around 45 minutes. Flexibility and economy is achieved in this way by varying the kiln's size according to the current requirement. Being an updraught design there is no need for an extended fire-box or a chimney. The pots are fed in and removed from the open top of the kiln with tongs – removing a few bricks when necessary. Stoking the kiln with small pieces of dry waste-wood from a carpentry shop brings the first load to 900°C in roughly 45 minutes – each subsequent load taking 15–20 minutes. In this way many pots can be fired in a day, and the kiln, once cool, is dismantled and stored away. An excellent idea for groups of students.

I once built a similar kiln on a beach in Turkey for an Iranian refugee; an art student who was making little clay statues, but didn't know how to fire them. We gathered whatever bricks from building sites we could find. Having no grate, we used shish-kebab skewers: burning twigs and branches, cob corms etc. – and the kiln fired excellently.

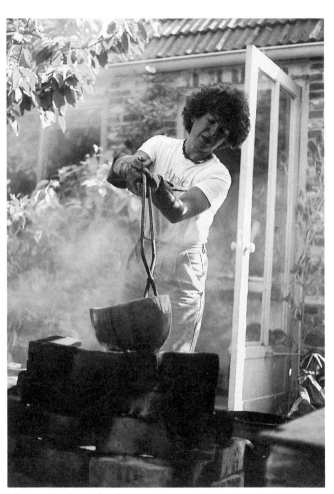

Nesrin During raku firing.

Bruce Chivers – UK – Australia

Australian potter Bruce Chivers has been established in Great Britain for the last nine years or so. Most of his work in that time has concentrated on high-fired porcelain but more recently he has developed a unique style of raku and become interested in using the latest kiln technology to fire it.

The pot featured is thrown in porcelain, bisque-fired to 930°C and then raku-fired to 1020°C. My own work is a direct response to the firing technique in my small, efficient kiln (see page 32). The glaze is a glassy, high-copper lustre glaze which has the ability to pool when gas pressure and reduction is applied. A smooth lustre, a development of fine lines, or a complete pooling of the glaze can be achieved this way.

When ready, the pots are taken from the kiln and placed, rather than buried, in sawdust: allowing the flame to lip across the pot. The right type of sawdust is also essential. I usually use a fine grade. New sawdust precipitates a large flame mark whereas smouldering ash creates subtle pink blushes. I always leave the pieces to cool in the sawdust and find no need to quench them in water.

Essentially the accidental becomes technique – one tries to reproduce the conditions under which a certain effect happened. Of course subsequent pots will always be slightly different, but that's the joy of fire. Seeing and knowing is as much a part of the potter's art as the making.

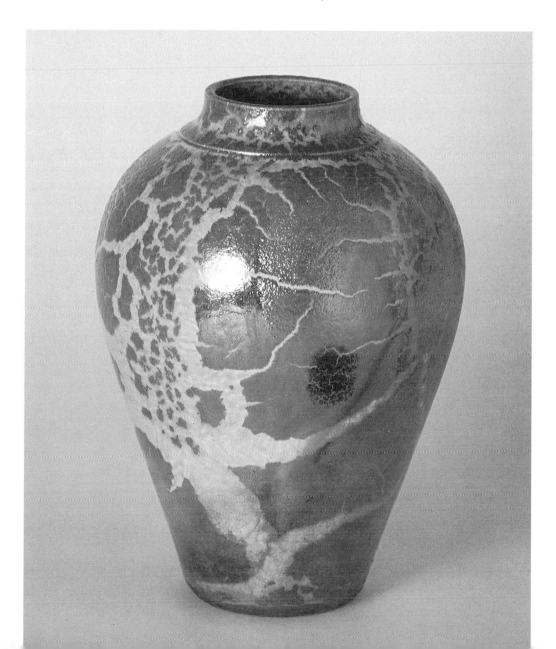

Vase by Bruce Chivers, h. 22 cm. Porcelain with copper lustre glaze.

Hildegard Anstice – Australia

Largely self-taught, Hildegard Anstice works from her own studio, situated one hour north of Sydney, Australia. She has been involved with raku for more than 15 years, making pots and teaching the technique alongside other low-temperature firing methods.

> The clay I use requires 1020° C in the bisque – for which I use an electric kiln. I fire raku with gas, wood or electricity, employing four different methods:
>
> 1. 'Clean melt'. In this firing, I take the temperature up to 950° C in an oxidised atmosphere, then cool it to 800° C, and remove the pots from the kiln.
>
> 2. I melt the glazes, and then reduce the pots at the top temperature of 950° C for 20 minutes by cutting back the primary air to the gas burner.
>
> 3. I melt the glazes at 950° C, then cool to 700° C, and reduce pots in the kiln by placing sticks amongst the pots for one hour. After every reduction, the temperature has to drop to 700° C before the next lot of wood is placed in the kiln. I also do this in the electric kiln, a three and a half cubic foot top-loader.
>
> 4. The pots are fired to 950° C, and reduced with a sump-oil drip during cooling. The kiln has to be clamped and slurried tightly, in order to avoid re-oxidation. The pots are left in the kiln to cool. This method is suitable for very difficult shapes, or for pots too large to handle.

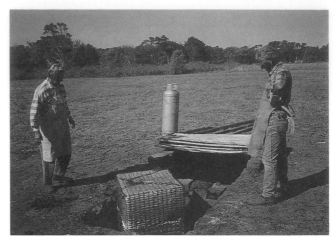

Firing in Australia – Hildegard Anstice.

In addition to electric and gas kilns, Hildegard uses an 'Olsen fast-fire' kiln for wood-firing. Her gas kiln is homemade in three sections of varied sizes. A pulley system lifts the lid so pieces can be easily removed. Pieces up to 5ft tall can be accommodated, and the sections can also be used to make a second kiln for group firings.

Hildegard favours pine needles for her main combustible material in post-firing reduction. Dry grass is second choice, sawdust also being used.

> The pots are lifted from the kiln with tongs. I have various types of tongs, to suit a variety of shapes. The smoking chambers must relate in size to the piece to be reduced. My favourite ones are old tin trunks brought to Australia by early settlers. I also use metal garbage bins or tubes, specially made in a variety of sizes, which can be slipped over tall pieces and a lid placed on top.

Each bin is lined with pine needles which catch fire when the glowing pot is put in. After a period of smoking with the lid on, the tin is then 'burped', letting in more air, and re-igniting the needles. A handful or two of sawdust is then thrown on to the glazed areas of the pot to cause strong crazing. The piece may have to be turned over to receive this treatment on both sides. Cooling takes place in the bin before the pot is cleaned with steel wool and water, and dried in the still warm kiln overnight.

> I usually only fire one lot of pots in a day – loading them into a cold kiln makes it safe. A relaxed happy atmosphere remains during the process, which I think is important.

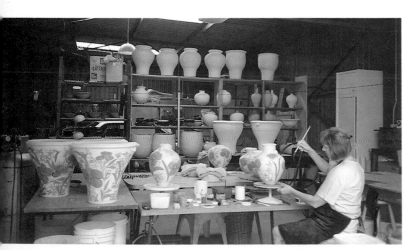

Hildegard Anstice in the workshop decorating raw pots with underglaze stains.

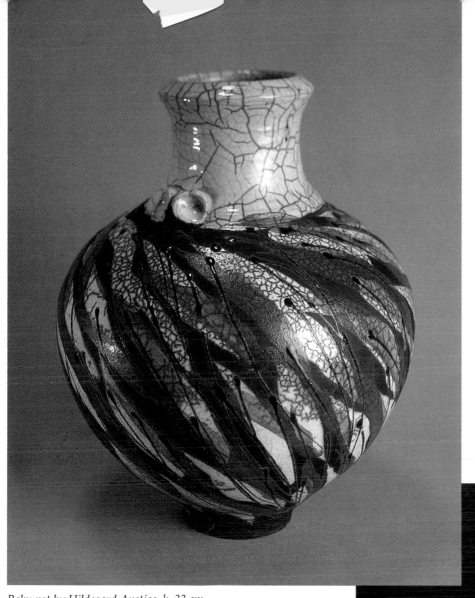

Raku pot by Hildegard Anstice, h. 33 cm.
Sprayed white slip, brushed and trailed glazes. Fired in
electric kiln and reduced at 700°C.

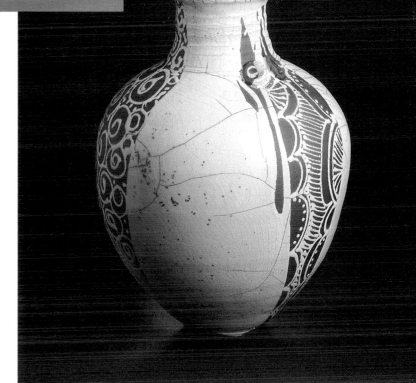

Thrown raku pot by Hildegard Anstice, h. 40 cm.
White slip, poured and trailed glazes. Oxidised firing.

Monique Bourbonnais – Canada

Predominantly made of slab construction, Monique's striking pieces show a desire to use the raku technique in an immediate, spontaneous way. Monumental wall plaques are assembled from variously shaped slabs. Impressed marks and applied relief shapes provide complex patterns of surface texture in a deceptively haphazard manner. References to Aztec art, North American Indian cave painting, and even modern graffiti are apparent – the whole combining to make imposing, thought-provoking sculpture.

> Raku is more than just fast results. It is a complicated and difficult technique to master, with a large component of philosophy thrown in. As I was stubbornly working to develop my technique I was also led into the aesthetic and cultural aspects that are an essential part of the process.

This combination of the philosophical and technical leads Monique to innovation and discovery.

> I try to leave enough 'space' in my work so the imagination can wander about in it; it is the feeling each individual has about the piece that is important. My own attitude towards my production varies. For instance, a series of vessels I made reminded me of images I had of ships: ships that had travelled far, over many oceans, and were old and weathered. They also reminded me, at the same time, of more mundane vessels; utensils that had been battered by everyday use in their long and useful lives.

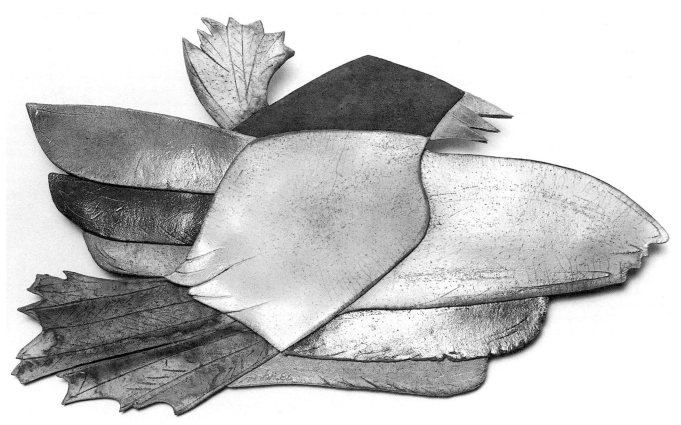

'The Road Runner' by Monique Bourbonnais,
92 cm × 55 cm, 1986.
Raku, glazes and oxides.
Collection of M. Koffler. Photograph by Kero.

108

But innovation and experiment comes at a cost:

Hours of work and planning can literally crumble in front of your eyes. There were, and are, moments of discouragement and frustration: moments when I slammed the door of my studio and vowed that it was the end – it was all over. But I always came back to it – total addiction!

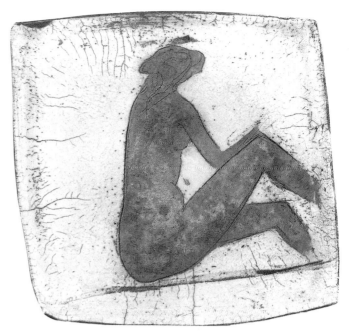

Wall plaque by Monique Bourbonnais, 30 cm × 30 cm, 1983. Raku, glazes and oxides.

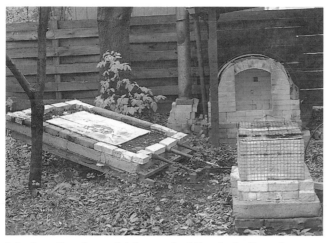

Monique Bourbonnais' three raku kilns including a large square kiln for firing murals.

'Myste' by Monique Bourbonnais, 90 cm × 122 cm, 1985. Raku wall piece. Raku, clay, glazes and oxides. Photograph by R. Max Tremblay.

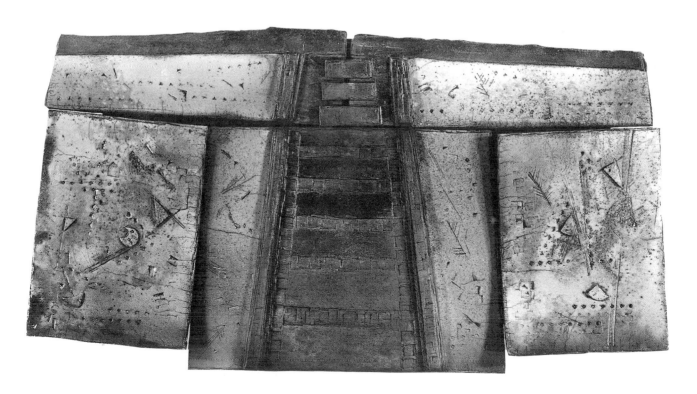

Christopher Wolff – USA

In 1989 Chris Wolff returned to university after a 15-year break in schooling. He had found that cone 10 reduction-firing was just too slow and predictable for him and felt the need for a change of direction. Encouraged by Dick Luster and others at the University of North Colorado, he rediscovered raku.

The results of the process are so immediate that new ideas can be tested. The outcome can be seen in a relatively short space of time, and then compared to the visualisation in one's 'mind's eye'. I think it was this immediacy, and the variables involved that really got me excited (. . . to the point of goose bumps at viewing some of the finished pieces!).

Other strong influences are the work of Allen Bales, Bob Smith (see page 71) and Joan Jarrett; the articles of Hal Reigger, and the philosophy presented by the late Marguerite Wildenhain.

The majority of Chris's pots feature a single, high-copper glaze which provides him with an infinite number of colour variations. Fired with natural gas in a front-loading soft brick kiln, the pots are then reduced in pine wood chips. 'Some experimentation with different particle sizes and types of wood showed substantial differences in the final results.'

Vase form with high copper glaze by Christopher Wolff, h. 14", w. 9½".

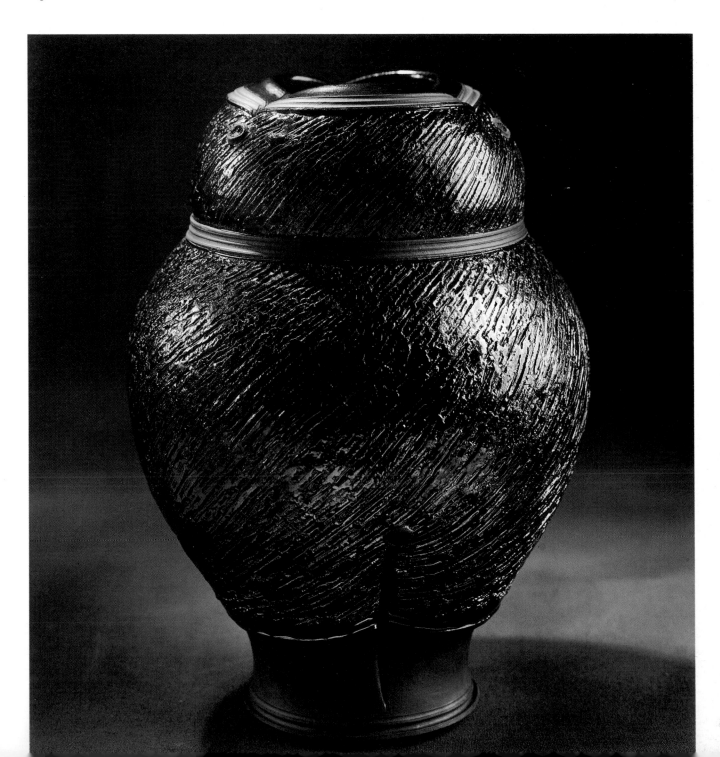

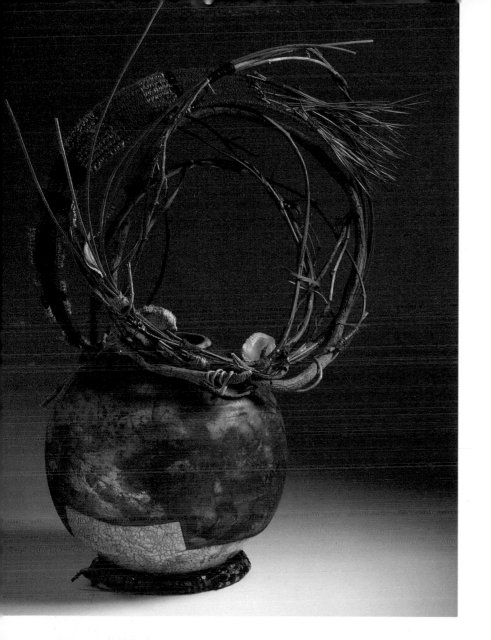

Michael Obranovich – USA

*Raku Basket by Michael Obranovich,
h. 26", 1986.*
A spherical raku pot with an
extravagant woven cane handle.
Fumed copper with crackle glazed
lower section.

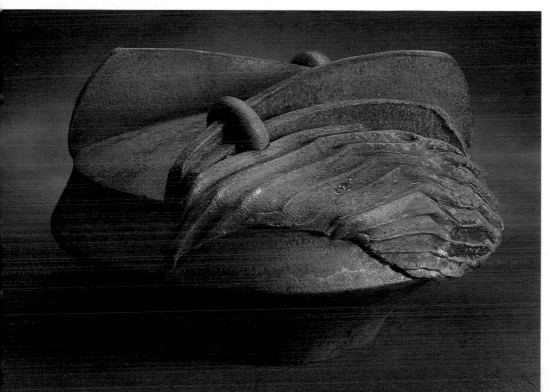

Jeff Mincham –
Australia

*'Neoteric Vessel' by
Jeff Mincham, w. 36".*
Wheel-thrown form, with
handbuilt additions.
Copper matt surface.
1000°C, raku-firing process.

111

Gertrud Båge – Sweden

Gertrud Båge fires her raku work at the workshop of Lena Andersson. Several times a year, loaded with boxes of bisque-fired plates, she boards a train to the countryside. There the two potters have built an oil-drum gas-fired raku kiln and the next four days are intensively spent firing a considerable volume of work.

The clay used contains 40–50% grog (chamotte) and has a very low quartz content. Many of the pieces are covered with a layer of terra sigillata: an extremely fine-grained engobe, or slip, which the Ancient Greeks employed for their black vases. Made by levigation, dry clay is added to water and left to stand for days, or even weeks. The heavier particles sink, leaving the 'cream' layer near the surface to be drawn off. The process may be repeated several times to obtain the finest possible particle size. 'For a shiny black surface I cover my pots with a very thin layer "two molecules" thick.'

Bert Mens – The Netherlands

Combining throwing, coiling and slab methods, Bert Mens often starts pieces on the wheel and then modifies them. Clay body stains, slips and oxides are routinely worked into the clay; or poured, brushed or sprayed, onto the surface. Under- and onglaze decoration is typically abstract in style.

A member of the Dutch Ceramists Association, Bert has work in a number of public and private collections, and he holds a teaching post at the creative centre in Almelo, and has guested at several workshops.

His own work is fired in a variety of ways, but normally he uses wood or gas kilns, often specifically custom-built for the pieces to be fired. Unusually, the pots are fired up to 1100°–1160°C which is an extremely high temperature for raku work, but which provides for greater strength in the finished pieces. All kinds of materials are used for post-firing.

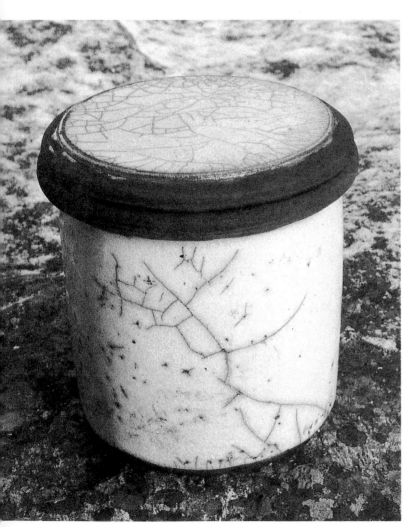

Lidded jar by Gertrud Båge.

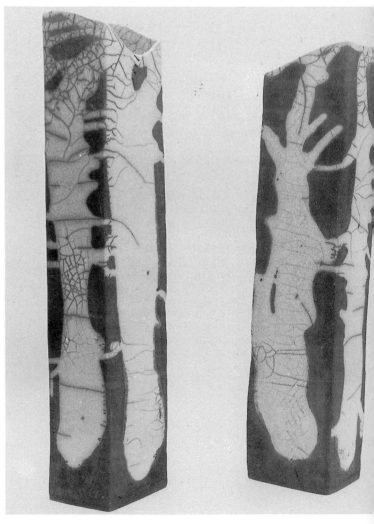

Tall slab-built pots by Bert Mens, h. 40 cm
Raku fired to 1100–1160°C with poured and trailed alkaline glaze decoration.
Photograph by Dick Elsenaar.

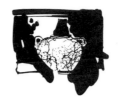

MAN AND BEAST IN RAKU

Raku is a vital medium. The physical act of firing and post-reduction involves finely-judged choreography and dexterity on the part of the potter and indeed has often been described by practitioners in terms of dance or theatre. Responding to the free-flowing continuity of movement from raw clay to finished piece it is little wonder that many artists choose raku as a sympathetic medium for figurative and animal sculpture. This short chapter contains a small selection of potters who choose to work in this diverse field.

Jill Crowley is a long-established and well-known UK potter. Over the years she has consistently and adventurously explored aspects of the human form and has built a reputation for her intimate and unconventional approach to apparently such unpromising themes as 'the hand' or 'the foot'.

Sarah Noël's two-dimensional pieces have a theatrical flavour, their rich surfaces decorated with dancers in extravagant poses or musicians and performers in colourful costumes.

Michael Flynn is an artist who fully exploits the medium of clay. His striking and thought-provoking figures and beasts impact on the viewer with their abundant raw energy and frequent injections of black comedy.

The work of Anna Noël is more lyrical. Many of her stylised animals reflect an interest in Celtic legends and mythology offering a more poetic approach to nature. In contrast Jennie Hale's work is very firmly rooted in reality. Working from field drawings she brings to her skilfully-made forms a spirit of wildness which she observes in the fauna around her home.

Michael Flynn – UK

The work of Michael Flynn seems to range over the whole gamut of human experience. Comedy and tragedy walk hand-in-hand with love, death, joy and sorrow. Impish dancing figures cavort around, their animated clownish bodies balanced on tip-toes. Ample 'Titianesque' ladies flaunt curves with gay abandon. Wild riders and horses, squatting pot-bellied men, bulls and vicious looking wild pigs sit alongside more overtly serious works.

Man in relationship with God is an ever-present theme. Contorted cockerels crow in portentious isolation or skirmish with a tormented male figure. One expressive series of the *Stations of the Cross* bears witness to Flynn's Irish Catholic upbringing, and Christianity is one subject which is explored repeatedly.

Animals feature as a major subject in Michael's work – particularly farm animals. His fourth-floor warehouse studio in Cardiff's city centre might seem a strange environment to produce such creative pieces. Perhaps to compensate, he surrounds himself with multifarious objects of inspiration – anything from a pith helmet to an evil-looking live green snapper turtle which swims around in a glass-fibre coffin! Drawings and paintings abound along with magazines and books. Literature is a great love and ancient mythology often spawns ideas for pieces. A recent series exploring the theme of the bull was initially inspired by a Greek myth and then augmented from observation and imagination.

'Earth and Air' by Michael Flynn.

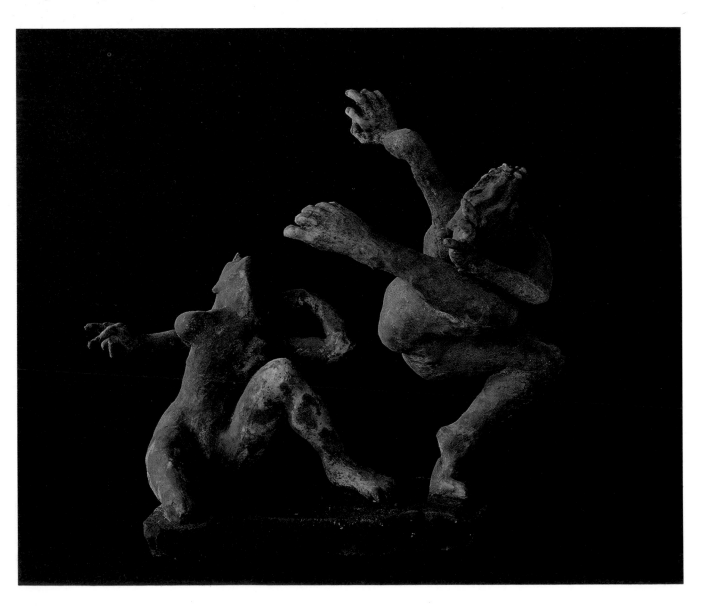

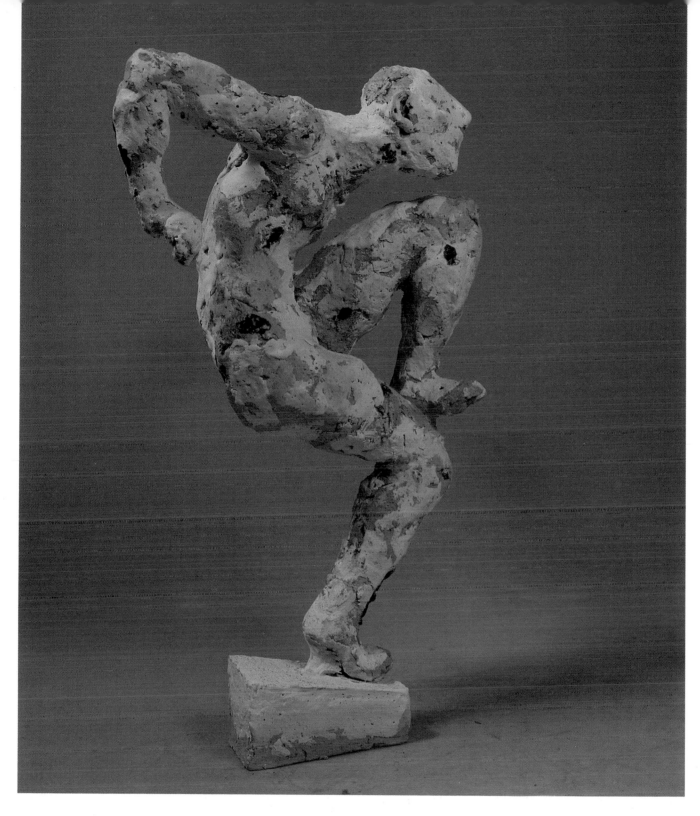

'Harlequin' by Michael Flynn.
Raku and 'dry' pastel glazes.

Michael Flynn works in clay at great speed – it is almost as if he is trying to remove his conscious mind from the piece in hand, and make it automatically. This burst of physical activity, however, comes after a long period of reflection – thinking through a theme: reading, sketching, drawing and painting. The idea is mentally honed and fashioned until he is ready to make the piece in clay – then it is 'released' with great energy.

Perhaps Flynn is the method-actor of pottery – the Marlon Brando of ceramics. He steeps himself in the part, almost becoming the sculpture which he is going to create. In this way the final 'performance' is kept fresh and unself-conscious.

Ceramic processes interest Michael greatly and he is not bound by tradition. He constantly experiments with materials and firing techniques. His raku kiln is a fibre-lined metal box bearing the scars of numerous trials and triumphs. Quite large pieces are regularly glazed and fired directly from the wet-clay state: the escaping water vapour seeming to form a protective cloak around the pot to prevent total destruction. Sometimes even finished sculptures are dismembered and then reassembled with glue in a different arrangement, perhaps using newly-fired arms or legs.

Michael Flynn's dynamic work imposes on many different levels of human emotion. He imbues his pieces with an intense, passionate celebration of life's physical energy. From the dark to the delightful, Flynn treads a dangerous path, taunting the observer with a serious joke. However, the joke is not the sculpture – it is the sculpture which is laughing at the observer: challenging him to laugh at himself and his own preposterous existence, and in doing so, release his own creative spirit.

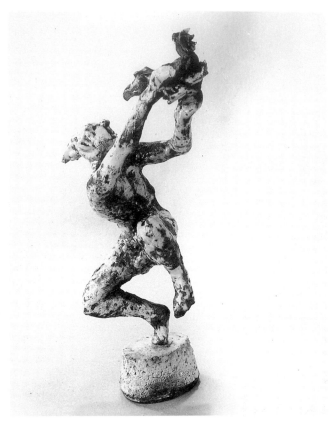

'Catching the Cock' by Michael Flynn, h. 18", 1988.

Michael Flynn in his warehouse studio.

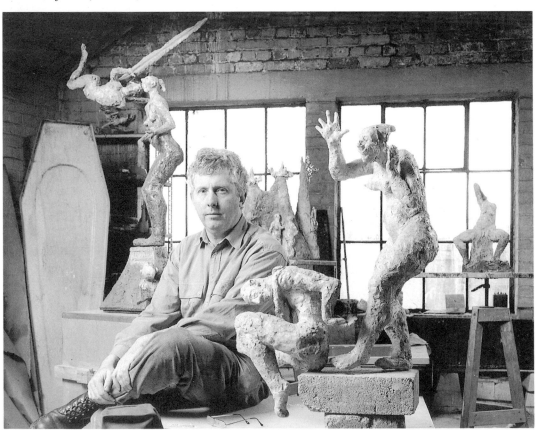

Jill Crowley – UK

Jill has been an influential figure in British ceramics for more than 20 years. In that time she has most consistently used raku as one of several ceramic processes for her work and it is this method for which she is probably best known. Her work appears in many public collections and she has exhibited all over the world.

Jill's imagery derives from many sources: animals, domestic objects and, perhaps most of all, the human form. The now familiar busts of her raku men of the 1970s and early 1980s were stylised and expressive, striking a subtly amusing but poignant chord with the observer. Later work has focused in on such themes as the female torso, and recently, a series of pieces which study intimately the human hand. Perhaps it is this feeling for the domestic and the immediate, combined with an in-depth knowledge of the materials she uses, which sets Jill apart from other sculptors in clay. She has somehow found and maintained the freedom to create something expressive out of the mundane and ordinary.

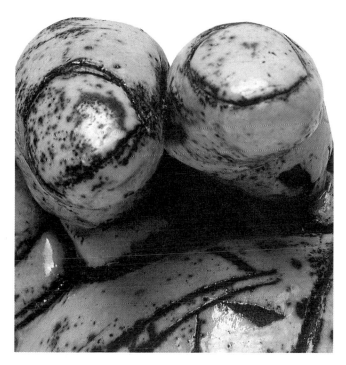

Close-ups of a raku hand by Jill Crowley. This piece is handbuilt with incised lines and a 'fleshy' glaze.

Raku hand by Jill Crowley.
Photograph by David Cripps

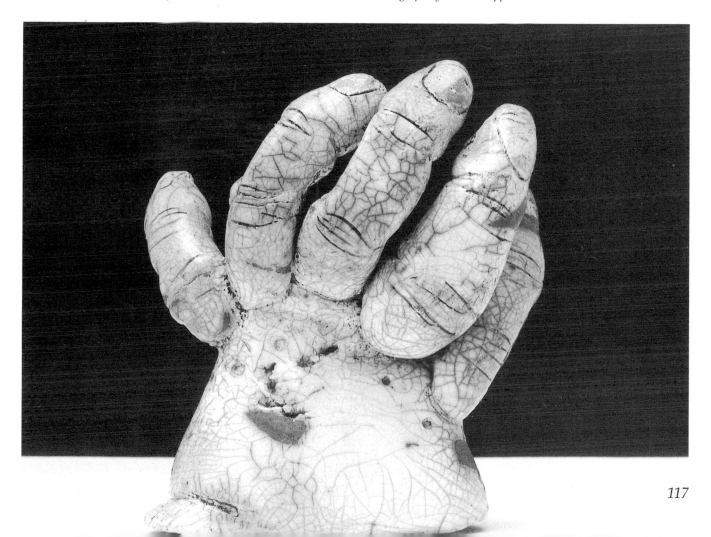

117

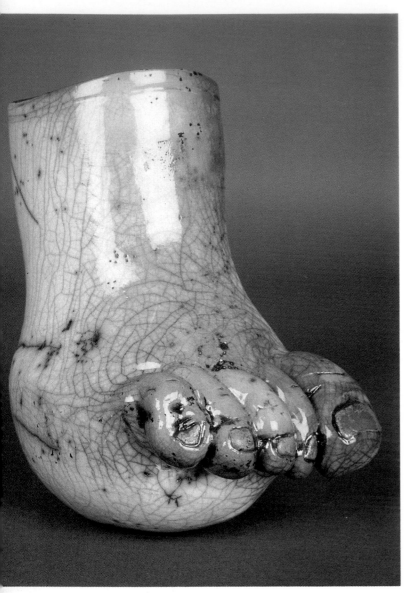

Raku foot by Jill Crowley.
White crackle glaze.

Jill has never been a mainstream artist. She was making figurative work at a time when much of the 'acceptable' sculpture was abstract. She has also stayed largely away from the traditional teaching haunts of degree courses, and has chosen instead to teach part-time adult education.

From Alison Britton:

Recognition of the absurd is something that has affected many people in the postwar generation. Redefinitions of faith and philosophy, and the growing popular awareness of psychology and the subconscious, were strong in the cultural climate that readjusted to the upheavals and losses of two world wars. In the writing of Samuel Beckett, there is a poignant balance between gaiety and gloom in his characters, wry mirth and irony in the face of desperation and decay; the wit and beauty of the language is juxtaposed with the ludicrous bleakness of the predicament. For me the depth and appeal that Jill Crowley's work summons, belongs somehow in this same territory. I respond to her imagery in the light of those books. Whether she is making mermaids, cats' heads on plinths, vegetables, teapots, hands, feet, goldfish bowls, flattened ladies for the wall, or busts of old men; in the way clay has been formed there is a mixture of the tender and the grotesque that evokes the Beckett tone. She avoids the sentimental entirely, and moves toward the humorous, but to say that these things are comic would be a superficial mistake.

Jill Crowley is an artist who disrupts conventions. In the current aesthetic culture, clay is not yet a mainstream sculptural material, but that matters little. Crowley has set herself her own boundaries, and has consistently cut away the edges of our preconceptions about what ceramics is. The most interesting role of the applied arts is in shaking categories, still.

icons and Indian miniatures with their economy of line, powerful features and sensitive decoration. Out of these influences come my ladies and gentlemen in extravagant costumes playing instruments or holding birds, and mermaids and mermen.

The other group of images is influenced by my enjoyment of old toys – especially tin toys. Living by the sea gives me the opportunity to draw the boats and ships in the nearby marina and docks. These sources result in my ceramic images of fishing boats and ships, some with sailors and seagulls, aeroplanes with begoggled pilots, hot-air balloons with passengers, and lighthouses and locomotives.

Sarah's double-sided ceramic pieces are made by drawing onto rolled-out slabs of clay with a knife and cutting out two identically shaped silhouettes. After decoration, the edges of the slabs are stuck together with slip, leaving a splayed gap for a base. The biscuit- and raku-firings are shared with her sister and are conducted in much the same way.

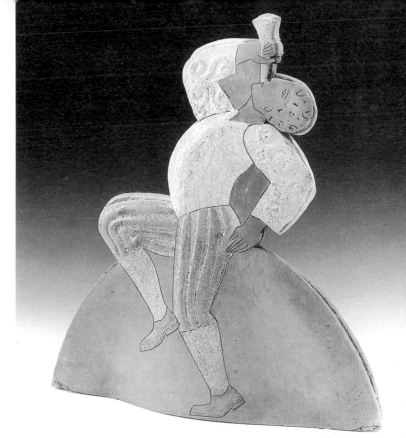

'Musician' by Sarah Noël, h. 22 cm.
Glazed and smoked raku.
Photograph by Peter Harper.

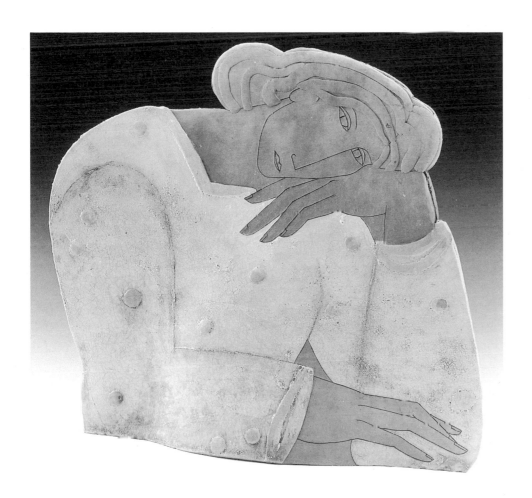

'Sinking Lady' by Sarah Noël,
42 cm × 42 cm.
Standing piece. Pink glaze
and smoked raku.
Photograph by Peter Harper.

123

Jennie Hale – UK

You might wonder what a potter is doing with her head stuck in the grass watching shrews belting around – but spend a day with Jennie Hale and the 'madness' reveals its method. She just loves animals. Her work is becoming recognised as some of the best-observed and interpreted animal studies in clay.

> Thinking back, it started early in life. Moments of indescribable excitement being near a wild creature. Seals basking on shingle beaches and rocks, dolphins leaping around the prow of a little dinghy, a wild cat creeping down a rockface in the Scottish highlands, watching sanderlings at the water's edge.

> Oddities in rockpools all had to be collected and transferred into my seawater aquarium. Bugs in jars festooned any corner available to me, tadpoles metamorphosed in the kitchen – and on one unfortunate night escaped into my mother's soup!

At first she was a hunter, collecting and capturing – perhaps believing that some of the mystery the creatures possessed would rub off on her. Legends of seal children and other Scottish folklore made it seem possible for her to join the creatures she felt so close to.

Now Jennie is an observer, spending hours and days in silence watching foxes, deer and badgers around her home, or studying estuary birds at the mouth of the river Exe.

Filling page after page of her sketchbook with drawings in pencil, ink and watercolour she closely observes and records detail of form and texture – steeping herself in every aspect of behaviour, movement and posture. All are stored, revisited, and then shared through her comic, fierce or tender manifestations of a lifelong passion.

Working methods

Fundamental to Jennie's approach is her drawing and painting. Quick sketches in ink or pencil are fleshed out with a watercolour wash and any details added in ink. These life studies made in the field are then developed back at the studio into working drawings from which ideas come that can be transferred to a three-dimensional form in clay. Very often each of these stages develops simultaneously and there is a strong continuity in the way that she works.

Working quickly, the pieces are coiled in sections. As the coils are added, the form is created by manipulating the clay, stretching, pushing and coercing it to arrive at roughly the desired shape. When the first section is complete, it is left to dry to the leatherhard stage before the next part is built-up. Several pieces are on the go at the same time and each one may take three or four sections before it is complete.

Once the basic building is done the piece is beaten with a wooden paddle and scraped to finalise and tighten up the form. It is then smoothed over with a rubber kidney to achieve a surface which will happily take a glaze without pinholing. Then, using additions of clay, coils, slabs, etc., features and characteristics begin to emerge. With a deft hand Jennie models eyes, noses, beaks and so on. This is the moment when hours of patient observation really pays off, as she breathes life into an inanimate lump of clay. Textures and details are 'drawn' or cut into the clay body with modelling tools. Working quickly and precisely keeps the lines fresh and unlaboured.

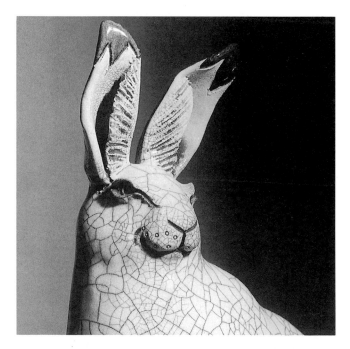

Raku Hare by Jennie Hale, h. 35 cm.
Coil-built.

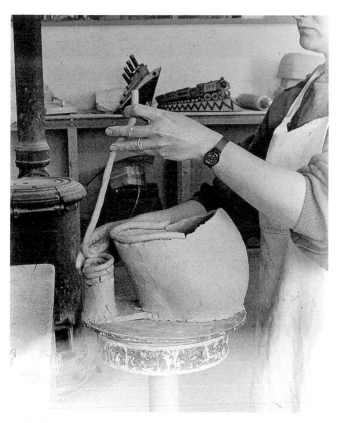

1. Coils are quickly assembled and the joints well smoothed down.

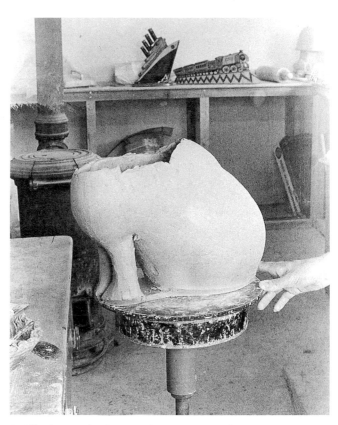

2. The form is built up and slowly refined.

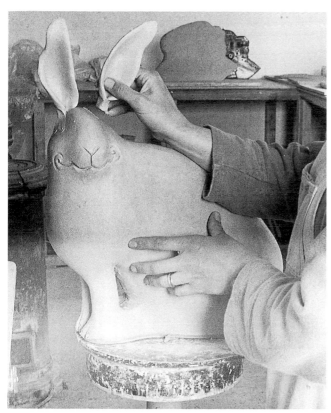

3. Clay is smoothed over to achieve the desired finish and the features drawn and modelled.

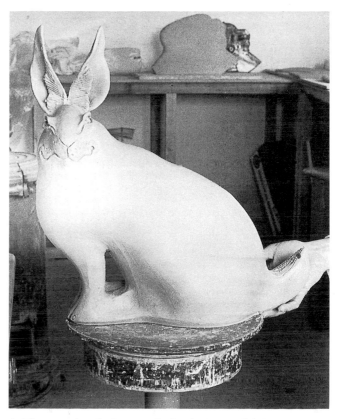

4. The completed piece ready for drying and firing.

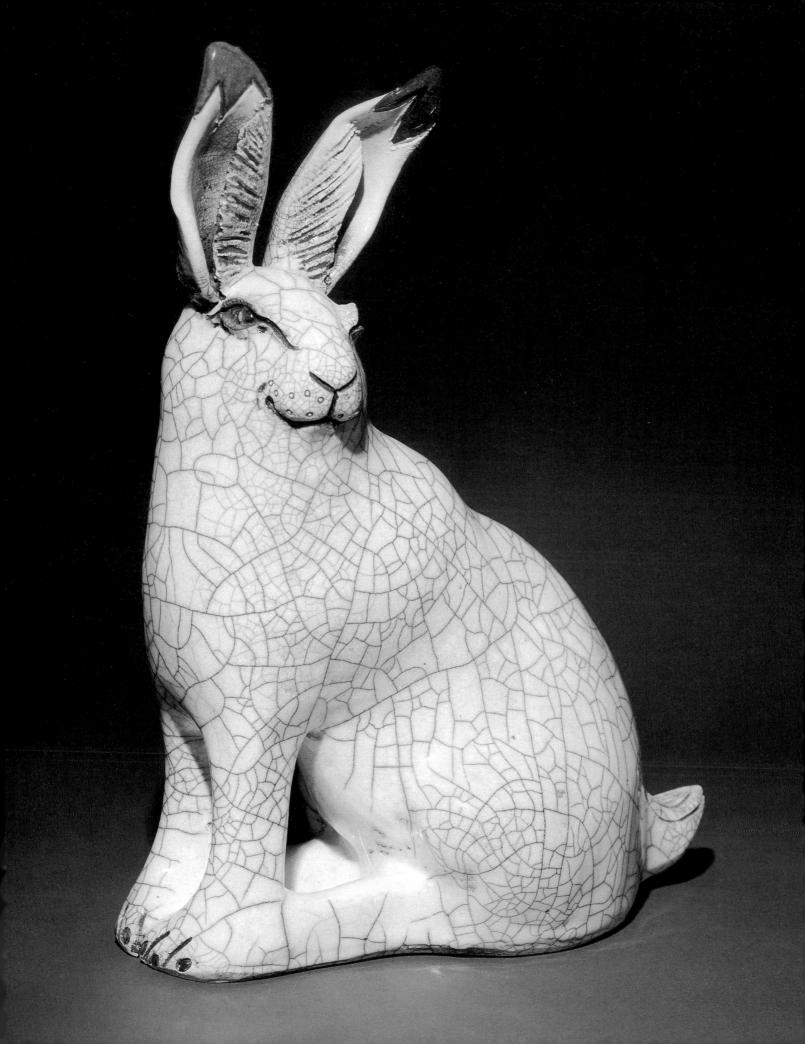

Decoration and firing

After thorough drying in a purpose-built drying cabinet, the form is decorated with stains, slips and underglazes which are brushed on. A few of the more temperamental underglaze colours have to be applied after the bisque-firing. A slow bisque to 1010°C is followed by the spraying of a high alkaline glaze which may be selectively applied with the use of a wax resist.

The propane-fired raku kiln is a fibre 'top-hat' type with an additional section which may be added to accommodate taller pieces. A slow rise of temperature to 600°C assures an even heat and the pots can then be taken up to around 1000°C quickly. Assessing the 'melt' mostly by eye, when ready, the pieces are removed and buried in sawdust for 20–30 minutes. When quite cold (possibly the next day), they are scrubbed clean.

Raku offers Jennie a range of qualities which are very much in sympathy with her approach to the work and to the subject matter. The soft, tactile glaze surface created with this technique lends itself to the expressive naturalism of the animal forms, with the crackle effect becoming fur and feathers. The immediacy and dangers of the technique matches the wildness of the beasts, for these are not domesticated or tame animals. Sometimes the method is as elusive as the animals themselves and she stalks them as much in the making as in the field, capturing and sharing their spirit in a true celebration of the creatures she delights in.

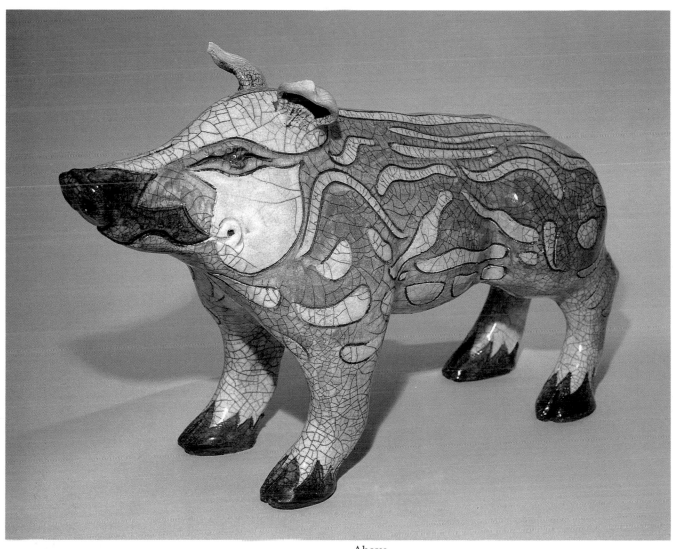

Opposite
Raku Hare by Jennie Hale, h. 35 cm.
White crackle glaze.

Above
Raku Boar by Jennie Hale, 50 cm × 30 cm.
Coil-built, underglaze colours with crackle glaze.

127

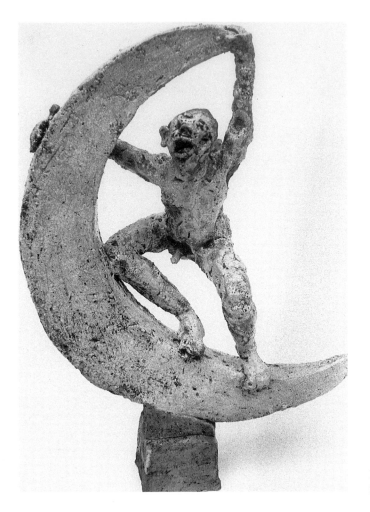

'Man in the Moon' by Ian Gregory, height 29".
Raku glazes fired to 950°C with salt vapour. Heavy
reduction, post-firing in straw.

Rosa Quy

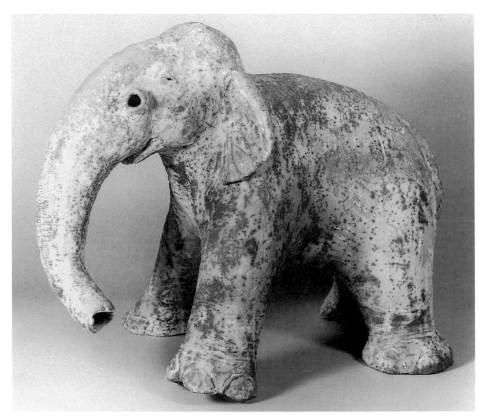

Elephant by Rosa Quy, w. 50 cm.
Raku with whitish glaze.
Courtesy of Bonhams.

Photograph by Thomas Ward.

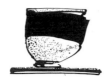

RAKU SCULPTURE AND A NEW APPROACH TO THE VESSEL

Including the word sculpture in the title of this chapter does not imply that the artists featured here are hanging onto the coat-tails of Henry Moore or that they have somehow elevated themselves to an imagined 'higher' level of artistic expression. In a sense all Western raku is to an extent sculptural in that it is for the most part non-functional.

But interestingly, many raku potters refer directly to the vessel as a source of inspiration, embracing rather than rejecting the notion of function. This stems from the legitimisation of the idea of the vessel as an 'Art object' by potters such as Peter Voulkos and Paul Soldner, who, in the 1960s, opened up a fertile plain which is now being enthusiastically cultivated by others.

Wayne Higby is one such figure in the US. His interest in landscape is apparent in the stylish, complicated sectional pieces made a few years ago. More recently the scenic imagery has been connected to an everyday object, a bowl which, although somewhat altered, provides a familiar physical structure enabling him to combine real and illusionary dimensions.

Domestic objects and the context in which they are used also holds a fascination for a leading UK potter, David Howard Jones whose sculptural 'English Tea-ceremony' vessels are 'seriously' humorous! And the notion of containment is explored in a very different way by the major British artist Martin Smith who continues to break fresh ground and set new standards in ceramics.

The travels of Canadian Agnes Olive have provided her with many powerful and poignant images. Deeply affected by tribal art, her work reflects in clay, many of the ceremonial vessels and offering baskets of Indonesia and the Far East. She also incorporates traditional materials such as bone, corn silk and horse hair to complete her pieces.

The influence of ancient artifacts is also apparent in the raku pots and sculptures of American Robert Piepenburg and indeed many of Elizabeth Raeburn's ideas originate from her own drawings of traditional pottery and prehistoric objects. Her striking pieces allude strongly to vessels, their basic shapes mostly confined to containers of various kinds. But the handbuilt bottles, raised bowls and dishes have evolved into very individual sculptural forms.

David Howard Jones – UK

There was a table set out under a tree in front of the house, and the March Hare and the Hatter were having tea at it; a Dormouse was sitting between them, fast asleep . . . The table was a large one but the three were all crowded together at one corner of it. 'No room! No room!' they cried out when they saw Alice coming.

'There's plenty of room!' said Alice indignantly, and she sat down in a large armchair at one end of the table.

(Excerpts from *Alice in Wonderland* by Lewis Carroll)

The topsy turvey world of Alice provides an appropriate paradoxical reference point from which to explore the pots and thoughts of David Jones. His work is widely recognised for its well-controlled structure, colourful iridescent glazes and complex linear designs. Articulating its three-dimensional qualities the patterns lead the observer on an engaging excursion around the lustrous surfaces.

Studying at Warwick University, David gained a degree in Philosophy and Literature followed by a diploma in ceramics at the Mid-Warwickshire College of Art. His academic background was augmented by an ongoing interest in 'hands-on' practical clay work and at university he was able to take over a ceramic workshop set up by an American he had met in the first year. After college David started teaching and making domestic ware, moving on later to porcelain.

In the early 1970s feedback from the new raku activity going on in the US was beginning to arrive in Britain. Paul Soldner and others were encouraging radical departures from accepted firing methods and materials, and even having fun with clay and fire. The idea of raku as a performance appealed to David, who had a theatrical bent, and so he embarked on the first pieces which led to a radical change of direction.

Since that time the work has evolved, becoming more complex in design as well as in concept. A pot-pourri of diverse influences includes elements from Post-Modernism and Deconstructionism (Derrida), American ceramics, Minoan artifacts and even the Epic of Gilgamesh (man seeking immortality). Appearing in many solo and joint exhibitions in the UK and Europe, his work features in several national collections including Liverpool Museum and Boymans Van Beunigen, Rotterdam.

The highly composed nature of the work might seem at odds with the unpredictable fire of the raku kiln but such apparently contradictory practice achieves a balance which is of great importance to David.

In my work I play. I establish ideas of great precision and allow them to be changed. The notion of control is central to a designer of forms; the pattern is drawn on the surface of the pot with exactitude; yet, for me, it is imperative that the outcome is determined by the fire. I have found this balance in the firing process of (American) raku where I can combine an interest in sculpture and painting – of the application of a glaze to a complex, three-dimensional surface – and then its testing in the kiln. This constitutes a tension between Apollonian and Dionysiac creative processes.

Apollo was a god of ancient Greece, taken by the Romans for a sun god and patron (amongst other things) of medicine and prophecy. Dionysus was the god of wine – representing emotional and sensual pleasure. Together they could be said to portray the 'head and the heart'.

The tradition of Japanese raku does appear to be much at odds with these ideas: there seems no place for the central concepts of quietness and restraint – but for the last 20 years I feel that I have been conducting a dialogue with the central tenets of the Raku-Zen philosophy – certainly with tricks to try to creep behind conscious thought processes. One of my major referents is the forms of the vessels of the Japanese 'Tea Ceremony'. My work is 'pots about pots': a commentary on tea bowls, kettles, vases, trays, etc.

The interest in Zen philosophy, the Japanese Tea Ceremony and its raku chawans (tea bowls) is particularly significant for David. In early years the notion of working within such a tradition appealed to him but gradually he felt that his work

Opposite
Raku lustre vessel by David Howard Jones, h. 23".

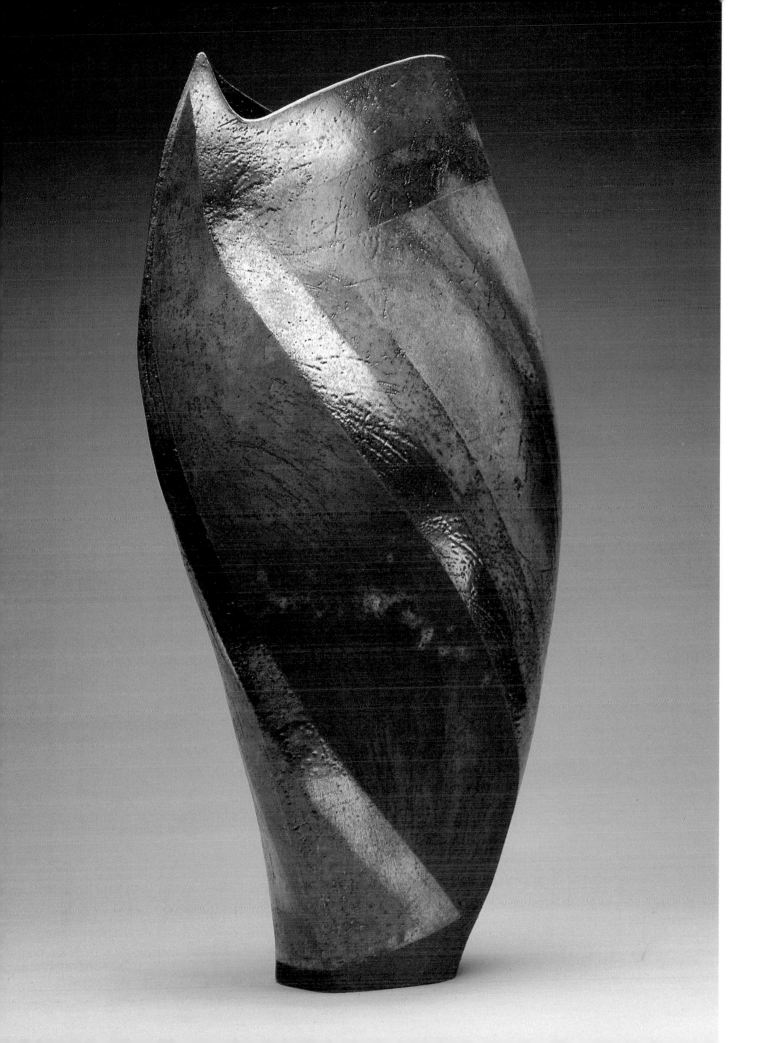

was more against the Japanese way than with it, so he decided to seek inspiration from nearer to home.

This over-conscious fealty to an alien (Japanese) culture, that I have never visited, struck a surreal note about six years ago. I then developed an interest in the objects and utensils of the 'English Tea ceremony', this I have perceived through the eyes of a favourite author – Lewis Carroll (Dodgson).

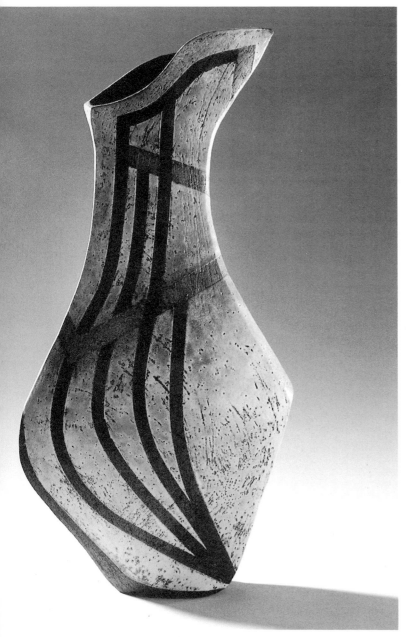

Vase form by David Howard Jones, d. 18".
Raku-fired lustres.
Photograph by Rod Dorling.

In *The Mad Hatter's Tea-Party*, Carroll paints an absurd and surreal picture of a very English institution. Replacing the contrived, polite conventions of the Victorian observance with the anarchic and nonsensical behaviour of the extraordinary company – March Hare, Hatter and Dormouse – he offers the reader a peculiar juxtaposition of the controlled and the maniacal.

It has continued to link to other obsessions – particularly the philosophical and aesthetic tradition that I studied as an undergraduate. A lot of philosophical thought works and reworks certain paradigmatic questions; I see my clay output as performing an analogous task. Two of the central issues that I see myself addressing are the essence of a thing or a concept e.g. the idea of a 'cup' or a tea bowl and the search for meaning in an absurd world. The former is best found in process – clay's mudness is a central rooting force and the marks (or lack of them), of fingers or tools, tell a history of the object – like geological strata revealed by an ebbing tide. The surreal world is discovered in determinants of scale, structure and the interrelationship of forms. By altering these parameters one can make the viewer see a familiar form with fresh eyes, and, perhaps more importantly in our discipline, feel with new hands.

At the time of writing, I am about to visit Japan having won the Inax Prize. I am very excited at the prospect of completing this particular circle through working in the actual country which previously was only known to me through books. I actually have an expectation of falling down a rabbit hole!

Like the characters created by Lewis Carroll, David's raku pieces can be perceived on many levels. But whether we are Hares, Hatters or 'intellectually challenged' Dormice, the pots are there to be enjoyed by all.

Technical information

David mixes Potclay's 1149 porcelain with T-material, leaving it to mature for six months. Building methods can involve a combination of slab and coil elements but most pieces are thrown and then altered. Each batch of work numbers around 15 pieces. Simple bowls may take a week or so to complete but more complicated pieces may be worked on for more than a month and then require a further two months to dry out slowly.

Wet clay decoration takes the form of controlled incised lines and textures derived from the process. Marks in the wet clay trap in an instant a moment of movement giving each piece a 'personal sense of history'.

After bisque firing the pieces are further decorated with glazes and colours using latex and masking tape resist techniques. The surface area is divided into positive and negative spaces and much thought and time goes into working out combinations of contrasting colours and interesting patterns.

Raku firing

Usually each batch of pots is fired in one day. Unlike many potters who prefer to fire alone, David likes to share the occasion with friends enjoying the drama of the unpredictable method. 'I was always interested in theatre and raku offered a different audience.'

Sometimes bowls will be fired on their edge to encourage deformation. Large pieces take up to two hours to reach temperature but small items may only require ten minutes or so. A temperature of 1080°–1100°C is reached – quite high for raku. The pieces are taken out of the kiln and put straight into the reduction chamber. Smoking is achieved in sawdust – softwood is preferred for heavy reduction but usually hardwood is used. Cooling takes place in the sawdust and then in the air. No water is used at all.

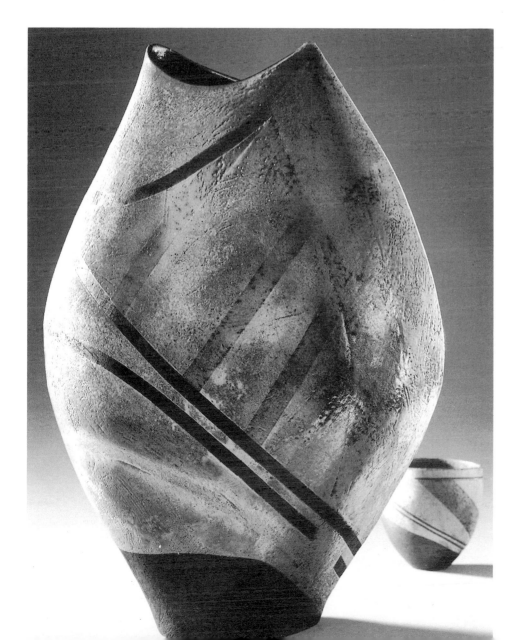

'Throne Bowl' by
David Howard Jones, d. 20".
Raku-fired lustres.
Photograph by Rod Dorling.

133

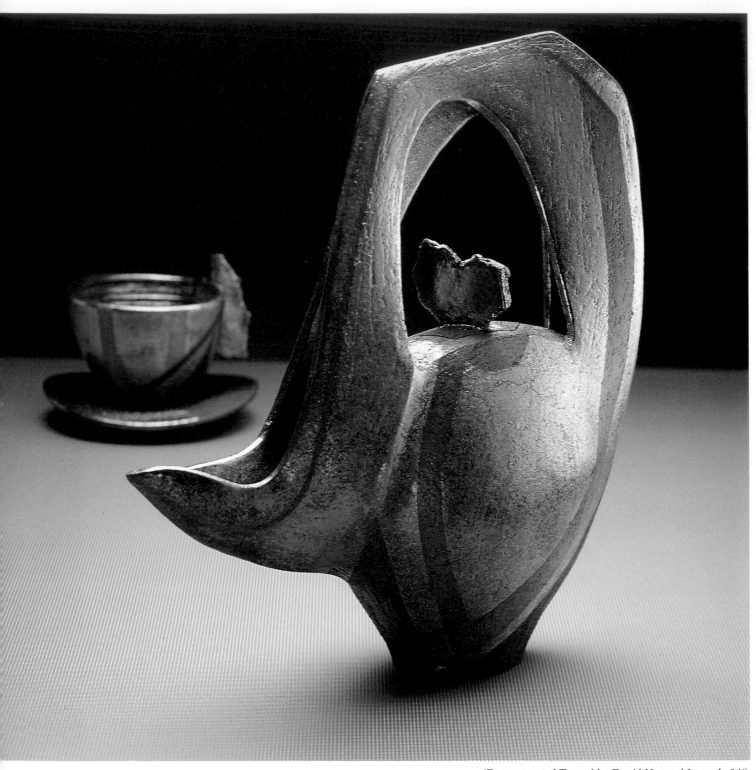

'Deconstructed Teapot' by David Howard Jones, h. 14".
Raku-fired lustre.
Photograph by Rod Dorling.

Wayne Higby – USA

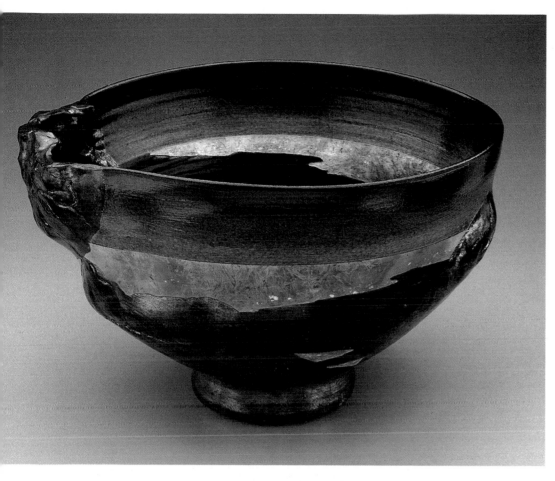

'Night Tide Inlet' landscape
bowl by Wayne Higby,
11 ¾″ × 19″ × 16″.
Earthenware, raku technique.
Collection of Mr Ed Roberts.
Photograph by John White.

(Wayne Higby)

Below
'Emerald Lake' landscape
container (5 boxes with lids)
by Wayne Higby,
14 ¾″ × 32 3P/4″ × 9″.
Earthenware, raku technique.
Collection of Dr George Andros.
Photograph by Steve Myers.

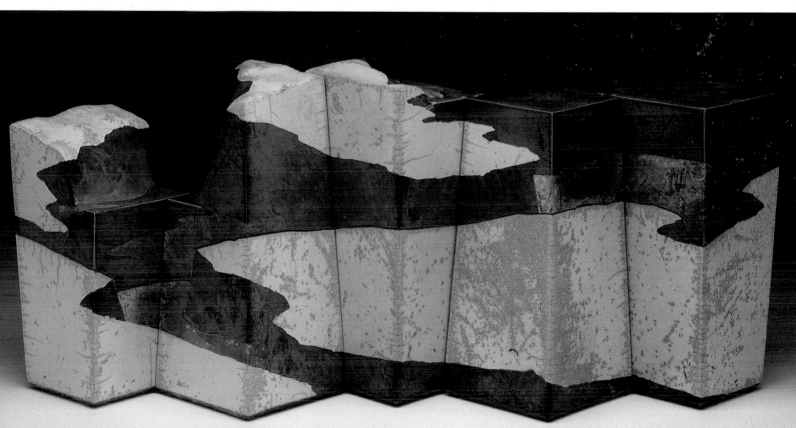

Wayne Higby has been an influential figure in American ceramics for a number of years; two decades of teaching at New York State College of Ceramics at Alfred University and numerous workshops and lectures have brought wide recognition. His now familiar multiple landscape boxes fascinate and tantalise the viewer with a complex play of space and perspective. Higby's long fascination and concern with landscape and environmental issues has been reflected for many years in the development of his work.

As the work began to surface in exhibitions I was often disappointed to hear of it referred to as 'Higby's sculpture'. I didn't want to make sculpture; I was making pots, but it seemed that others wanted pots to be sculpture and felt that they were complimenting my work. Of course, pottery operates in the realm of sculpture. It is three-dimensional, and deals with both positive and negative space.

Technical information

Bisque firing (cone 08 – 950°C)

The idea is to match the firing temperature of the clay with that of the glaze. Wayne tries to formulate a clay which will reach a certain density at bisque temperature, so that after glaze-firing the resulting ware will be fairly hard. The bisque must leave the ware porous enough to withstand rapid expansion and contraction, and yet be dense enough to be strong. For this reason a clay especially made for raku is used, rather than a stoneware body with additional grog or sand.

Glaze firing

I do not use cones, so this is somewhat of a guess. However, I have tried my glazes in an electric kiln, and they usually mature at about cone 8 (950°C), so the bisque temperature is the same or higher than the glaze-firing.

The glaze is applied with a brush using a rubber resist material to mark areas. This material is somewhat like rubber cement or the material watercolour artists use to 'save' white areas of the paper. It is removed before firing.

The ware is fired only once after the bisque. When the piece is hot (glaze is shiny) it is removed from the kiln. Simple tongs and asbestos gloves are used to get the ware out of the kiln, which is a front loader. Timing is especially important, and a variety of glaze effects can be achieved by removing pieces at different degrees of heat or glaze melt. The temperature of the air plays an important role. The quality of reduction depends on the amount of heat retained in the piece when it begins the reduction process. Judgements must therefore be made in relation to the outside ambient temperature as well as that inside the kiln.

After removing the piece, it is placed in a box lined with damp straw and then covered with more damp straw. The straw contacting the surface of the piece modulates the glazed surface but avoids heavy smoking, which Wayne does not want. The dampness of the straw helps cool the piece without exposing it to oxygen, thus avoiding both oxidation and an extended period of strong reduction.

In order to speed cooling and crackle the glaze, Wayne often briefly exposes the pot to the air after it has been in the straw for 30 seconds or so. He then re-covers it in the pit for an extended cooling and gentle reducing sometimes lasting up to half an hour.

When the piece is completely cool, out of the straw, and back to normal room temperature, it is scrubbed vigorously with soap, water and steel wool to remove any surface effects that are not permanently fused into the glaze or slipped surface.

I keep no records, so each time I fire it is entirely a sensing experience. There are many variables which challenge my control. I enjoy this challenge each time I match wits with the 'forces' of the fire. Sometimes the magic works. Often it doesn't. I demand a great deal and success is often the result of suddenly achieving a moment of fine-edged balance between the realm of material facts and intuitive push.

Jerome Heck – USA

Jerome Heck's unique raku pieces are individually created in his North Shore studio on Oahu, Hawaii. His imaginative use of self-designed textural impressions in the clay injects an additional dimension to his singular style.

In 1991 Jerome retired after 31 years as a career naval officer. A specialist in explosive ordnance disposal, perhaps firing with raku was an appropriate direction to take! He was first introduced to the technique at the Hawaiian Craftsmen's annual gathering.

The work that has evolved since that first experience is fundamentally sculptural, but derives strongly from functional items, notably teapots. The pieces are dominated by the use of heavily-textured surfaces and modelling. Some are architectural in construction, alluding perhaps to Oriental or South American temples. Others are very much more animal in nature. Quadrupedal teapots featuring skin-like folds of clay, engender visions of desert lizards or marching pachyderms.

Jerome has a strong feel for the subtle, earthy tones brought about through the use of copper matt glazes. They give his pieces a sense of antiquity, and further enhance the textural treatment which springs to life through the raku-firing process.

> I like to think about Japanese raku by making tea bowls but my work does not reflect their traditions. Clay allows me to do something that is truly my own expression, and reap the pleasure when others enjoy the work. For me, raku was an awakening of a spirit inside – something unexplainable.

Some technical observations

Many of Jerome's pots are created from rough 'idea sketches' but he allows the clay to help drive the final design during the making. Construction often involves thrown, slab and coil components. He uses a high-grog sculpture mix for hand-building, and a prepared raku body for wheel work. The slabs are impressed using carved wooden rollers or stamps, in a random fashion prior to cutting the clay for building the piece. Painstaking care is taken at all assembly points. Joints are strengthened with added coils and well-paddled to ensure a good bond which will handle the heat stresses.

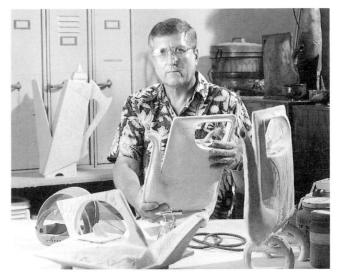

Jerome Heck in his studio.

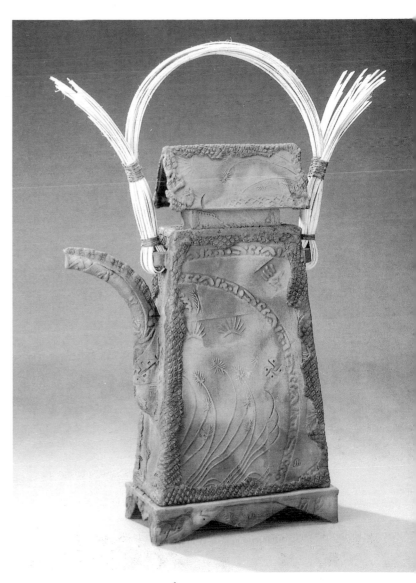

'August Tea' by Jerome Heck, 28 ½" × 6", 1992.
Slab built with cane handle, fumed copper effect.

Occasionally a porcelain slip is applied to ensure whiteness of the clay but almost no under-glaze is used. Jerome relies on the fumed copper effects to highlight his clay decoration. Bisque-firing is to about 1000°C and glazes are mostly common recipes, sometimes with small additions of oxides.

The raku-firing is achieved in a fibre-lined oil-drum kiln which has been sectioned to adjust for the height of each piece.

My experience with the copper glazes means a fast pull from the kiln followed by fairly heavy reduction. When I use a high proportion of copper carbonate (90%) to 10% frit, I like to reoxidise and quench with water using a sprayer that can be pressurised. I have used a lot of reduction materials: paper, various tree leaves and needles, straw/hay and used motor oil – but if I have a preference it would be banana leaves, which seem to give the best colours.

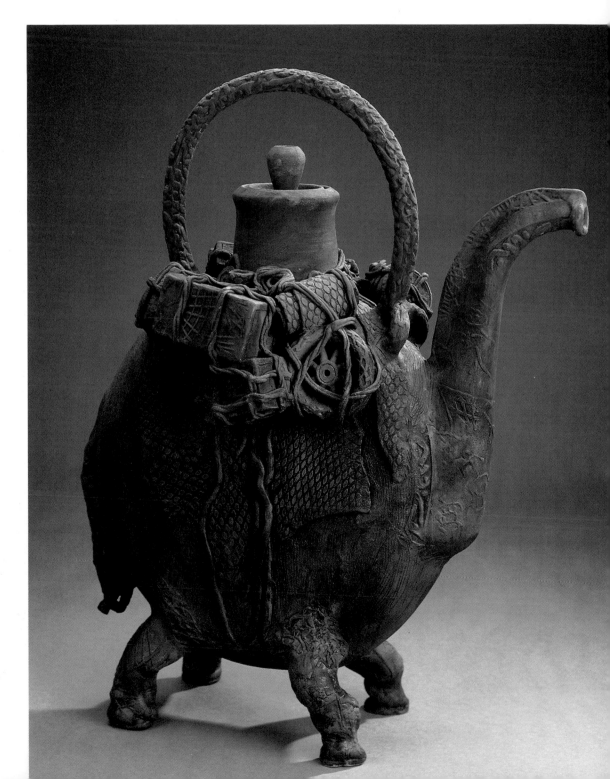

'Desert Pack' by Jerome Heck, 24" × 18" × 11". Fumed copper glaze, reduced in banana leaves.

138

Agnes Olive – Canada

During one summer, I spent several weeks exploring many countries of the Far East. In Bali, Indonesia, I was fascinated with the offering baskets for the 'Bad Gods'. These small baskets were made, daily and simply, from palm fronds and thin sticks, and were set out on the ground with offerings of food or flowers to appease the 'Bad Gods'. I have borrowed from these baskets and am using them as a starting point for an exploration into new forms and surfaces. The transition from the medium of palm leaves to that of clay is very challenging and exciting. I am attempting to retain the sense of spontancity and joy which the baskets initially provoked, and which I feel is entirely compatible with the history and essence of raku.

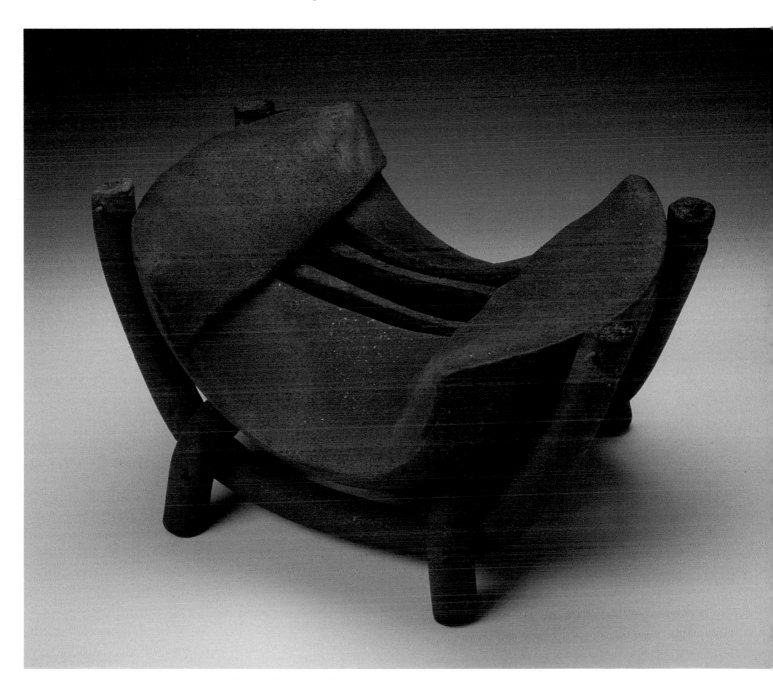

'Repository for Transient Souls' by Agnes Olive, 10" × 9" × 12".
Raku-fired slab and separate coil base.

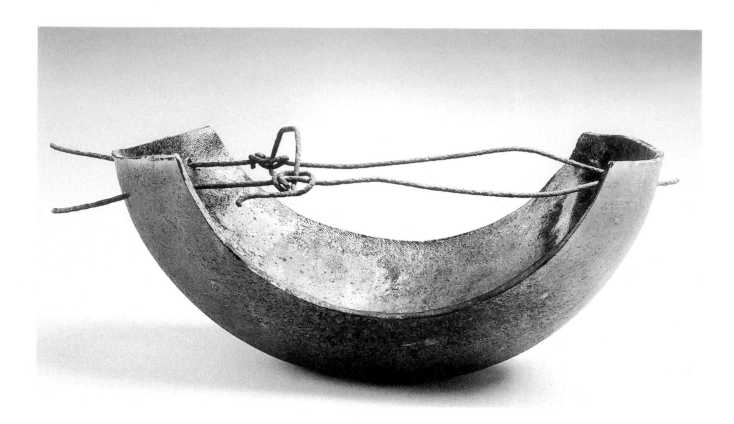

Agnes Olive is as much an archaeologist at heart as a potter. She has travelled extensively, spending time studying remote peoples across the world – their cultures, art, philosophy and religions. During her sojourns she has reacted with deep emotion to many of the indigenous forms and textures used in tribal art and religion, leading her to investigate their cultural history and current usage.

Landscape vessel with fence wire by Agnes Olive, approximately 15" × 8".
Raku, slab mould construction, copper saturated glaze inside, underglazed outside, post-fired in sawdust.
Photograph by Ben Hogan.

> My experiences culminate in the wish, and attempt, to carry a vital aspect of an earlier culture into the world of today. Whether I am surrounded by ancient ruins, sitting quietly in a Buddhist garden or watching an old village woman grinding corn, I am filled with a sense of reverence for all these aspects of life. I attempt to carry this felt sense into my work.

A 'convert' to raku in the late 1970s, Agnes was previously a porcelain potter. She writes:

> At this time I was bonded to a notion of porcelain as a precious medium. A long and established tradition distinguished it. Moreover, it had a very vivid memory and therefore demanded to be treated with great respect. As a result, my work was becoming too tight, too controlled – and all the while, it seemed as though there were a person inside me kicking and screaming to break loose. I was willing and eager to take some risks. I wanted to be less of a technician and more of an artist – less rigid and certainly more spontaneous. One morning I said to myself: 'I want to have more fun with my work.' I stored away my porcelain, and immediately made the first of my 'crazy teapots'. Unimpeded by past rules and traditions, I purposely did not wedge the clay. As I allowed it to lead me on the wheel, the child in me drifted to the surface and I experienced a marvellous sense of freedom. After many years, the long struggle for communion with the clay was complete. I had finally listened to myself.

Working from an old forge in her home village of Terra Cotta, Ontario, Canada, Agnes has continued to develop her work experimenting with clay, glaze and firing technology. Because the designs are extemporary and spontaneous, the technique of making or firing has to be worked out later to achieve the desired result. This method of working constantly challenges Agnes to come up with new ideas, keeping her work always moving on.

Some throwing is done but the majority of the pieces are formed by slab and coil. A specially-built slab roller and an old hand-turned extruder help her to make some of the larger pieces. Water is drawn from the small river which passes the forge and, until recently, Agnes dug the local clay for her pots – leaching out the lime which would not tolerate the firings.

The raku firing technique allows Agnes to monitor and control the process at every stage. She tests the glazes at various temperatures, often preferring the texture of an underfired or overfired glaze.

I was very excited years ago when I discovered that by underfiring certain glazes, I could achieve the look of historic pots unearthed from ancient civilisations. For this reason I prefer to do my firings by myself without distractions, just me and the pots talking.

The biscuited pieces are fired one at a time in a temporary kiln fashioned out of soft fire bricks. Recent trials using a glass-fibre furnace liner are encouraging and enable the pieces to be fired more quickly. Post-firing is usually done with sawdust which is selectively dropped on to the hot piece rather than covering it completely. She describes this as 'painting with sawdust'.

Glazes are all lead-free and are applied by dipping or spraying. An old shop vacuum cleaner has taken the place of expensive spray guns which often became clogged with glaze.

Agnes Olive's personal spiritual quest has led to a profound transformation of her life which she expresses and shares through her work. The images she creates are strong, intriguing, some-times celebratory, occasionally disturbing, almost always alluding to 'primitive' art – usually vessels. She is a potter of courage and integrity who is prepared to take risks in order to express her per-ceived reality of the world. 'Someone told me recently that I look like my work. I'm still not sure if that is a compliment.'

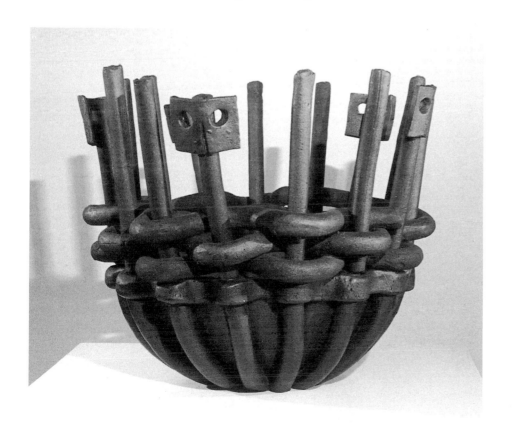

'From the Earth' by Agnes Olive,
h. 406 cm, w. 51 cm.
Slab and coil construction.
Photograph by David Olive.

Elizabeth Raeburn – UK

Having worked in music publishing, Liz trained as a nursery and primary school teacher taking pottery as the main subject. Evening classes provided an opportunity to make her own work and in 1973, feeling the need to break from teaching, she successfully applied for a place at Harrow School of Art. Harrow had by then built up a reputation for domestic pottery and many excellent potters had successfully set up workshops after training there.

Many students at Harrow (and indeed other colleges) were taken on to help in the workshops of established craftsmen during the summer vacation. Hands-on experience was vital to potential professional full-time potters. Liz spent a happy and influential period with David Leach. He was perhaps the most experienced workshop manager at the time providing a disciplined, intensive approach and a lot of basic know-how.

In 1975 Liz established a workshop in a converted Somerset chapel with her potter partner Rodney Lawrence. She concentrated on domestic pottery with some teaching, but a few years of production left her feeling disappointed with her rather functional work, and looking for another direction. In 1981 she decided to try some raku.

The very first pieces were quite successful and excited the owner of a prestigious gallery who offered an exhibition.

> From then on every piece of work was a disaster. Slips peeled, pots cracked – the more I read on the subject, the more it went wrong. For two months I threw away every piece I made. Then one day a neighbour knocked over my little 'kiln god'* which guarded the firings. I made a new one, decided to throw away the books and the very next pots worked! ...
>
> ... I enjoy using methods which give me time, and my natural inclination is to work very precisely. At first I found that I was frequently disappointed with the results, because I was always trying to gain finer control over the technique. It gradually came to me that the most creative way to work was to use the unpredictability of the process rather than to fight it. Raku seemed an ideal medium. It is a creative way to use ceramic possibilities.

Seduced by the many possibilities of a new and different technique, she became hooked. A close comparison with the ancient Japanese raku potters would be false, but certainly Liz is inspired by them.

A sketchbook travels with her to exhibitions and museums. Drawings of all manner of things fill its pages: armorial forms, shields, swords, axes and helmets provide a rich source of strong images. A simple observation such as the angle of an axe-head to its handle is enough to spark off an idea which may evolve into a whole range of new forms. Boat-shapes emerge in her pots – reminiscent of the rice barns of Papua New Guinea. The human body shows its influence as waists, shoulders and feet are much in evidence. As a musician, the proportions and lines of old musical instruments is an obvious influence for her; even something as trivial as the way a spade leans against a shed may be incorporated into a later piece of work. All this information is inwardly digested, nurtured and developed. 'I don't see things clearly at first. Ideas go round and round in my mind then something comes out. It all takes a long time.'

Technical information

Liz takes up to several days to make some of the bigger pieces. To finish five in a week would be a good record for her. A major exhibition would involve the best part of a year's work. Initial construction of the pots is done quite quickly. The clay (T-material and sand mixture) is rolled out into slabs, cut to the desired shapes and assembled. Each piece is then worked on painstakingly: cutting away, modelling and scraping. Up to three pieces may be in production at any one time. Any more than this breaks her concentration. By standing the pots on a thick piece of foam rubber, the pots can be modelled and refined without any distortion. Decoration in the wet stage is restricted to the use of scored lines and textures, and the application of slips to the leatherhard pots. Drying time is dependent on the weather as the pieces are left to dry naturally in the workshop. 'I hate the

Tall vase by Elizabeth Raeburn, h. 34 cm. Raku, white glaze.
By kind permission of Galerie Besson.

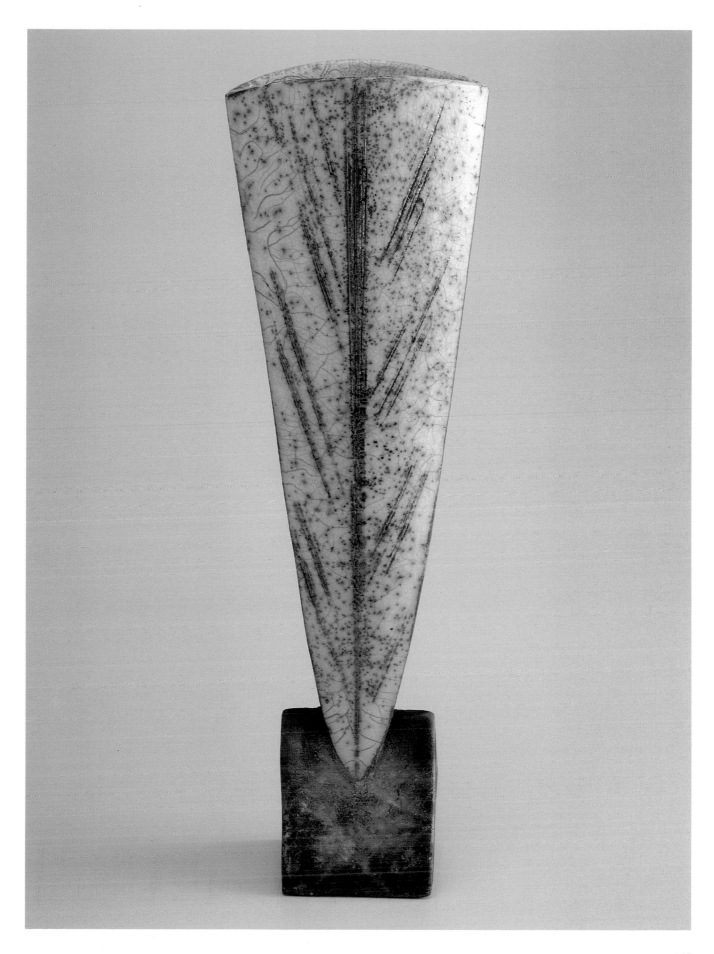

pots when they are drying and usually throw away ten per cent or so.'

When biscuit fired, some pieces have a resist-slip applied before the pots are glazed. A range of slips and glazes have been developed and the workshop is usually littered with the latest trials. Liz simply dips her pots to glaze them, accepting the pinholing which sometimes occurs as the glaze dries. Rubbing the dry glaze surface with a finger helps eradicate this problem. Areas of the biscuited pot may be made glaze-free with the use of a liquid wax emulsion which is brushed on.

The raku-firing experience to Liz is a theatrical one. A batch of work has been made and is ready glazed. The kiln, which is semi-portable, is brought out and prepared. The firers must be mentally alert and emotionally geared up for a couple of days of hot, dirty, smoky work. Several weeks' work now depends on careful judgment and split-second timing. After the many hours spent making, it is a dangerous time. Valuable pieces could be lost and yet, on a good day, when the kiln god is smiling, an unexpected gem could be created. 'I love the excitement of the process and the possibilities of the results. It counterbalances the precision-work that went before.'

*The kiln god is part of the Shinto tradition in Japan. A small idol is made by the potter to guard the firings, and offerings of rice wine and food are made to it before each firing. Some Western potters have adopted the tradition in a light-hearted manner as an acknowledgement to Japan's cultural influence.

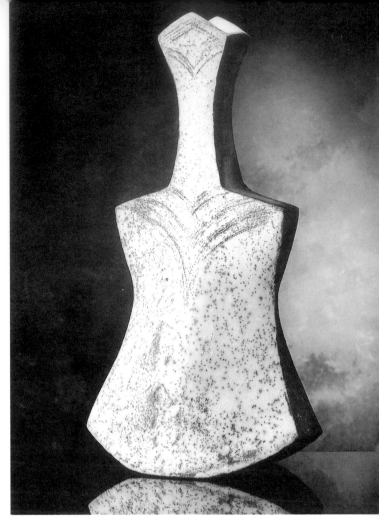

Tall vase by Elizabeth Raeburn, h. 34 cm.
Raku, white glaze.
From collection of Miss C. Halstead. Photograph by Peter Harper.

Group of three raku sculptures by Elizabeth Raeburn, tallest approximately 35 cm.
Courtesy of Bonhams. Photograph by Thomas Ward.

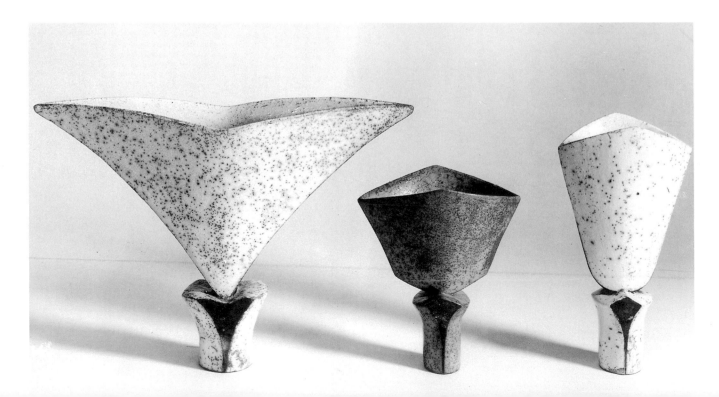

Martin Smith – UK

Martin Smith attempts feats with clay that would be folly in a less safe pair of hands. He chooses a complicated process with great purpose but the technique is not an end in itself. Martin has been described as 'one of Britain's most pioneering ceramic artists' and, after nearly 20 years of exploring clay, is recognised by many as being at the leading edge of the art, pointing the way forward into the next century.

The work has many of the characteristics of the best modern sculpture: great visual strength, calmness, intrigue and above all, a truly three-dimensional quality. But it is not elevated to the point where we ordinary mortals are unable to appreciate or identify with it. Martin fully acknowledges human experience and tradition, drawing on it freely. 'I've never made functional ceramic tableware but I find that the formal limitations of working within a vessel constraint is very important to me.' The essence of his interest in the vessel is the notion of containment. Although self-constrained by this tradition, Martin is not bound by it and, with integrity and humility, he challenges our perception of familiar objects, and the relationship of their disparate elements.

Martin has only recently returned to raku (although not exclusively) after a break of several years. His interest began in the 1970s whilst a student at the Royal College of Art, where he is now a senior tutor. His work from that early period was mainly raku bowls and cylinders with geometric surface patterns. The method of firing was just a 'process to be exploited'. Japanese Zen origins were of little interest to him. The 1980s saw a move to other techniques and a wide variety of materials, such as glass, wood, brick, metal and terracotta. One result of this experimentation was a series of tables made in 1988 incorporating many of these elements. His latest work returns to the use of clay as the principal element, either in the form of unglazed black raku or in red terracotta. Some of these pieces are complemented by the expansive use of applied copper and silver leaf. This new body of work reflects his continued preoccupation with the ordering of space and the nature of formal relationships.

His mastery of technique is outstanding but he also offers an understanding of space, line and plane, resulting in a deceptively simple appearance to his forms. He shows awareness of the way light falls on surfaces: the way a piece interacts with the surface it is sitting on; everything is considered, nothing spontaneous, and yet, the first-time observer is affected immediately by the freshness of the objects. As with the best sculptures, they do not appear laboured or overworked but quietly occupy their space with a presence which demands attention.

The process begins with the smallest of ideas. A font in a church in Parma, northern Italy, or perhaps just an emotional reaction to a piece of architecture. It is often something quite insignificant in itself. Charcoal drawings are made and then progressively refined; the relationship of wall thickness to the interior space and base are all considered as he explores his ideas of space and proportion.

The drawings are usually made in plan view, and are very carefully and mathematically developed. Progressions of size, increasing or decreasing, are tried until he considers the finely-judged combination of integrated planes to be complete.

Internal and external lines are given equal importance – sometimes mirroring each other: sometimes offering opposing themes such as hardness and softness. Arcs and curves are juxtaposed and echoed. Vertical walls are met by curling waves of clay, setting up a tension of line often seen in nature but rarely achieved in handmade objects.

A running theme is his concentration on the meeting point of the internal wall of the pot with its base. Martin has chosen to confuse this normally safe intersection by leaving a gap, a dark shadowy line which makes the massive walls of the pot appear to float, hovering above the base. With the outside lines of the piece firmly sitting on the table, an optical illusion is created, reminiscent of the drawings of Escher and his everlasting staircase.

Technical information

Using cut templates, either pivoted or dragged along a former (a technique known as sledging), a plaster version of the piece is made. In turn, a plaster mould is made from this, into which is

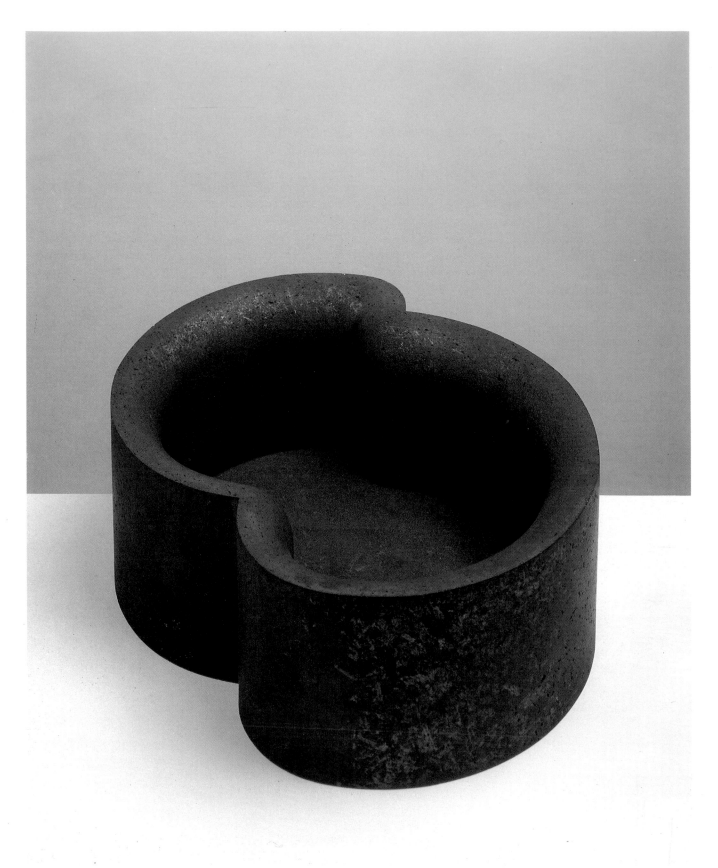

'Substance and Shadow No. 11' by Martin Smith, 16 × 40 × 33 cm. Courtesy of Contemporary Applied Arts. Photograph by David Cripps.

smeared the clay. Great care is taken to compress the clay as it is pushed into the mould, as any air pockets trapped or bad joins will result in the piece cracking. The use of soft clay makes the task easier. Martin uses T-material for the raku pieces, kneading in wet wood chippings (roughly two litres of chippings to a 25 kg bag of clay). Using the wood wet is an easy way of softening the clay body. This will eventually burn out to leave an open texture. When the piece has dried to a handle-able state it is removed from the mould. A certain amount of tidying up is required, filling in any little areas that may have been missed, and fettling off superfluous material. A long, slow drying period is followed by a careful biscuit-firing to around 1000°C.

By now, most potters would have completed the making process and would be concentrating on the firing. Martin Smith's mind is still firmly on form. The fired piece is worked on relentlessly.

Using grinders, diamond pads, files and saws, he fashions the surfaces to a perfect, machined finish which is wonderfully smooth to the touch.

The raku firing itself is carefully controlled. A slow rise of temperature up to around 800°C is followed by the removal of the piece into a dustbin of sawdust, where it is covered and allowed to cool completely before being scrubbed clean with wire wool.

Martin imposes on himself the formal limitations of the vessel and feels himself very much part of 'a ceramic tradition that has to do with domestic scale and the vessel form'. Within his self-imposed discipline, he finds great freedom to explore, and indeed exploit, the various states of raw and fired clay – pushing at accepted boundaries and revealing a new dynamism in the material that has been relatively unexplored by others.

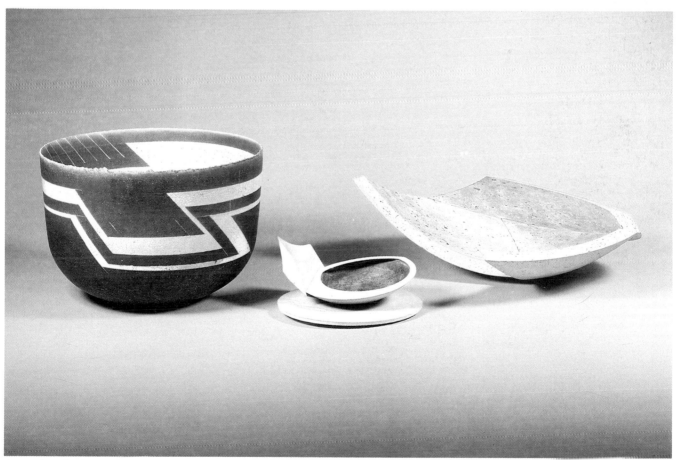

An early raku bowl, salmon pink and black, d. 28 cm, a cup and saucer, orange with painted interior, w. of saucer 17 cm, and a cut sectioned earthenware form with an off-white interior by Martin Smith.
Courtesy of Bonhams. Photograph by Thomas Ward.

Wim Hos – The Netherlands

The armoured head of a Samurai soldier, a Japanese woman with *Kanzashi* (chopstick-type hair adornments) and a mask from the Japanese *No* theatre – all have influenced the work of Wim Hos. He first became involved with raku through a film shown by the Japanese Embassy in the Netherlands, and indeed, the Japanese culture and philosophy is central to his inspiration.

Multiple thrown forms are radically distorted, assembled and vigorously modelled. Linear designs are applied to some pieces which may be left unglazed, becoming black after firing.

I try to get contrasting elements in one piece: rough and smooth, black and white, shiny and matt. I use different thicknesses of glaze to achieve different sizes of crackle.

One basic glaze is used. This is poured on, and resisted by a wax emulsion previously applied to the desired areas.

Loosely hanging beads added to the sculptures allude to the netsuke carvings Japanese used to hang from their belts.

I complete the pieces by adding stone, iron and other materials which are painted with acrylics. In this way, I can get the colour combination: black, white and red – which in Japan suggests Life, Death and the Erotic.

Wim is influenced by US potters such as Wayne Higby and Jim Romberg, and UK potter, Dave Roberts. Although the designs are largely Japanese-inspired, the pots have the free-form feel of the more relaxed, American-style raku.

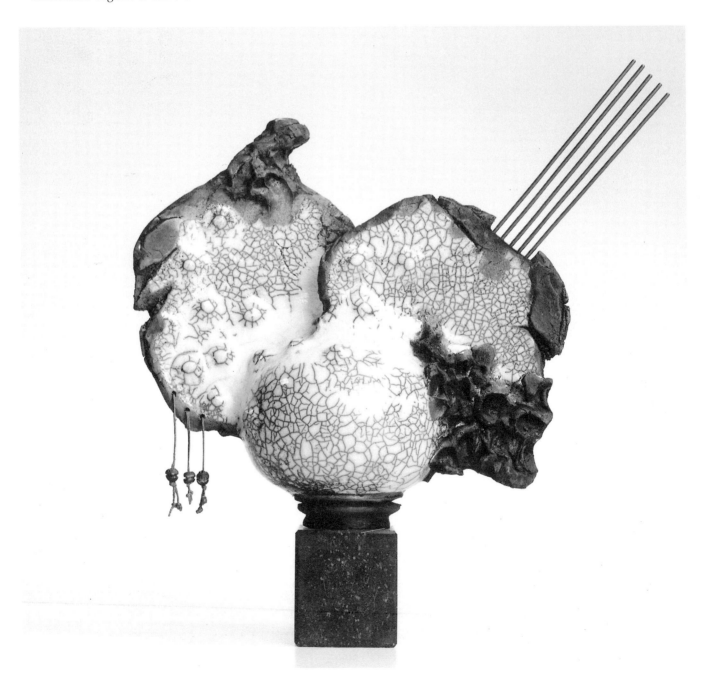

Robert Piepenburg – USA

Robert Piepenburg has been involved with raku since the mid-1960s. He says that he was 'romantically attracted to the process and the results in some primitive/primal way'. Certainly some of his pieces, particularly from the mid-1980s, seem to allude to ancient tomb vessels or burial pots from so-called 'primitive' cultures. These pieces were developed for 'the rich and timeless surface qualities that the firing technique brings to the clay'.

More recent work continues to emphasise surface treatment, but is applied to extended sculptural forms, hinting at, but less obviously based on function. 'The raku process forces me to work from an art aesthetic rather than a functional one and also keeps the scale of my work down to a manageable size.' He does, however, test his building skills to the extreme. Tall, narrow cone shapes support precariously balanced structures. Set at odd angles the sharply textured appendages offer, to the viewer, suggestions of unearthed and eroded Iron Age or Celtic weapons and tools.

In my clay work I often compose sculptural form from parts, each with their own aesthetic; like words, each with their own meaning, to create a sculptural sentence sensually infused with a spirit of humanness.

Technical information

Robert's glazes produce generally 'dry' non-shiny surfaces. One example is 'Piepenburg Patena':

Gerstley borate	4 parts
Nepheline syenite	3 parts
Bone ash	2 parts
Copper carbonate	1 part

I reduce for one minute in the kiln just prior to removal of the pots. Post-firing reduction treatment follows, using hay and sawdust as combustibles.

Thrown form with fumed copper glaze by Robert Piepenburg.

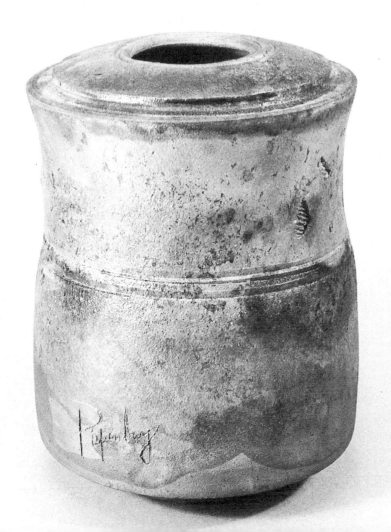

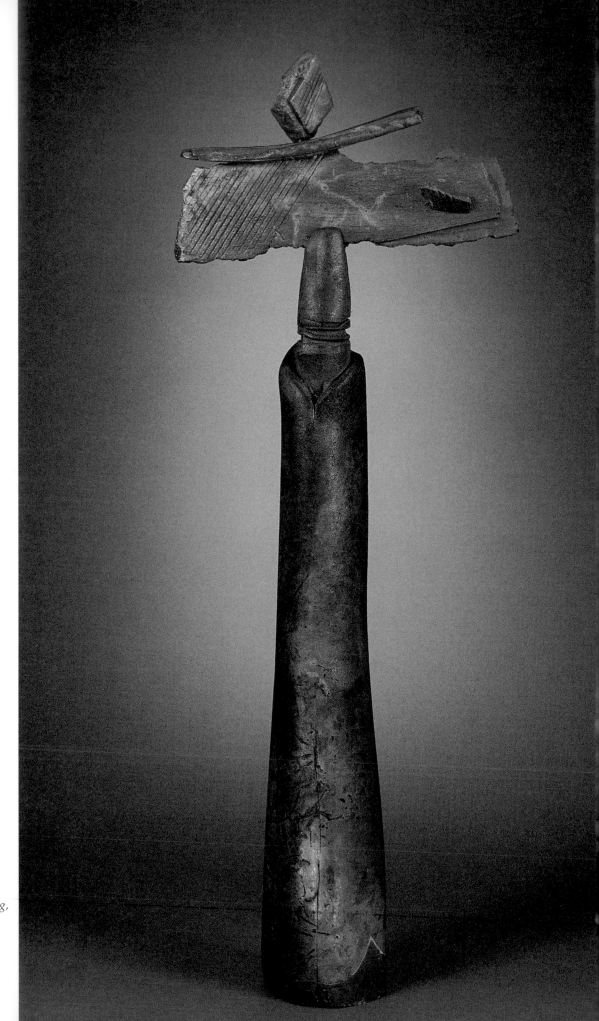

Tall raku sculpture by Robert Piepenburg, h. 31¼".

Gail Yurasek – USA

Michigan potter Gail Yurasek works exclusively with slab sculptures. The pieces are constructed by layering slabs together over a former, then drawing into and texturing the clay. Edges are torn or left 'organic' producing interesting profiles and matching the vitality of the calligraphic designs. The pieces are often sectional, the component parts sometimes linked only visually but making up an integrated whole.

When I work with clay, it is the creative process that absorbs me. Expressing my feelings and emotions with the clay as a canvas, makes it a powerful medium through which I can transform the quality of my life from an inherited, to a preferred state of being.

'Shield' by Gail Yurasek, 29" × 36".

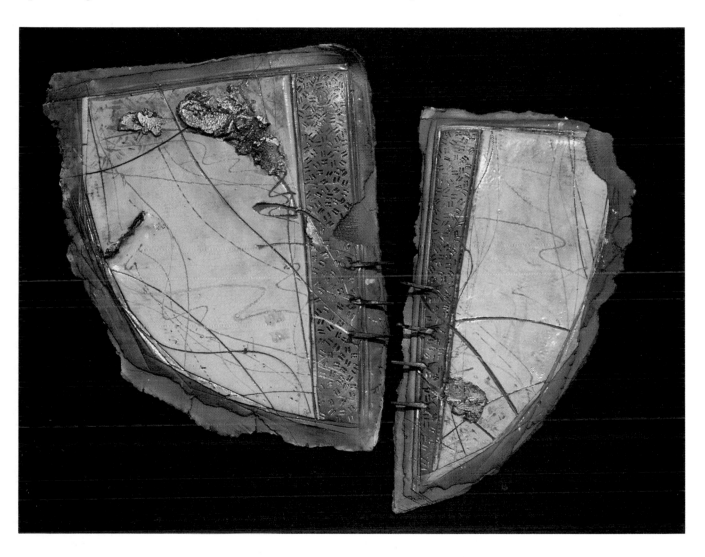

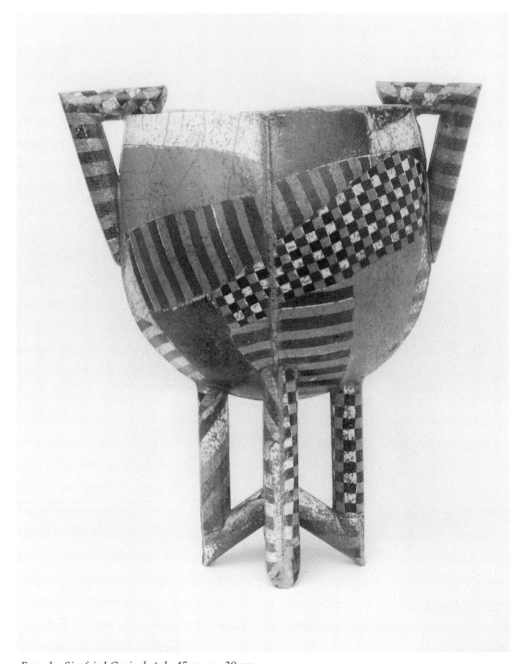

Form by Siegfried Gorinskat, h. 45 cm, w. 30 cm.
Handbuilt with coloured slip decoration, raku fired in the
presence of soda.

Conclusion

I find myself in sympathy with the 19th-century writer, Samuel Butler, who said: 'Life is the art of drawing sufficient conclusions from insufficient premises.' Perhaps it is in the nature of raku that it is difficult to sum up and perhaps also it would be foolish to draw too many conclusions from such a collection of techniques and the potters who practise them.

In this book I have described the roots of raku in ancient Japan and looked at some of the political and cultural reasons for its emergence in that country. I have considered its adoption and transformation in the West by Bernard Leach and later by Paul Soldner and others in the USA. Many of these modern variations and adaptations are described in the technical chapters and under the names of the individual craftsmen.

Some have a purely practical approach and use raku only as a means to an end, choosing it because it offers surface textures, colours and other effects which complement their particular work. However, there are those who turn to raku because they find themselves perhaps dissatisfied or unfulfilled in some way and feel that their work has become too safe.

Robert Herrick (1591–1674) summed-up this feeling concisely:

A winning wave (deserving note)
In the tempestuous petticoat
A careless shoestring in whose tie
I see a wild civility
Do more bewitch me than when art
Is too precise in every part.

Potters have revelled in the new freedom to explore fresh ideas which raku has opened up to them. Some move happily in and out of techniques such as salt, vapour-glaze, sawdust-firing, pit-firing and lustres etc., not wishing to be confined to what is perceived as 'true' raku.

For myself I would rather see the word 'raku', as a generic term, slowly disappear from the potter's vocabulary. For hundreds of years the Japanese style has remained largely the same and deserves to retain the title 'raku' for itself. Now, after only three decades, I believe modern, or American-style raku has come of age and outgrown its 'borrowed' name. Perhaps in the West, it should be replaced with a range of more apposite terms to cover what is now a very diverse range of making and firing techniques. Soldner suggests instead that pots may display a 'raku-ness' – the essence of raku – which could describe the imbuing of any pots with some of the spontaneity, asymmetry and freshness of the original spirit.

Raku has for many opened up previously unexplored territory. It breaks down conventions and appeals to those who seek a real challenge in their work. It combines a demand for great skill together with a conscious submission to chance. These opposing notions of man being in control and yet being also at the mercy of the four elements touch on fundamental issues dealing with our own existence in this world.

Who *is* the potter, pray, and who the pot?
Edward Fitzgerald 1809–1883

RAKU GLAZE RECIPES

All recipes are shown as parts by weight

Elizabeth Raeburn

Red Glaze:

Frit (Podmore 2251)	80
Garden clay	20

Alkaline crackle glaze:

Flint	20
China clay	5
Alkaline frit	75
Bentonite	2

Borax glaze:

Borax frit (2958)	85
China clay	15
Zinc oxide	7

Jennie Hale

Borax frit	24
Calcium borate frit or alkaline frit	48
China clay	8
Flint (quartz)	20

Bruce Chivers

Gerstley borate	20/25
Frit 3110	80/75

Frit 3110 can be replaced by any alkaline borax frit

Frit 3110	37
Gerstley borate	37
Nepheline syenite	11
Ball clay	5
Silica	5
Kaolin (China clay)	3
Tin oxide	2

8–10% copper oxide is added for the copper lustre glaze.

Chris Thompson

White glaze

Frit (3110)	30
Nepheline syenite	20
Gerstley borate	50

Black glaze
Base glaze as above with the addition of:

Manganese dioxide	4.5
Cobalt oxide	4.0
Copper oxide	4.5
Black iron oxide	3.5

David Miller

Gerstley borate	80
Ball clay	20
Tin oxide	5

White opaque crackle glaze

Boro-calcite frit	70
Soft alkaline frit	10
Ball clay	20
Tin oxide	10%

Karin Heeman

Basic glaze recipe

Standard borax frit	40
Calcium borate frit	40
China clay (kaolin)	15
Tin oxide	5

To this base glaze are added various oxides to colour the glaze.

Martin Mindermann

Transparent base glazes

Frit 1233 M&M	90.74
China clay	3.24
Quartz	6.02
Frit 1233 M&M	86.10
Quartz	10.40
Lithium carbonate	3.50
Frit 1233 M&M	77.39
Talc	15.48
China Clay	7.13
Frit 1233 M&M	58.1
Quartz	34.9
China clay	6.9
Frit 1233 M&M	57.35
Quartz	18.38
China clay	13.24
Zinc oxide	11.03

The frit comes from Mondre & Manz, Troisdorf.

Michael Parry

White crackle glaze

Colemanite	80
Nepheline syenite	20
EPK	4
Zircopax	2

Copper Matt Glaze

Copper carbonate	90 grams
Frit 3110 or borax frit	15 grams
Bentonite	0.5 grams

Nesrin During

Base glaze

Alkaline frit	70
Kaolin (China clay)	30

0.5–3% Addition of synthetic iron oxide (Fe_2O_3) gives light-pink to pomegranate-red in oxidation, or tones of grey in reduction.

2–3% Addition of copper carbonate ($CuCO_3$) gives Granny Smith apple green in oxidation to Bordeaux red in reduction.

Other combinations such as iron plus copper or iron plus manganese are also good.

Robert Piepenburg

'Piepenburg Patena'

Gerstley borate	4
Nepheline syenite	3
Bone ash	2
Copper carbonate	1

Wayne Higby

1, 2, 3, White (clear)

Silica	1
EPK	2
Gerstley borate	3

Blue – Green

1 cup of 1, 2, 3 wet and 1 teaspoon copper carbonate

Green

1 cup of 1, 2, 3 wet and 2 teaspoons copper carbonate

Dark Green etc. as above plus 3 tsp and so on.

Rocks and cliffs (orange brown)

1 part 1, 2, 3 wet and 1 part copper carbonate
or
6 parts 1, 2, 3
1 part tin oxide
4 parts copper carbonate

Coil water blue

Frit 3110	70 grams
Gerstley borate	8 grams
Silica	6 grams
Kaolin	10 grams
Copper carbonate	6%
Zinc oxide	3%

Wim Hos

Colemanite	82
Cornish stone	18
CMC	1 tsp

David Howard Jones

Base glaze – 1080°–1100°C

Frit FP 3006	85
China clay	10
Bentonite	5

For a range of iridescent and coloured glazes add the following in amounts of 1–2% each: silver nitrate, gold chloride, cobalt oxide, copper carbonate.

For a white glaze add 7% tin oxide

Lithium carbonate	40
Frit	45
China clay	10
Bentonite	5

James Lawton

Basic crackle clear glaze

Gerstley borate	70
Nepheline syenite	20
Kaolin (China clay)	10

Sandy Scott raku base

Gerstley borate	28
Lepidolite	14
Spodumene	14
Lithium carbonate	14
Ultrox	14

add 4% copper carbonate for green/turquoise/pink to orange.

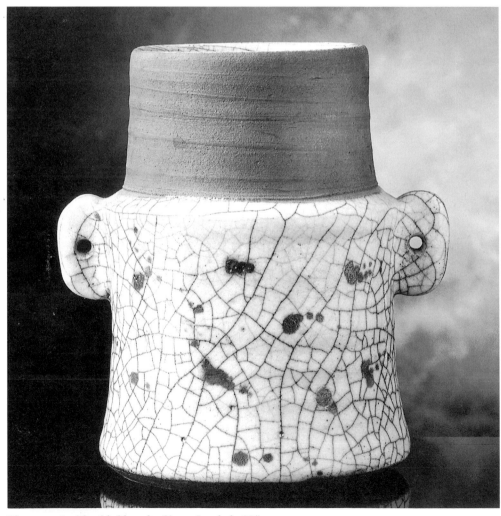

Thrown pot with added lugs by Simon Leach, h. 10".
Creamy white crackle glaze with spots of reduced copper and unglazed upper section.
Photograph by Peter Harper.

Materials – UK/USA equivalents

Here is a list of materials that can substituted for UK or USA products which may not be available. They may not produce exactly the same results and should be thoroughly tested.

USA	UK
Tennessee ball clay	TWVD ball clay from Watts Blake and Bearne
Goldart	Super Strength NDK from Watts Blake and Bearne
OM4 ball clay	Most standard ball clays
Albany type clay	Fremington red clay
Missouri fireclay	Any good fireclay
AP green fireclay	Glenboig fireclay
PBX fireclay	Potclays fireclay No. 6
Redart	Etruria marl
EPK	China clay
Ferro 3134 / Pemco P-54	Standard borax frit
Ferro 3110 984°C / Ferro 3124 1031°C	High-alkaline frits
Gerstley borate	Now available in UK from Potclays
Cornwall stone	Cornish stone, China stone
Custer feldspar	Potash feldspar
Zircopax, Opax	Zirconium silicate (zircon)
Superpax	Any commercial opacifier

Temperature conversion

Fahrenheit/Centigrade (Celsius) conversion

Degrees Fahrenheit	Degrees Centigrade (Celsius)
122	50
212	100
392	200
572	300
752	400
932	500
1112	600
1292	700
1472	800
1652	900
1832	1000
1922	1050
2012	1100
2102	1150
2192	1200
2283	1250
2372	1300
2462	1350
2552	1400

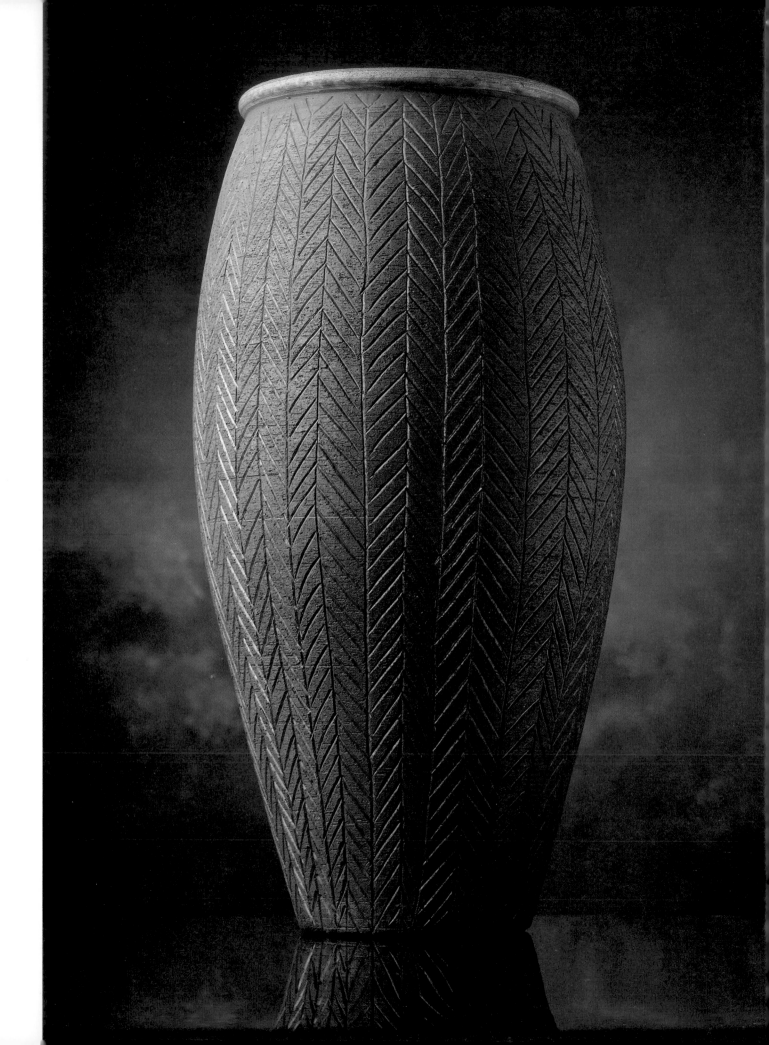

Bibliography
(Selected)

Books

Branfman, Steve. *Raku, A Practical Approach*. A&C Black, London 1991.

Leach, Bernard. *A Potter's Book*. Faber and Faber, London, 1973.

Smith, Lawrence, Harris, Victor and Clarke, Timothy. *Japanese Art – Masterpieces in the British Museum*. Oxford University Press, New York, 1990.

Gombrich E.H. *The Story of Art*. Phaidon, London.

Toulouse, Betty. *Pueblo Pottery of the New Mexico Indians*. Museum of New Mexico Press, 1977.

Lynggard, Finn. *Pottery: Raku Technique*. Van Nostrand Reinhold Company Ltd. 1973.

Holden, Andrew. *The Self Reliant Potter*. A&C Black, 1982.

Byers, Ian. *The Complete Potter, Raku*. B.T. Batsford Ltd. 1990.

Hamer, Frank. *The Potter's Dictionary of Materials and Techniques*. A&C Black London, 1975.

Magazines

Ceramic Review. 21 Carnaby St. London, W 1, UK.

Ceramics Monthly. Professional Publications, Inc. Box 12448, Columbus, Ohio, 43212, USA.

Ceramics: Art and Perception. 35 William St, Paddington, Sydney, NSW 2021, Australia.

Chanoyu Quarterly. Urasenke Foundation. Kyoto, Japan.

Opposite
Tall incised pot by Tim Andrews, h. 20"
Unglazed smoked raku with gold lustre rim.
Collection of Miss C. Halstead. Photograph by Peter Harper.

INDEX